Stockholding in Europe

Stockholding in Europe

Edited by

Luigi Guiso, Michael Haliassos and Tullio Jappelli

palgrave
macmillan

oee
Observatoire de l'Epargne Européenne

First published 2003 by
PALGRAVE MACMILLAN
Houndmills, Basignstoke, Hampshire RG21 6XS and
175 Fifth Avenue, New York, N.Y. 10010
Companies and representatives throughout the world

PALGRAVE MACMILLAN is the global academic imprint of the Palgrave Macmillan division of St. Martin's Press, LLC and of Palgrave Macmillan Ltd. Macmillan® is a registered trademark in the United States, United Kingdom and other countries. Palgrave is a registered trademark in the European Union and other countries.

ISBN 1–4039–0471–5 hardback

This book is printed on paper suitable for recycling and made from fully managed and sustained forest sources.

A catalogue record for this book is available from the British Library.

Library of Congress Cataloging-in-Publication Data
Stockholding in Europe / edited by Luigi Guiso, Michael Haliassos, Tullio Jappelli.
p. cm.
Includes bibliographical references and index.
ISBN 1–4039–0471–5
1. Stock ownership – Europe. 2. Stocks – Europe. 3. Portfolio management – Europe. 4. Investments – Europe. I. Guiso, Luigi. II. Haliassos, Michael. III. Jappelli, Tullio.

HG5422 .S73 2002
332.63'22'094–dc21 2002027085

10 9 8 7 6 5 4 3 2 1
12 11 10 09 08 07 06 05 04 03

Printed and bound in Great Britain by
Antony Rowe Ltd, Chippenham and Eastbourne

Contents

Contributors

Rob Alessie (Free University of Amsterdam, Tinbergen Institute and CentER)

Luc Arrondel (CNRS-DELTA, Paris)

James Banks (Institute for Fiscal Studies, London)

Axel Börsch-Supan (MEA, University of Mannheim and NBER)

Lothar Essig (MEA, University of Mannheim)

Luigi Guiso (University of Sassari, Ente Luigi Einaudi, and CEPR)

Michael Haliassos (University of Cyprus, HERMES and IMOP)

Stefan Hochguertel (European University Institute, Florence)

Tullio Jappelli (CSEF, University of Salerno and CEPR)

André Masson (CNRS-DELTA, Paris)

Raffaele Miniaci (University of Padova)

Matthew Wakefield (Institute for Fiscal Studies, London)

Guglielmo Weber (University of Padova, IFS and CEPR)

Preface

In the Fall of 2000 the European Savings Institute (Observatoire de l'Epargne Européenne – OEE) launched a research project with the aim of providing an in-depth study of households' direct and indirect holdings of shares, focused on demographic groups of particular interest for policy design, such as those based on age, education, and wealth levels. The research was coordinated by Luigi Guiso, Michael Haliassos, and Tullio Jappelli.

The current book is the outcome of this two-year research effort. It offers a comparative analysis of household stockholding decisions in France, Germany, Italy, the Netherlands, and the United Kingdom based on household-level data of high quality. In addition, it presents theoretical findings and methodological achievements in the area of stockholding in a way that is accessible to a wide audience of students, practitioners, and policy makers. We are most grateful to all contributors for preparing careful and stimulating analyses, and for numerous discussions over the past two years.

The financial support, professional advice, and encouragement of OEE were instrumental in ensuring the success of this project. We are especially indebted to André Babeau and Didier Davydoff for valuable input, advice, and suggestions at various stages of the project. Preliminary versions of the papers were presented at a special Conference on Stockholding in Europe organized and financed by the OEE for this purpose. The conference was held on 14 May 2001 at Euronext in Paris and was well attended by practitioners in the financial sector.

On the production side, we are indebted to Lia Ambrosio, who managed the manuscript submission, and to the Palgrave Macmillan editors and staff for their high degree of professionalism, efficiency, and courteousness.

The European Savings Institute was created in 1999 with two main goals: collecting European savings-related information, encouraging studies and research contributing to the public debate. The OEE is a forum for exchanges between public and professional bodies. Members of the Institute include representatives from Central Banks, Stock Exchanges, financial institutions, a rating agency, administrative bodies, and professional organizations.

Part I

Overview and Tools of Analysis

1
Stockholding: A European Comparison*

Luigi Guiso, Michael Haliassos and Tullio Jappelli

1.1 Introduction

The 1990s witnessed significant increases in stock market participation by households, both in Europe and in the United States. This participation took the form both of direct involvement in stock market trading of individual stocks and of indirect stockholding through participation in managed investment accounts. By the end of the 1990s, 17.3 per cent of the households in five major European countries (France, Germany, Italy, the Netherlands, and the United Kingdom) were holding stocks directly. Direct participation was highest in the United Kingdom (27.9 per cent) and lowest in Italy (7.9 per cent), with values for France, Germany and the Netherlands in the 15–17 per cent range. Including indirect stockownership through mutual funds sets the overall stock market participation at 23 per cent for France, 15 per cent for Italy, 20 per cent for Germany, 33 per cent in the Netherlands, and almost 50 per cent in the United Kingdom and the United States.

This book is intended to describe the phenomenon of the spread of equity culture to European households and to compare the extent to which equity culture has affected different European countries and different policy-relevant demographic groups within each country. In the Introduction, we discuss the background to the spread of equity culture and provide an overview of stockholding behaviour across European countries, focusing on demographic groups defined in terms of education,

* We are grateful to the Observatoire de l'Epargne Européenne for its generous support of the project, and to all project participants (Luc Arrondel, James Banks, Axel Börsch-Supan, Lothar Essig, Stefan Hochguertel, Andrè Masson, Raffaele Miniaci, Matt Wakefield, and Guglielmo Weber) for their work on individual country data on which many of our remarks in this chapter are based.

age, and position in the distributions of income and of financial wealth. We analyse separately two major issues, namely the participation rate of each group and the average shares of financial assets devoted to stocks by those members of each group that do hold stocks. Our main objective is to identify common patterns across countries and to point to major differences in their stockholding in view also of the experience in the United States.

Chapter 2, written by Michael Haliassos, explains the intuition behind theoretical results in recent, state-of-the-art models of household portfolio choice that can help us understand the major forces shaping stockholding behaviour of European households. In Chapter 3, Raffaele Miniaci and Guglielmo Weber describe the main features of household-level databases that contain substantial amounts of information on household portfolios, demographics, and attitudes, as well as the main instruments of econometric investigation of stockholding behaviour. The overall objective of this first part of the book is to provide readers with the background necessary to make sense of individual country experiences with stockholding that are described in the second part.

The second part of the book is devoted to country studies. Authors use data to identify the extent of household participation in the stock market of their own country and the degree of exposure to stockholding risk. The former amounts to examining the proportions of households engaged in direct stockholding, and in indirect stockownership through mutual funds and retirement accounts. The latter entails estimation of the portfolio shares devoted to stocks among those households that do participate in the stock market. In both cases, authors report figures for the entire population and for a number of demographic groups of policy and professional interest (e.g. age groups, education categories, and various parts of the wealth distribution). Authors try to uncover the role of a number of socio-economic variables in determining stock market participation and portfolio shares. They are careful to present not only figures for each country, but also brief reviews of the overall policy and institutional background that are relevant to understanding stockholding behaviour in the country they examine.

Chapter 4, written by Luc Arrondel and André Masson makes use of newly available portfolio data for France. Axel Börsch-Supan and Lothar Essig report on stockholding behaviour in Germany in Chapter 5, utilizing a variety of available sources. Luigi Guiso and Tullio Jappelli use the detailed Bank of Italy survey of household income and wealth (SHIW) to study stockholding behaviour in Italy in Chapter 6. Chapter 7, written by Rob Alessie and Stefan Hochguertel, is devoted to the Netherlands and makes use of rich data sets on portfolios of Dutch households. James Banks and Matthew Wakefield overcome major deficiencies of stockholding data in the United Kingdom to report on the spread of equity culture in that country in Chapter 8.

1.2 The background

Although the good performance of stock markets, relatively to bond markets, has undoubtedly contributed to the high participation figures by the end of the decade, the underlying causes can be found in the confluence of several factors – some policy-induced and some promoted by the actions of the private sector. Among these factors, increasing competition in the financial sector, privatization of public utilities, and pension reforms played a prominent role.

One type of policies that seem to have contributed to stock market participation fit into the more general European policy framework that promoted development and competition in the financial sector. This framework includes the European Union directives on financial integration, financial liberalization and removal of remaining capital controls, and the policy coordination necessitated by the Maastricht treaty and preparations for adoption of a common currency.

These efforts were accompanied by policies aimed at privatization of public utilities, which produced a supply of stocks in newly privatized companies that needed to be taken up by the household sector. Governments had an incentive to draw a larger number of households into the stock market to accomplish this aim. In the United Kingdom and Italy, for example, this led to the government advertising on a large scale in an effort to educate households on the many attractions of stock market participation and more specifically on the good prospects of newly privatized companies.

All European countries have, in various degrees, undertaken programmes of privatization of public utilities and state-owned firms. In some countries, such as the United Kingdom and Italy, where revenues have been very substantial, the privatization process and the number of firms going public have increased stock market capitalization. These privatizations were accompanied by massive publicity, through which households got acquainted with stocks and their return and risk characteristics. It is likely that this dissemination of information has permanently increased stockholding. The relatively low speed of the privatization process in Germany, where State ownership of public utilities remains relevant, suggests that the process of privatization is still far from being completed. Thus, future privatizations will likely be an important factor in spurring stockownership in the coming decade.

Pension reform was yet another way in which government policy influenced the spread of equity culture among households. The overall demographic picture still is one of an aging Europe, in which contributions of the young no longer suffice to finance retirement of the numerous old. Since Europe can no longer rely on unfunded social security systems to support the large numbers of its pensioners, public debate and government-sponsored financial education programmes focus attention on individual retirement accounts and on how households could rely partly on stocks in saving for retirement.

A major source of inspiration for European policy makers was the tremendous success of individual retirement accounts (IRAs) in the United States and the move from traditional, defined-benefit pension systems to defined-contribution pension funds where benefits depend, among other things, on stock market performance.

In all countries, there has been an increase in the importance of assets in pension funds, although their relevance differs markedly across European countries and between Europe and the United States Pension funds assets are over 90 per cent of GDP in the Netherlands and around 60 per cent in the US; they are less than 10 per cent in France, Italy and Germany. The main reason for these differences is the dominant role of public pension schemes in the countries where the development of pension funds is still limited. Again, this suggests that this channel of stockownership promotion is still at its infancy in continental Europe (with the important exception of the Netherlands).

In addition to government policies, the financial sector also contributed to promote household participation in the stock market. Gone were the days in which stock market participation required each household to choose the stocks it would invest in, to find out how to trade, to do the bookkeeping, and to hold an un-diversified portfolio unless it could secure considerable funds. With the advent of mutual funds, portfolio selection and trading could be left to professionals, resources could be pooled with other smaller or bigger investors, and qualified account managers could provide financial advice and bookkeeping services reliably and efficiently. Moreover, mutual funds developed in great variety. This provided households with considerable choice and possibilities for diversification across funds, but also made them targets of aggressive advertising as part of the effort by mutual funds to expand their clientele base and their market share. A by-product of advertising campaigns was increased awareness of households regarding the stock market and the number of options facing stockholders.

The extent to which equity culture has spread among different demographic groups in each country, and the degree to which these groups expose themselves to stockholding risk cannot be analysed with aggregate financial data. This is because increases in the aggregate value of stocks and even in the overall share of stocks in aggregate wealth do not necessarily signal higher participation rates by households, nor do they reveal the demographic composition of the stockholder pool. Luckily, these developments were accompanied by the collection of detailed household-level data on portfolios in a (still small but significant) number of European countries. Our project makes use of precisely these data to analyse the portfolio of European stockholders.

1.3 Why is the demographic pattern of stockholding important?

We saw above that government policies and private advertising efforts have been directed towards encouraging new stockholders to participate in the stock market, either directly or indirectly. We also saw that equity culture has spread to significant population segments in European countries, but it is still far from encompassing all European households. Indeed, in none of the countries we consider has stock market participation spread to the majority of households. Given that equity culture has spread to new households, stockholder behaviour of the past cannot be taken for granted in the future, as the demographic composition of the stockholder pool is likely to have changed with the addition of newcomers. It is thus important to uncover not only the composition of the new stockholder pool but also differences in stockholding patterns across demographic groups of policy interest.

An important reason for uncovering this demographic composition is that stockholders can contribute to market instability in response to various signals. Direct stockholders can influence markets directly through trading, but indirect stockholders can also influence fund managers if they tend to follow fads and to respond to market signals in a symmetric way. This factor is particularly important in stock market downturns, as those that characterize European stock exchanges in 2002 following the collapse of dot coms and of the high technology sector. In such an environment, it is natural to ask how European stockholders in the household sector will interpret market signals and to what extent they will be able to withstand the pressure on their finances before they jump off the ship. Concern with the possible contribution of new and old stockholders to market instability is likely to characterize both governments interested in stock market performance and the private sector that depends on movements in stock prices.

Policy makers follow stock market indices closely, but they are also concerned about broader indicators of economic performance, welfare, and possibilities of re-election. If they are to design government policy targeted at redistribution and risk sharing across different groups, it is important for them to know which segments of their population tend to absorb most of the stockholding risk. Financial practitioners are also likely to take interest in the composition of the stockholder base for a different reason. They typically have to make choices on groups to target in marketing financial products, and knowledge of the current profile of stockholders allows them to identify groups that are likely to be responsive to opportunities for stock market participation, as well as those that are currently underrepresented.

1.4 The data sets used in this volume

In this volume, we use survey data for five European countries: France, Germany, Italy, the Netherlands, and the United Kingdom. In this introductory section we also rely for comparison on the 1998 Survey of Consumer Finances for the United States. The discussion below is based in part on Miniaci and Weber (Chapter 3), to which we refer readers interested in the statistical design and quality of the data used.

Table 1.1 reports the main data sources used in the individual country chapters. The French data are drawn from Patrimoine 97, a large survey run by the central statistical office, which involves over 10 000 households. By design, Patrimoine 97 oversamples wealthy households and collects good quality information on many of the socio-economic variables of interest, both at household and individual level.

The German data are drawn from the 1998 income and expenditure survey (EVS), a very large survey run by the central statistical office (Statistiche Bundesamt), involving over 50 000 households. Miniaci and Weber explain that there is evidence that the household income distribution of the EVS sample is too concentrated toward central income classes, which has consequences on ownership rates and on the overall coverage of wealth if compared to the flow-of-funds statistics.

The Italian data are drawn from the 1998 survey of household income and wealth (SHIW), a survey run by the Bank of Italy involving some

Table 1.1 Portfolio information in major household surveys

	Survey name					
	INSEE survey on wealth	**Income and expenditure survey**	**Survey of household income and wealth**	**Center saving survey**	**Family resources survey**	**Survey of consumer finances**
	France	**Germany**	**Italy**	**Netherlands**	**United Kingdom**	**United States**
Participation in the stock market	Yes	Yes	Yes	Yes	Yes	Yes
Participation in mutual funds	Yes	No	Yes	Yes	Yes	Yes
Total stock market participation	Yes	No	Yes	Yes	Yes	Yes
Amount in stocks	Yes	Yes	Yes	Yes	No	Yes
Amount in mutual funds	Yes	No	Yes	Yes	No	Yes
Total financial assets invested in stocks	Yes	No	Yes	Yes	No	Yes
Total financial assets	Yes	Yes	Yes	Yes	No	Yes
Household income	Yes	Yes	Yes	Yes	Yes	Yes
Number of observations	10 200	50 000	7 100	2 800	22 900	4 327

Note: In all countries except the United States total financial assets invested in stocks is defined as directly held stocks and mutual funds. Data refer to 1998.

7000 households, half of which have been participating in the same survey in earlier years. The financial wealth section of the questionnaire is fairly detailed and it is organized in such a way that respondents are first asked whether they know the existence of the various financial assets.

The Dutch data are drawn from the CentER saving survey (CSS) panel, a survey run by CentER (Tilburg University), involving some 2000 households who were interviewed online (every participating household had been equipped with a PC and modem). CSS is targeted at the structure of individual and household wealth and saving behaviour. Therefore, unlike all the other surveys used in this volume, CSS collects detailed information on individual portfolios. Potentially, this gives the most precise picture of household portfolios, but aggregating to household-level or to broader asset categories might be a problem if some member of the household refuses to participate in the survey or does not respond to any specific question on some of the 44 assets and debts categories considered.

The British data are drawn from the 1998 family resources survey (FRS), a large survey run by the Central Statistical Office and involving some 23 000 households in Great Britain. Information on individual income is of excellent quality, but for most of the households the data on portfolio allocation is limited to ownership information for broad categories of assets and a banded variable on total amount of liquid financial assets.

In short, the data sets have some common features but differ in a number of important aspects that require some assumptions for international comparison. As explained in Table 1.1, each survey has information on direct stockholding, which provides a lower bound of financial assets invested in stocks. In fact, in all countries, a significant amount of shares is held through mutual funds and other investment accounts. However, the distinction between categories of mutual funds is seldom available.[1] Moreover, in many instances, the investor is aware of the general investment strategy of the account, but at each point in time has no details as to the exact composition of the account. To provide an estimate of the total amount of financial assets invested in stocks we therefore supplement the analysis by considering participation in mutual funds. Since a considerable portion of mutual funds is invested in stocks, this represents an upper bound of total financial assets invested in stocks. Except for Germany, mutual funds are singled out in each of the surveys that we analyse.

As for asset amounts, in the United Kingdom, existing surveys do not provide data on financial asset amounts, so the analysis relies mainly on direct and indirect participation in the stock market. In Germany, statistics on stock amounts are available, but not on mutual funds. Therefore, in this country we do not attempt to provide an upper bound for total financial assets invested directly and indirectly in stocks.

1.5 How does stockholding participation differ across demographic groups?

In Table 1.2, we report total stockholding participation rates, but we also distinguish between participation rates in direct stockholding and in mutual funds.[2] Looking at the entire population of households, we confirm that the United Kingdom exhibits the highest participation rate in stockholding among European countries, but it still falls short of the participation rate in the United States that is very close to half the population. The Netherlands and France come next, being very close to each other, while Italy is a more distant third. Unfortunately, total participation for Germany cannot be assessed, because 1998 figures for stockholding through mutual fund participation are not available.

Table 1.2 also reveals another difference across European countries, namely in the relative popularity of direct stockholding versus mutual fund participation. We observe, for instance, that UK households tend to participate substantially more in direct stockholding than in mutual funds, unlike what happens in the Netherlands or in Italy. The UK experience is probably related to the massive advertising campaign that the government undertook in order to promote stockholding in privatized

Table 1.2 Stock market, mutual funds and total participation: total sample, no college and college education

	France	Germany	Italy	Netherlands	UK	US
Total sample						
Stocks	0.15	0.17	0.07	0.14	0.27	0.19
Mutual fund	0.13	—	0.11	0.16	0.16	0.16
Total participation	0.23	—	0.15	0.24	0.34	0.48
No college education						
Stocks	0.13	0.14	0.06	0.08	0.22	0.13
Mutual fund	0.12	—	0.09	0.11	0.11	0.10
Total participation	0.21	—	0.13	0.16	0.27	0.39
College education						
Stocks	0.23	0.28	0.22	0.22	0.40	0.31
Mutual fund	0.18	—	0.28	0.23	0.27	0.29
Total participation	0.32	—	0.37	0.35	0.50	0.69

public utilities. Mutual funds are also more popular than direct stockholding among French households, though the difference is much less marked than in the case of the United Kingdom.

Mutual fund participation typically entails substantially more diversification of stockholding risk across different stocks than direct stockholding. Households engaged in direct stockholding usually find it difficult to hold an optimally balanced variety of stocks, both because they usually lack the expertise required for design of optimal portfolios and because purchase of an optimal portfolio of directly held stocks requires substantial investment of funds due to indivisibilities. Households that invest in mutual funds face neither problem and are thus more likely to be better diversified across stocks.

Since the profile of European investors is important both for policy makers and for financial practitioners, it is useful to compare stockholding participation between groups that differ in terms of a particular demographic characteristic that economic theory suggests is relevant for stockholding behaviour. We focus on four such demographic characteristics in what follows: investor's education, income, financial wealth and age.

1.5.1 Stockholding participation across education groups

An important characteristic for stockholding behaviour is the level of educational attainment of the household, as proxied by the education of the household head responsible for managing finances. Education correlates not only with income and employment prospects of the household, but also with its ability to process stock market signals and other information on how to trade in the stock market. Thus, education can affect both the appropriateness of household response to stock market signals and the ability of households to withstand pressure on finances imposed by stock market downturns.

A very robust finding in recent household portfolio research is that education correlates positively with stock market participation, even controlling for other factors such as income and employment status. The effects of this positive correlation are highly visible in our data on European stockholders. As we consider progressively higher educational levels, the extent of household participation in stockholding increases, often more than doubling as education moves from below high-school to college degree.

To summarize the broad patterns offered by the data, we distinguish between two educational categories. In the first, we include households without a college degree, while the second consists of all college graduates, including those that have obtained postgraduate degrees. The second and third panels of Table 1.2 report participation according to this sample split. The most striking difference between the two panels is in the levels of participation. These are substantially higher for college graduates than for those without a college degree.

In the United Kingdom, 41 per cent of college graduates are stockholders (50 per cent including mutual funds), while only 22 per cent (28 per cent including mutual funds) of those without college degree participate in the stock market. In France, the corresponding figures are 23 and 13 per cent, respectively (32 and 21 including mutual funds). Perhaps the most dramatic difference among education groups is observed in Italy, where less than 7 per cent (13 including mutual funds) of those without college degree are stockholders while among college graduates participation exceeds 22 per cent (37 including mutual funds). It is probably not surprising that this striking difference is observed in the country where the overall stock market participation of households, and hence familiarity with the stock market, is more limited than in all other countries we considered.

Given that participation in mutual funds imposes less informational requirements on households, one might expect that lower-education households would tend to prefer this indirect form of stockholding to holding stocks directly. Interestingly, as panels 2 and 3 reveal, both education classes in each country display the same pattern of relative preference for the two forms of stockholding. For example, direct stockholding is more popular than mutual fund participation among UK households, regardless of whether their heads have a college degree or not. Thus, any effect that education has turns out to be insufficient to reverse the popularity ranking of these two forms of stockholding among households in the countries examined, though in the case of the Netherlands college graduates come close to being indifferent between the two forms of stockholding.

These findings also point to the fact that stockholding by European households is not confined among the most highly educated households, but it has spread to all education classes. This means, in turn, that there are now significant contingents of European stockholders with limited educational background. To the extent that education correlates positively with financial sophistication and familiarity with financial instruments, this observation implies the presence of a group of unsophisticated and potentially unpredictable investors.

The ability of European households to withstand stock market pressures is likely to be influenced by education, since education plays a key role in their earnings prospects and in their potential to adapt to stock market fluctuations by varying their labour supply or moving across sectors. Perhaps a more crucial factor in this respect is the amount of financial resources (or 'cash in hand') that is available to the household. Cash in hand consists of income and financial assets. We next examine how stock market participation is related to these two characteristics of the household.

1.5.2 Stockholding participation across the income distribution

Table 1.3 shows how direct stock market participation differs across households at different points in the income distribution. Households are grouped according to the decile in the income distribution to which they belong, and participation rates among households in each decile are reported. The clear picture that emerges from this table is that higher-income households are more likely to be holding stocks directly in all European countries considered and in the United States.

In all countries, households in the top income decile exhibit significantly higher participation rates in direct stockholding than their counterparts in the low income deciles. In fact, participation rates increase significantly faster as we move from the eighth or ninth decile to the top one, compared to how much they vary across lower successive income deciles.[3] The significantly higher participation rates among the rich segments of the population emphasize the point that the rich in each country are not simply 'scaled-up' versions of the poor. In other words, we should not expect to find that households with half the income of their rich counterparts should also have half their direct stockholding. As this table shows, they are much more likely to have no stocks at all.

Table 1.3 Stock market participation, by income decile

Income decile	France	Germany	Italy	Netherlands	UK	US
I	0.03	0.45	0.03	0.08	0.14	0.04
II	0.01	0.51	0.02	0.03	0.10	0.03
III	0.96	0.77	0.01	0.05	0.15	0.06
IV	0.10	0.12	0.02	0.12	0.16	0.12
V	0.10	0.13	0.04	0.08	0.21	0.15
VI	0.14	0.15	0.05	0.12	0.27	0.20
VII	0.14	0.19	0.07	0.15	0.33	0.17
VIII	0.20	0.22	0.10	0.14	0.38	0.26
IX	0.22	0.32	0.11	0.27	0.45	0.31
X	0.39	0.41	0.29	0.40	0.56	0.54

Comparing across countries, we find that participation rates of households low in the income distribution are quite similar despite marked country differences in overall participation rates in the population. Participation rates of the rich also show similarities across countries, though the high participation rates of the rich in the United States and in the United Kingdom do stand out. Country differences in overall participation rates seem to arise largely from differences in the extent to which direct stock market participation has spread to the middle-income deciles. The table shows that Italy is one extreme, with very low participation rates and an almost flat income-participation profile for most of the income distribution. At the other extreme, we witness substantial direct participation in the stock market by the bulk of middle-income households in the United Kingdom.

The general flavour of these remarks, with some qualifications, applies to the case of total stock market participation, defined as participation either through direct holdings of stock or through mutual funds. The relationship between total stock market participation and income decile of the household is depicted in Table 1.4. Inclusion of mutual fund participation appears to induce a more visible positive relationship between income decile and participation even among middle-income households in Italy, a sign that indirect stockholding has managed to spread to this segment of the population.

The most striking aspects of this table are two. First, we note the very high total participation rates among the very rich in the United States and in the United Kingdom compared to those in the other three countries. Second, the table provides evidence that equity culture has spread much more among the middle-income classes of these two countries than among the middle-income classes of France, Italy, and the Netherlands.

Table 1.4 Total participation, by income decile

Income decile	France	Italy	Netherlands	UK	US
I	0.05	0.04	0.14	0.18	0.08
II	0.07	0.04	0.06	0.14	0.12
III	0.15	0.05	0.10	0.19	0.21
IV	0.15	0.07	0.16	0.21	0.39
V	0.17	0.08	0.17	0.27	0.44
VI	0.24	0.13	0.22	0.35	0.56
VII	0.26	0.15	0.30	0.40	0.62
VIII	0.30	0.22	0.32	0.46	0.75
IX	0.36	0.24	0.43	0.55	0.78
X	0.52	0.45	0.54	0.67	0.91

1.5.3 Stockholding participation across the distribution of financial wealth

We now turn to the relevance of the distribution of wealth for participation in stockholding. A clear finding across all countries we consider is that participation in stockholding, direct or indirect, is stronger among wealthier groups of European households. Indeed, there are dramatic differences in participation between households in the lowest wealth deciles and in the top of the wealth distribution.

The top of the wealth distribution contains relatively small numbers of households. Still, because of the skewness of the distribution, these small numbers of households hold very large amounts of stocks and control a disproportionate amount of stocks. The data reveal that participation rates in direct or indirect stockholding at the top of the wealth distribution are of the order of 50 per cent or higher in virtually all countries we considered.

Tables 1.5 and 1.6 take a close look at stockholding across the wealth distribution by distinguishing between distribution deciles. Table 1.5 exhibits direct stock market participation, while Table 1.6 adds participation through mutual funds. The tables do not report figures for the United Kingdom where wealth deciles cannot be calculated. The picture that emerges is quite similar to that in the case of income deciles. In the case of direct stockholding (Table 1.5), we observe a smoother relationship between wealth deciles and participation than the one observed for income deciles. Ultimately, an important factor determining stock market participation is the level of overall resources of the household. As we move towards higher deciles of the distribution of cash in hand, financial

Table 1.5 Stock market participation, by financial wealth decile

Financial wealth decile	France	Germany	Italy	Netherlands	US
I	0	0.00	0.00	0.00	0.00
II	0.02	0.02	0.00	0.00	0.02
III	0.04	0.05	0.00	0.01	0.03
IV	0.07	0.08	0.00	0.04	0.05
V	0.07	0.12	0.02	0.03	0.10
VI	0.10	0.16	0.03	0.08	0.14
VII	0.15	0.20	0.04	0.12	0.23
VIII	0.20	0.26	0.07	0.18	0.27
IX	0.27	0.33	0.22	0.34	0.43
X	0.54	0.48	0.37	0.59	0.61

Table 1.6 Total participation, by financial wealth decile

Financial wealth decile	France	Italy	Netherlands	US
I	0	0.01	0	0
II	0.04	0	0.01	0.06
III	0.08	0	0.02	0.14
IV	0.11	0.01	0.06	0.40
V	0.14	0.04	0.10	0.49
VI	0.18	0.05	0.15	0.57
VII	0.25	0.10	0.23	0.66
VIII	0.34	0.19	0.43	0.75
IX	0.43	0.42	0.58	0.86
X	0.69	0.63	0.78	0.93

wealth tends to represent a higher proportion of these overall resources and thus to be a better proxy for the 'rich'.

We should also recall that the end of the 1990s were years of good stock market performance. Stockholders experienced significant capital gains relative to those not holding stocks and were thus more likely to be included in the higher deciles of the financial wealth distribution because they held stocks. Thus, part of this clear positive association between financial wealth and participation is due to this composition effect.

Table 1.6 reports total stock market participation. We see again that participation among the very rich is somewhat lower in Italy and in France than in the United States and the Netherlands, but not all that much different. Perhaps the clearest difference between European countries and the United States is in the acceleration in participation rates observed among the higher wealth classes. Although total stock market participation is almost linear in wealth in the United States, it is clearly convex in wealth in European countries, with the rich displaying substantially higher participation rates than the poor and the middle-wealth households. This feature is most pronounced in Italy and least pronounced in France among the European countries shown.

Wide differences in participation rates between the very wealthy and the rest of the population do have positive aspects. It seems that a large component of European stockholders belong to groups with considerable amounts of overall financial wealth, probably including other assets that could act as buffers to stock market fluctuations, while the less wealthy tend to shy away from stockholding risk.

Of course, the nature of other, non-financial assets held is important for the overall ability of households to withstand stock market pressures. For example, the rich often tend to tie up large amounts of their wealth in risky private businesses, wherefrom they also derive much of their labour income. This results not only in portfolios with substantial risk overall, but also in positive correlation between earnings and stock returns. This positive correlation should temper the notion that as long as the rich hold most of the stocks, there is limited possibility that they will sell off stock or even withdraw from the stock market during downturns.

1.5.4 Stockholding participation across age groups

The fourth and final demographic characteristic we consider is the age of the household head. When we split the population of European households in each country according to this criterion and distinguish between households in their thirties, forties, and so on, we find for all countries that stock market participation follows a hump-shaped pattern when plotted against age. In general, participation rates tend to peak in the 50–59 age group, and they are lower in the younger and in the older age groups.

Tables 1.7 and 1.8 report the relationship between age and stock market participation rates, first for direct stockholding (Table 1.7) and then including also mutual funds (Table 1.8). Inclusion of mutual funds does not appear to have pronounced effects on the main message of these tables, except of course for changing the observed levels of participation.[4] The overall picture is clearly one of a hump-shaped profile of participation using either definition of stockholding, with the exception of the Netherlands where one observes an upward trend in participation as age increases.

Table 1.7 Stock market participation, by age

Age of household head	France	Germany	Italy	Netherlands	UK	US
21–25	0.07	0.14	0	0.08	0.14	0.08
26–30	0.10	0.17	0.04	0.03	0.20	0.13
31–35	0.15	0.19	0.10	0.06	0.24	0.15
36–40	0.14	0.18	0.09	0.07	0.25	0.20
41–45	0.16	0.18	0.08	0.13	0.29	0.18
46–50	0.15	0.19	0.07	0.14	0.34	0.22
51–55	0.22	0.20	0.11	0.19	0.36	0.25
56–60	0.19	0.22	0.10	0.18	0.33	0.25
61–65	0.15	0.18	0.07	0.16	0.33	0.21
66–70	0.17	0.16	0.06	0.20	0.29	0.25
72–75	0.16	0.11	0.05	0.18	0.25	0.19
76–80	0.10	0.09	0.03	0.23	0.20	0.16

Table 1.8 Total participation, by age

Age of household head	France	Italy	Netherlands	UK	US
21–25	0.10	0.04	0.15	0.17	0.24
26–30	0.18	0.09	0.06	0.25	0.43
31–35	0.25	0.23	0.14	0.31	0.50
36–40	0.22	0.18	0.16	0.32	0.57
41–45	0.25	0.14	0.21	0.36	0.56
46–50	0.24	0.15	0.22	0.42	0.58
51–55	0.31	0.20	0.30	0.45	0.63
56–60	0.26	0.19	0.29	0.43	0.58
61–65	0.22	0.14	0.30	0.43	0.43
66–70	0.25	0.12	0.33	0.38	0.47
72–75	0.24	0.10	0.26	0.32	0.34
76–80	0.18	0.06	0.37	0.24	0.29

The pattern of the Netherlands is consistent with theoretical models that assume a more-or-less constant probability of receiving information regarding how to invest in stocks throughout life and thus imply an increased probability that the household will come across such information as it ages. Hump-shaped participation rates that are observed in the rest of the countries are more challenging to explain. They tend to be consistent with an important role for fixed costs of stock market participation in determining whether a household will undertake stockholding or not. In the face of such a fixed cost, which can be a composite of objective participation costs and perceived costs, households that would undertake limited stockholding might not find it worthwhile to pay the cost and enter the stock market. Young households tend to fall in this category because of their limited resources and difficulties in obtaining loans. Elderly households can also fall in this category, mainly because their lack of a prospective labour income stream with some guaranteed minimum value makes it optimal for them to hold limited amounts in the risky asset.

Whether an upward sloping age-participation profile is observed (as in the Netherlands) or a hump-shaped profile with a peak in the later years of working life, aging of populations in European countries implies that the majority of European stockholders tend to be at the later stages of their working lifetime. This suggests in turn that they tend to have more stable jobs, lower unemployment risks, and a larger buffer of other assets than what would have been implied by a younger group of stockholders. Indeed, this conclusion is consistent with the figures we reported when we examined income and wealth distributions. Since education is also positively correlated with participation in stockholding, it appears that European stockholders should have both the sophistication and the resources to withstand moderate swings in stock markets.

In interpreting the age-profiles reported in Tables 1.7 and 1.8, one should keep in mind that with pure cross-sectional data it is not possible to distinguish a pure age-profile from cohort effects. That is, it might well be that older households invest less in stocks because they belong to a different generation, not because of a genuine age effect. Repeated cross-sectional data can be used to purge the cross-sectional age-profile from cohort effects.

Several of the country reports use repeated cross-sectional data to explore if cohort effects contaminate the cross-sectional profile. Given the collinearity between age, time and cohort, with repeated cross-sectional data we can identify only two of these effects. In principle, there are two plausible identifying assumptions. One is to explain the raw data in terms of cohort and age effects. This decomposition disregards time effects, or assumes that they reflect idiosyncratic macro shocks that sum to zero and are orthogonal to a time trend. The other is to interpret the data as a combination of age and unrestricted time effects. We experimented with both to see which provides a more plausible description of the data and found that the interpretation in terms of age and unrestricted time effects is far more plausible.

1.6 How do portfolio shares of stocks differ across demographic groups?

Up to now we have presented findings regarding the decision of households as to whether they ought to hold any stocks or not. In what follows, we focus on those households that have decided to undertake stockholding, and we examine the proportion of their financial assets that they hold in the form of stocks.[5] Technically, we focus on portfolio shares of stocks, conditional on participation in stockholding, and we examine how these differ across demographic groups defined in terms of education, financial wealth, and age. For each household, we compute two conditional portfolio shares: one that includes only direct holdings of stocks, and another that includes both direct stock holdings and investments in mutual funds.[6]

The first panel in Table 1.9 presents asset shares of stocks, both narrowly and broadly defined, for various countries. If we focus on the asset share of stocks that are directly held, we observe that this does not differ markedly between the United States and European countries, though France and Italy do exhibit somewhat lower conditional portfolio shares

Table 1.9 Conditional asset share of stocks, asset share of mutual funds and total asset share invested in stocks: total sample, no college and college education

	France	Germany	Italy	Netherlands	US
Total sample					
Asset share of stocks	0.14	0.04	0.14	0.19	0.17
Asset share of mutual funds	0.14	—	0.32	0.15	0.17
Total share	0.28	—	0.46	0.35	0.52
No college education					
Asset share of stocks	0.13	0.03	0.13	0.19	0.19
Asset share of mutual funds	0.14	—	0.32	0.16	0.18
Total share	0.28	—	0.46	0.35	0.48
College education					
Asset share of stocks	0.15	0.07	0.15	0.19	0.16
Asset share of mutual funds	0.12	—	0.31	0.15	0.17
Total share	0.28	—	0.46	0.35	0.56

than the rest. In other words, households that do invest in the stock market directly tend to invest in stocks similar proportions of their assets, despite the substantial differences in stock market participation noted above.

Differences are much greater, however, when we also allow for investments in mutual funds. There is a large difference between the total portfolio share of stocks in the United States and in European countries.[7] This occurs, despite the virtual lack of difference in the portfolio share devoted to direct holdings of stock and, strikingly, despite the fact that reported mutual fund holdings in European countries overstate actual stock holdings through mutual funds (see previous footnote). Based on this, there may be considerable scope for European mutual funds to boost investments by their current customers, even before they attempt to expand their customer base.

Among the European countries considered, the highest conditional portfolio share of stocks and mutual funds is observed in Italy, a country in which direct and overall stock market participation is rather limited. This is not unreasonable in a country with limited tradition in direct stockholding. Households take advantage of the expertise of mutual fund managers in selecting portfolios and opt for this easier way to diversify their portfolios than attempting to do so via direct holdings of a large number of appropriately selected stocks. The apparent success of Italian mutual funds in attracting large investments of investors that have chosen to participate in them should be encouraging for European fund managers more generally. Large investments in mutual funds are not to be expected only in countries with high overall participation rates such as the United States, but also in those with limited tradition of stockholding.

As we shall see, explaining the conditional asset share with demographic variables, income and wealth, is much more difficult than predicting participation.

1.6.1 Conditional asset shares across education groups

The second and third panels of Table 1.9 repeat the same conditional portfolio shares for two sub-samples: one includes only households whose heads have no college degree and the other is comprised of those whose heads are college graduates. Splitting the sample by education reveals relatively small differences across education groups. For instance, in France, the conditional total asset share is close to 30 per cent for both education categories. In Italy the share is only slightly higher for investors with college education. In the United States, the overall share of assets invested in stocks is close to 50 per cent, regardless of the educational attainment of the head. These patterns should be contrasted with the dramatic differences in stock market participation highlighted in Table 1.2.

1.6.2 Conditional asset shares across the income distribution

Table 1.10 reports average conditional asset shares in directly held stocks for each decile of the income distribution of the household. In France and Italy, the share invested in stocks is flat, while in Germany it is slightly increasing across deciles. In the Netherlands the share exhibits considerable variability, while in the United States it is decreasing.

Table 1.11 repeats the analysis for the average conditional share of assets invested directly or indirectly in stocks. We see again constancy of the share in Italy and France, and a variable profile in the Netherlands. Contrary to the profile of the asset share invested in stocks, the total profile is slightly increasing in the United States. In short, the income profile of the conditional asset share does not exhibit a clear tendency to vary across the income distribution.

1.6.3 Conditional asset shares across the distribution of financial wealth

Table 1.12 reports average conditional asset shares in directly held stocks for each decile of the financial wealth distribution. There is again

Table 1.10 Conditional asset share of stocks, by income decile

Income decile	France	Italy	Netherlands	US
I	0.18	0.19	0.15	0.33
II	0.14	0.17	0.10	0.30
III	0.15	0.14	0.34	0.21
IV	0.15	0.09	0.27	0.17
V	0.12	0.12	0.15	0.22
VI	0.13	0.10	0.16	0.17
VII	0.12	0.13	0.18	0.16
VIII	0.14	0.09	0.09	0.12
IX	0.13	0.14	0.20	0.14
X	0.15	0.17	0.24	0.20

Table 1.11 Total asset share, by income decile

Income decile	France	Italy	Netherlands	US
I	0.33	0.62	0.31	0.51
II	0.28	0.43	0.26	0.53
III	0.30	0.48	0.55	0.48
IV	0.27	0.47	0.46	0.39
V	0.30	0.42	0.32	0.53
VI	0.27	0.45	0.30	0.45
VII	0.27	0.46	0.36	0.46
VIII	0.25	0.44	0.26	0.51
IX	0.27	0.44	0.36	0.55
X	0.28	0.47	0.35	0.60

Table 1.12 Conditional asset share of stocks, by financial wealth decile

Financial wealth decile	France	Italy	Netherlands	US
I	0.06	0.00	0.00	0.00
II	0.30	0.20	0.44	0.44
III	0.17	0.10	0.26	0.34
IV	0.18	0.15	0.24	0.18
V	0.12	0.24	0.08	0.19
VI	0.14	0.17	0.13	0.17
VII	0.12	0.16	0.17	0.16
VIII	0.10	0.12	0.15	0.14
IX	0.10	0.15	0.12	0.17
X	0.16	0.12	0.28	0.19

considerable heterogeneity in the observed patterns. In Germany, there appears to be a mildly positive relationship between financial wealth and conditional asset shares, whereas in the Netherlands we observe a marked negative relationship for a wide range of financial wealth. In France, the negative relationship is less marked, while no clear pattern emerges for Italy and for the United States.

Modern portfolio theory predicts an inverse relationship between the portfolio share of stocks and current cash on hand that consists of current financial assets and current labour income (Haliassos, Chapter 2). It is, thus, consistent with the negatively sloped relationship at low levels of financial wealth that is observed in all countries except for Germany.

The intuition behind this theoretical prediction is that, at low levels of resources, most of future consumption is financed through labour income rather than through portfolio holdings. Moreover, even high portfolio shares of stock represent small amounts of stocks. For both reasons, households of limited resources should be willing to invest a larger proportion of their financial assets in stocks.

Two further considerations may intensify this tendency. First, low-wealth households have more of a reason to rely on the wealth-generating potential of the equity premium, namely the higher expected return offered by stocks compared to relatively riskless assets. Second, if low-wealth households are concerned at all about holding reasonably diversified portfolios, indivisibilities in stocks (i.e. the fact that they cannot buy fractions of each stock) may induce them to invest larger amounts in directly held stocks than in the absence of a diversification objective.

With the exception of Italy, all countries display a visible increase in the conditional portfolio share of directly held stocks as we move to the top decile of the wealth distribution. Carroll (2002) has recently noted a tendency of the very rich to hold financial portfolios that are considerably riskier than the rest of the population. This is all the more surprising, because the very rich typically combine highly undiversified holdings of risky enterprises and investment real estate with these risky financial portfolios.

There is some econometric evidence that increases in wealth make households more tolerant towards asset risk. The theoretical literature has also proposed models that attempt to account for such wealth effects on risk aversion.[8] It is still premature, however, to pronounce judgment on what is the major driving force behind the peculiar composition of the portfolios of the very rich.

Leaving the two tails of the financial asset distribution aside, one notices in Table 1.12 that there is no clear relationship between financial

Table 1.13 Total asset share of stocks, by financial wealth decile

Financial wealth decile	France	Italy	Netherlands	US
I	0.43	0.00	0.00	0.00
II	0.53	0.40	0.59	0.44
III	0.38	0.38	0.33	0.43
IV	0.31	0.48	0.33	0.48
V	0.28	0.45	0.31	0.48
VI	0.30	0.51	0.35	0.53
VII	0.27	0.47	0.34	0.47
VIII	0.24	0.42	0.35	0.49
IX	0.22	0.42	0.30	0.57
X	0.29	0.49	0.40	0.54

assets and the asset share of directly held stocks for the middle segment of the distribution of financial assets. In contrast to our findings regarding stock market participation, conditional asset shares do not seem to vary in any systematic way across middle-class households in different deciles of the financial asset distribution. It, thus, appears that changes in financial wealth tend to induce households to reconsider their choice of whether to participate directly in the stock market or not, but not to alter their asset share of stocks if they do hold stocks.

These conclusions remain in force when we include in stockholding not only direct holdings of stocks but also investments in mutual funds. Table 1.13 shows the asset share of direct holdings of stocks plus mutual fund holdings in the four countries for which such data exist. Besides the increase in reported portfolio shares, perhaps the only change worth noting is that inclusion of mutual funds appears to induce a mildly positive relationship between financial wealth and conditional asset shares in the case of the United States.

1.6.4 Conditional asset shares across age groups

Table 1.14 reports mean conditional asset shares of directly held stocks for various age groups. With the possible exception of the United States, it is hard to discern any relationship between asset shares and age. In the case of the United States, there appears to be a weak positive relationship. These findings are at odds not only with standard economic theory, but also with the practical advice given to stockholders by financial advisors. Both theory and advisors suggest that conditional portfolio shares invested in stocks should be falling as the household ages.

Table 1.14 Conditional asset share of stocks, by age

Age of household head	France	Germany	Italy	Netherlands	US
21–25	0.15	0.06	0.00	0.10	0.19
26–30	0.11	0.05	0.11	0.25	0.16
31–35	0.14	0.05	0.11	0.12	0.12
36–40	0.13	0.04	0.14	0.17	0.19
41–45	0.16	0.03	0.13	0.13	0.14
46–50	0.12	0.04	0.14	0.17	0.15
51–55	0.13	0.03	0.13	0.15	0.14
56–60	0.14	0.04	0.18	0.23	0.19
61–65	0.15	0.04	0.13	0.21	0.27
66–70	0.14	0.04	0.13	0.22	0.16
72–75	0.14	0.03	0.13	0.21	0.22
76–80	0.13	0.03	0.17	0.34	0.24

Perhaps the key consideration behind this suggestion is that households become progressively less able to handle stockholding risk as they age. There are various reasons for this. The number of working years ahead of them diminishes (or is already zero). Thus, households' access to some minimum guaranteed level of labour income is reduced (or lost altogether). For younger households, this minimum guaranteed income acts as a surrogate safe asset, offering at least some guaranteed payment in each period. As households age, they need to replace this surrogate safe asset with actual holdings of safe assets in their portfolios. Moreover, older households may find it more difficult to borrow or to work more hours than their younger counterparts when faced with stock market downturns.

Whatever the intuition behind the models or the advice, it does not appear however, to be consistent with the observed failure of households to adjust their portfolio shares as they age, let alone with the apparent (weak) tendency of US households to increase them. When contrasted with the hump-shaped relationship between age and participation rates, this finding leads to the conclusion that age may induce households to consider investing in stocks or not, but that households are not preoccupied with recalculating optimal portfolio shares and rebalancing their portfolios. In some sense, this is not too surprising, since it imposes much heavier computational requirements on households with limited time and perhaps knowledge of how to make these calculations.

Interestingly, no clearer picture emerges when we add mutual fund investments to those held directly in stocks in Table 1.15. Perhaps the

Table 1.15 Total asset share of stocks, by age

Age of household head	France	Italy	Netherlands	US
21–25	0.22	0.27	0.26	0.50
26–30	0.26	0.40	0.38	0.54
31–35	0.25	0.41	0.33	0.49
36–40	0.27	0.41	0.30	0.55
41–45	0.30	0.43	0.27	0.52
46–50	0.27	0.42	0.33	0.57
51–55	0.26	0.49	0.31	0.58
56–60	0.27	0.47	0.36	0.49
61–65	0.28	0.54	0.35	0.58
66–70	0.28	0.54	0.41	0.45
72–75	0.31	0.48	0.33	0.44
76–80	0.31	0.48	0.58	0.42

only improvement (in terms of correspondence with theory and financial advice) is that at least in two countries (Italy and the United States) there is a drop in the asset share at very old ages. However, this may well be due to our inability to distinguish between effects due to aging and effects due to the fact that households of different ages in a cross section belong to different population cohorts. It is quite possible that the oldest households in the sample never caught on to the existence and usefulness of mutual funds because these funds became known and popular when these cohorts were already past their prime years of economic activity. All in all, the picture that emerges suggests that households that do hold stocks do not engage in substantial rebalancing of their portfolios as they age.

1.7 Summary

The research reported in this book has revealed considerable growth in participation in European stock markets during the last decade and significant regularities in how households allocate their savings among different assets. One of the main findings is that, in all countries examined, stock market participation is strongly correlated with financial wealth. At the bottom of the wealth distribution very few households invest in stocks, either directly or through mutual funds and other managed investment accounts. We take this as firm evidence that entry costs, minimum investment requirements, and participation costs limit stock market participation severely.

We also observe that among the richest segment of the population (even in the top 10 per cent of the wealth distribution) many households do not invest in stocks. Can this feature be fully accounted for by entry and management costs? Or should one bring information costs explicitly into the picture?

Evidence on this issue is provided by the strong correlation between education and stock market participation. Better-educated households are more likely to hold stocks because they are better informed about the existence and properties of different assets, and are thus better able to take advantage of investment opportunities. Overall, research in this book suggests that entry costs and information costs still represent important barriers to entry to European stock markets, despite the spreading of an equity culture in the last decade. Lessons from this volume are therefore relevant not only to economists in understanding the effect of market instability, but also to the financial community interested in marketing financial products to targeted groups. Finally, the still incomplete process of privatization in most European countries together with the likely increase in the importance of private pensions funds as a response to the inevitable pension reforms, imply that in the future the still significant gap in stockownership will be partly filled in.

Turning to shares of stocks as a proportion of total financial assets of those who do hold stocks, we find a number of interesting results. Among those who do hold stocks, the average asset share devoted to stocks is quite similar in all the European countries considered and in the United States, despite differences in participation rates. Substantial differences are observed, however, when we also include investments in mutual funds. These show that United States households tend to invest much larger proportions of their financial assets than Europeans in this indirect form of stockholding, suggesting that there may be considerable scope for expansion along this intensive margin, together with prospects for expansion of the customer base.

Conditional asset shares invested in stocks drop at low levels of financial wealth but rise at high wealth levels. They tend to be relatively flat for the middle range of the financial wealth distribution, suggesting that changes in financial wealth do not induce substantial portfolio rebalancing across this middle range. Similarly, there seems to be no clear relationship between age and conditional asset shares.

All in all, our findings on participation in stockholding and on shares of stocks conditional on participation suggest that various demographic groups, defined according to education, age, and financial resources, exhibit important differences in stock market participation but much less important differences in conditional asset shares of stocks or differences that are much more difficult to explain with state-of-the-art analytical models. Still, comparison with the United States suggests that there is plenty of room for financial practitioners to expand both the number of stockholders and the shares of stocks in their financial portfolios.

References

Alessie, R. and S. Hochguertel (2002) 'Stockholding in the Netherlands', Chapter 7, this volume.

Arrondel, L. and A. Masson (2002) 'Stockholding in France', Chapter 4, this volume.

Banks, J. and M. Wakefield (2002) 'Stockholding in the United Kingdom', Chapter 8, this volume.

Bertaut, C. C. and M. S. McCluer (2002) 'Household portfolios in the United States', in L. Guiso, M. Haliassos and T. Jappelli (eds), *Household Portfolios*, Cambridge, MA: MIT Press.

Börsch-Supan, A. and L. Essig (2002) 'Stockholding in Germany', Chapter 5, this volume.

Carroll, C. (2002) 'Portfolios of the rich', in L. Guiso, M. Haliassos and T. Jappelli (eds), *Household Portfolios*, Cambridge, MA: MIT Press.

Guiso, L. and T. Jappelli (2002) 'Stockholding in Italy', Chapter 6, this volume.

Haliassos, M. (2002) 'Stockholding: recent lessons from theory and computations', Chapter 2, this volume.

Miniaci, R. and G. Weber (2002) 'Survey design and estimation of portfolio models', Chapter 3, this volume.

2

Stockholding: Recent Lessons from Theory and Computations*

Michael Haliassos

2.1 Introduction

This chapter presents recent developments in the theory of optimal portfolio design in a non-technical manner, provides the intuition behind these results, and uses them to interpret important findings in the empirical literature based on high-quality, household-level portfolio data. Where theoretical predictions are confirmed by empirical observation, theory provides a way to interpret empirical findings. Where the two disagree, the mechanisms stressed by theory serve as a first step towards identifying the full set of factors at work and the extent to which household behaviour can be modified to fit objectives better.

Household-level portfolio data show a tendency of the majority of households in each country to hold no stocks despite a historical expected-return premium on equity relative to riskless assets. The chapter first explains why such a tendency constitutes a puzzle in economic theory (the 'stockholding puzzle'). It discusses why popular notions regarding the source of non-participation (risk aversion, risky labour income, and borrowing constraints) are not confirmed by careful analysis of portfolio models and presents the state-of-the-art view on what

* I am grateful to Luigi Guiso for insightful comments on a previous draft, and to Carol Bertaut, Christis Hassapis, Tullio Jappelli, and Alexander Michaelides for discussions, over the recent years, that contributed to shaping the ideas presented here. I would like to give special thanks to the Observatoire de l'Epargne Européenne, Paris, France for financial support of this research project. I have benefited from interactions with OEE project participants in preparing this chapter. I also thank the HERMES Center on Computational Finance and Economics and the Leventis Foundation for supporting some of the original research reported in this paper.

causes non-participation. Based on this, it revisits the popular view on non-participation and shows how it can be qualified to be consistent with lessons from economic theory. It also explains how this view can be extended to account for exits from the stock market and for limited diversification.

Then, the chapter describes three unsolved empirical puzzles concerning the share of stocks in portfolios of households that do participate in the stock market. It points to the sources of theoretical results on optimal portfolio composition[1] and discusses briefly possible future directions for research that may help resolve the puzzles. Finally, the chapter draws lessons from theory that can be of use to practitioners in their efforts to expand the stockholder base.

Section 2.2 discusses the main factors that are likely to prevent households from participating in the stock market. Section 2.3 examines what might cause households that previously held stocks to exit the stock market, while Section 2.4 distinguishes stock market participation from portfolio diversification. Section 2.5 investigates whether households that do participate in the stock market choose an optimal portfolio share of stocks as the latter is implied by theory. Section 2.6 draws lessons from the theory of household portfolios that can be useful to practitioners.

2.2 The stock market participation puzzle

2.2.1 What is the participation puzzle and why do we care?

Despite substantial increases in stock market participation among households over the last decade, there is no country in the world where the majority of households hold stocks. This is true not only for European countries surveyed in the current project, but also for the United States where only 19 per cent of households hold stocks directly according to the 1998 *Survey of Consumer Finances*. It remains true even when we allow for indirect holdings of stock through mutual funds and defined-contribution pension funds: the participation rate for the United States then rises to just under 49 per cent. This happens in the face of substantial realized stock returns in the later part of the 1990s, and despite estimates of an expected-return premium on equity based on long historical time series (of the order of 4 to 6 percentage points in the United States). The puzzle can be stated simply: if one can expect to earn more by holding stocks than by holding essentially riskless financial assets (such as bank deposits), what is it that keeps the majority of households out of the stock market?

Resolving this puzzle is not simply a matter of intellectual curiosity, but can suggest important profit opportunities for financial institutions, practitioners, and even governments. If we understand what keeps people out of the stock market, we can expand the customer base by designing financial products that appeal to the average household. We can also market financial products more effectively by targeting appropriate segments of the population. Governments can ensure the maximum effectiveness of their efforts to float stock of newly privatized companies. Finally, we may be able to speculate about the likely reactions of households to recent reversals in stock market performance on both sides of the Atlantic: are the new stockholders likely to stay in the market or are they likely to abandon ship in bad weather?

2.2.2 The source of the participation puzzle

Most people are unlikely to perceive a serious stock market participation puzzle. The most common instinctive reaction to this puzzle is that households tend not to participate in the stock market because they do not like to assume substantial financial risk. This view is strengthened by two observations. First, households face background risk arising from uncertain labour income or unpredictable health expenditures that they are unable to insure against. Assuming stockholding risk on top of this probably seems excessive to most households. Second, households face borrowing limits and may not be able to borrow against future earnings. If they cannot borrow, why should they sacrifice their precious current resources on stockholding, especially when they are also unlikely to be able to borrow in the future in order to offset consumption effects of bad stock market outcomes? A clear lesson from economic theory, whether based on analytical or on computational methods, is that such instinctive answers are too simplistic. Let us see why.

A risk-averse household that maximizes expected utility will always want to invest some, albeit small, amount in stocks if stocks offer an expected-return premium over the riskless asset.[2] The intuition behind this result stems from the idea that a risk-averse household dislikes riskiness of its consumption stream. It will, therefore, evaluate all assets not only according to their expected returns but also according to the *contribution* each asset makes to the riskiness of the consumption stream. If a risky asset offers a higher expected return than a riskless asset, then it will be deemed superior to the riskless asset unless the household values its contribution to riskiness of consumption more than its contribution to the expected return on the portfolio.

Consider a household with riskless labour income and no stocks in its portfolio that contemplates adding a small amount of stocks versus adding an equal amount of the riskless asset. Since there is an expected-return premium on stocks, stocks are more attractive than the riskless asset in this respect. If the household is to be discouraged from undertaking stock investment, stocks must contribute to the riskiness of consumption. But since the household holds no stocks, stock returns are not correlated with the household's consumption and a marginal addition of stocks does not contribute to consumption riskiness. A marginal addition of stocks should be preferred to a marginal addition of the riskless asset by someone that holds no stocks. Of course, this holds for small additions of stocks starting from no stocks. Once households include stocks in their portfolios, their risk aversion will clearly influence the amount they do invest in stocks. Risk aversion is irrelevant for *whether* they hold stocks in this basic setup, not for *the portfolio share* of stocks among stockholders.

The argument holds even when labour income is risky or when the household faces other sources of background risk, as long as such risk is uncorrelated with stock returns.[3] It continues to hold even if the household is not allowed to be a net borrower (in the sense of having negative net wealth) in any period of life. This is because constraints on net wealth (the algebraic sum of assets and liabilities) treat each component of this sum symmetrically, and they fail to reverse the superiority of stocks to riskless assets for a household that has no holdings of stock.[4]

Thus, usual notions of risk aversion and standard types of risky labour income and borrowing constraints cannot induce an optimizing household to adopt a zero position in stocks in the face of a perceived expected-return premium over riskless assets (Haliassos and Bertaut, 1995). On the basis of the discussion so far, there seems to be no basis for the popular belief that non-participation in the stock market can be attributed to these reasons. But, later on, we will see how this popular belief can be modified to be consistent with our theoretical understanding of stockholding behaviour.

2.2.3 Could a different type of risk aversion account for non-participation?

Realization that the standard notion of aversion to financial risk embodied in expected-utility models of portfolio choice cannot account for non-participation in the stock market has encouraged attempts to consider alternative specifications of household preferences. Put simply, researchers have explored the idea that grandma may be right in attributing non-participation to risk aversion but we may have been too conservative in the way we model risk aversion.

In standard models, households are assumed to compute the utility of each possible consumption outcome and weight it by the probability of its occurrence. The optimal portfolio is then chosen so as to maximize expected utility of consumption. Note that this specification is flexible enough to allow for very low utility in bad states of the world. The investor may be quite miserable if his portfolio returns end up being very bad, but he is still assumed to weight the probability of such misery by its objective probability of occurrence.

What could happen if the investor weighted the probability of misery much more heavily than its objective probability of occurrence (with suitable modifications to the rest of the probability weights so that they sum to unity)? A first reaction may be to say that not much will happen. After all, what matters for a household is the weight assigned to each outcome *times* the utility arising from the outcome. Standard preferences allow us to consider cases where the investor experiences very low utility in bad outcomes, so the ability to manipulate the first term in the product, the weight, may not seem to add much to our ability to explain zero stockholding. Yet, such a reaction would be wrong. Powerful portfolio effects emerge when weights (and hence the household's objective function) depend on the *ranking* of outcomes that can be influenced by portfolio choices. Depending on the particular assumptions underlying the weighting scheme, this approach has been termed 'rank-dependent utility', 'dual theory of choice', and 'probability weighting'.[5]

Consider a simple example in which stock returns can either take a high or a low value, and this is the only source of uncertainty facing the household with zero stocks in its portfolio. The household contemplates investing a positive amount in stocks. If it does so, then the good outcome for the household is to experience a high stock return, and the bad is to experience a low stock return. Suppose that the household can also short stocks, that is, borrow an amount today by offering to deliver a certain number of stocks tomorrow. In this case, the household borrows at the risky stock return rate, and the good outcome is for stock returns to turn out low. This means that, starting from zero stockholding, a household with non-standard preferences will be using different weights to evaluate the utility resulting from positive investment in stocks than the weights it will be using to evaluate the results from short sales of stock. It thus becomes possible for the household to prefer zero stockholding to either positive holdings or short sales (Epstein and Zin, 1990).[6]

This novel type of aversion to risk, termed 'first-order risk aversion' seemed capable of generating and justifying zero stockholding. However, it turns out that labour income risk invalidates this possibility for resolving the stock market participation puzzle. As the simple example without background labour income risk illustrated, stockholding levels at which the household can be 'stuck' are those around which reversals in rankings of outcomes take place. The crucial question is whether the objective function changes at zero stockholding, thus justifying non-participation in the stock market. When the labour income realization also matters for the ranking of outcomes, it can be shown that reversals in rankings do not in general occur at zero stockholding.[7] Recent computational research has indeed demonstrated that overweighting of the worst state cannot justify by itself non-participation in the stock market (Haliassos and Hassapis, 2001). Other weighting schemes that overweight the worst and the best states relative to their objective probabilities of occurrence have also been shown to result in predictions of positive stockholdings (Donkers, 2000).

Overall, rank-dependent utility can lower predicted stockholding considerably, but it cannot by itself account for non-participation in the stock market of households that do face uninsurable background risk (such as earnings risk). However, the tendency of such preferences to lower predicted stockholding can be useful when combined with a different fundamental explanation for zero stockholding, as will be discussed below.

2.2.4 How about correlation between labour incomes and stock returns?

We saw above that risky labour income does not justify zero stockholding when earnings shocks are uncorrelated to stock returns, because it does not induce correlation between stock returns and household consumption. Other households with risky labour income that tends to move in the opposite direction from stock returns can even reduce consumption risk by including stocks in their portfolios. However, households whose labour incomes tend to move in the same direction as stock returns lower their demand for stocks for this reason. Theory tells us that such households may well find it optimal to sell stocks short, that is, to borrow at the risky rate of return on stocks. For those who engage in short sales of stock, having low stock returns is the 'good' outcome and high stock returns the 'bad' outcome. If low (high) stock returns tend to occur when earnings are also low (high), short sales of stock can help mitigate some of the adverse consequences of low earnings. Still, short sales are far from implying abstention from the stock market. If anything, they require more stock market involvement by households and impose heavy informational requirements on them, since the process and the rules governing short sales tend to be quite involved.

Thus, positive correlation between earnings and stock returns cannot be used by itself as an explanation for zero stockholding. Theory and computational studies indicate, however, that we can obtain optimal portfolios with zero stockholding if the household faces sufficiently high positive correlation between labour income and stock returns *combined with* restrictions preventing households from engaging in short sales of stock (Heaton and Lucas, 2000a,b; Haliassos and Michaelides, 1999).

A theoretical possibility is not necessarily a valid explanation of an observed phenomenon. Despite the mathematical sophistication of portfolio models with positive correlation, the relevance of positive correlation and short-sales constraints as an explanation of the zero stockholding puzzle is ultimately an empirical matter. Survey data in many countries have established that households that do not participate in the stock market tend to have low-education, low-income, low-wealth, and are more risk averse than those that do participate. On a purely introspective level, it is hard to imagine that such households hold no stocks because they tried to sell stocks short and found out that they were unable to do so.

Luckily, there is more to rely on than mere introspection. The few existing empirical studies of the correlation between earnings shocks and stock returns at the household level find rather small, if any, positive correlation and more importantly a pattern of estimated correlations across household groups that is inconsistent with their relative tendencies to abstain from the stock market. Davis and Willen (2000) obtain correlation estimates ranging between .1 and .3 over most of the working life for college-educated males and around −.25 at all ages for male high school dropouts. Heaton and Lucas (2000b) estimate positive correlation of entrepreneurial risk with stock returns at levels around .2. Besides being fairly small, these numbers imply at best that zero stockholding should be predominant among college graduates or entrepreneurs who in fact tend to hold stocks, and that low-education households should actually hold stocks as a hedging instrument when in fact they tend not to do so. Thus, the theoretical possibility notwithstanding, it does not seem that positive correlation between earnings and stock returns can account for the observed pattern of zero stockholding across different population segments.

Further empirical support to the notion that earnings–return correlations are not central to stockholding behaviour is provided by Vissing-Jorgensen (2002). She uses income data from the PSID (1983–92), and three observations of portfolio choice from the 1984, 1989, and 1994 PSID wealth supplements. She applies a two-step procedure, first estimating relevant moments of the income processes and then using them as regressors to explain portfolio choice. She finds no evidence of an effect of the earnings–return correlation on portfolio composition.

2.2.5 Can borrowing constraints justify zero stockholding?

The third commonly invoked factor for stock market non-participation is the inability of some households to borrow as much as is warranted by their expected lifetime earnings and any accumulated wealth. Such borrowing constraints can arise from various types of imperfections in the credit market; they can take various forms (such as quantity constraints, wedges between borrowing and saving interest rates, down-payment ratios), and they have been extensively explored in the literature on saving.

Why would a constraint on *borrowing* preclude somebody from *investing* in stocks? The idea is that people with low current resources, especially the young among them, would like to borrow both in order to consume and to invest in stocks, in view of higher expected future earnings and of the expected-return premium on equity. Restrictions on their ability to do so would force them to curtail both their consumption and their stock investment and might push them to a corner with zero stockholding.

It should already be clear that zero stockholding cannot arise from any arbitrary type of borrowing constraints faced by households. As mentioned above, a constraint that restricts overall financial net wealth to be non-negative does not induce zero stockholding. Since this constraint restricts the algebraic sum of assets and liabilities, it does not prevent positive stockholding financed entirely through borrowing in a way that leaves net financial wealth unaffected. More generally, a non-negativity constraint on net wealth allows stockholding as long as the size of debt outstanding is matched by the size of total asset holdings. More stringent borrowing constraints are needed if we are to justify zero stockholding.

What if the household is not allowed to borrow at all at the riskless rate, regardless of what it would do with the loan? Under this rather extreme type of borrowing constraint, young low-resource households that would have liked to short the riskless asset will end up holding none of it. Will they also end up holding no stocks? Not necessarily.

Computational studies (such as Heaton and Lucas, 1997, 2000a; and Haliassos and Michaelides, 1999, 2001) have found that young households that are particularly impatient (i.e. eager to boost their consumption by borrowing against their future earnings) may even seek to borrow by shorting stocks. Zero stockholding is not justified even by ruling out borrowing at the low riskless rate.

However, if there is an additional restriction preventing short sales of stock, then sufficiently impatient households will be eager to borrow at either the riskless or the risky rate and, prevented from doing so, they will end up with zero holdings of both assets.[8] Although it is the combination of these two severe borrowing restrictions that produces zero stockholding, the second assumption of no short sales of stock is not inconsistent with the first. Young households that are denied credit even at the riskless rate are unlikely to be allowed to engage in short sales at the stock exchange. The possibility seems both theoretically valid and intuitively plausible.

Is it also empirically relevant in accounting for observed non-stockholders? The computational models themselves provide some guidance as to the characteristics of optimizing households that could run into both short sales constraints and thus exhibit zero stockholding. Contributing factors are young age, low current cash on hand,[9] and considerable impatience that induces households to want to borrow at either rate. The findings of Cocco *et al.* (1999) and Haliassos and Michaelides (2001) imply that a crucial factor behind the influence of age on portfolios is the large ratio of human wealth (the present value of expected future earnings) to accumulated financial wealth typically observed when households are young.[10]

It should be stressed that this borrowing-constraint explanation of zero stockholding applies at best only to households that hold no assets at all, risky or riskless. Thus, it cannot explain the behaviour of households who choose to put all their savings in bank accounts and other riskless assets. Nor does it apply to households with large amounts of cash on hand because of high current incomes (or asset holdings), as these are predicted to invest positive amounts in stocks. This makes it virtually impossible to apply this explanation to savers, and especially the wealthier or middle- to high-income non-stockholders in household-level data. Moreover, the relevance of binding borrowing constraints tends to diminish as households age and climb the upward-sloping age-earnings profile. Binding borrowing constraints are far from being a universal explanation of the widespread non-participation in the stock market observed to different extents across age, income, and wealth groups.

2.2.6 Fixed entry and participation costs: Could grandma still have a point?

Economic theory serves to sharpen our understanding of economic phenomena but has seldom proved popular beliefs and intuition to be totally unfounded. While economic theory challenges the popular notion that risk aversion, uncertain earnings, and borrowing limitations are *sufficient* to account for zero stockholding in the face of an equity-return premium, it does not imply that these factors are irrelevant to stock market non-participation. Indeed, the prevailing current view in the theory of stock market participation seems to be that all these factors *contribute* to non-participation in the face of another, more fundamental factor.

This fundamental factor is fixed costs of entry or participation in the stock market, broadly interpreted. Households are assumed to decide whether to pay the cost of obtaining access to stocks or not based on a comparison of well being (expected lifetime utilities) under both options. One option is to gain access to stocks but to have to pay the costs, while the other saves the costs but gives access only to riskless assets (Haliassos and Bertaut, 1995; Haliassos and Michaelides, 1999; Polkovnichenko, 2000).

Some entry or participation costs are tangible and observable, while others are much more difficult to quantify. Households usually have to pay a certain fee to engage the services of brokers or to participate in a mutual fund. In addition, they need to spend some time selecting advisors and investment programmes, picking winners, and generally keeping up with developments in the stock market. We may be able to measure or at least approximate the value of a household's time spent on such activities, by considering the opportunity cost of this time. In practice, it will be quite difficult to have reliable estimates of the number of hours spent by the household on such activities, and this may contaminate estimates with sizeable measurement error.

Far more difficult to assess are household's *perceptions* as to how much it would cost to get involved in stockholding activities, monitor financial advisors or fund operators, and keep abreast of stock market developments. Yet, it is household perceptions that ultimately determine whether the household will enter the stock market, and exaggerated perceptions can generate inertia despite their inaccuracy.[11]

Thus, it seems almost impossible to infer the perceived entry/participation cost for each household. However, it is possible to compute the minimum level of entry cost that would keep a household of given characteristics out of the stock market (Haliassos and Michaelides, 1999;

Polkovnichenko, 2000; Paiella, 2000; Vissing-Jorgensen, 2002). The conclusion from existing computational and econometric work on this issue is that such threshold entry costs tend to be fairly small.

The main intuition for why small costs deter marginal investors from entry in the stock market is that, if these potential investors entered, they would invest very little in stocks anyway. If the planned stock investment is limited, then benefits from entry are relatively small, and small entry costs can discourage stock market participation. Although it is not possible to compare the computed costs to the objective costs of entry for each household, the low levels of such required costs for various household characteristics suggest that an entry cost explanation of the participation puzzle could apply to a wide range of households.

A bridge between popular beliefs about stock market non-participation and modern research on entry costs should now be apparent. Although risk aversion, earnings risk, and borrowing constraints are incapable of explaining widespread zero stockholding alone, they all serve to reduce the amount of stockholding that a household would undertake if it had access to the stock market. In so doing, they also serve to reduce the threshold entry costs sufficient to keep households out of the stock market. Thus, for any objective level of entry costs, households that are more risk averse, or disproportionately concerned about bad outcomes, or face considerable background earnings risk, or severe borrowing and short sales constraints are more likely to stay out of the stock market. Rather than being protagonists, as commonly thought, these factors are regarded by modern economic theory as supporting actors in a show produced by stock market entry and participation costs.

2.3 Accounting for stock market exits

Up to now, I have referred to 'entry' and 'participation' costs almost interchangeably. One is forced to draw a distinction between these two concepts when looking more closely at the evolution of stock market participation patterns of households over time. This exercise requires panel household-level data on portfolios that are less readily available than cross-sectional data. Although most of the observed transitions in stockholder status are from being a non-stockholder to being a stockholder, opposite transitions are also observed in panel data (Bertaut, 1998).

Transitions out of the stock market make it difficult to sustain the view that there are no costs associated with continued stock market participation. Entry fees are sunk costs for those who have participated in the stock market: once paid, they allow access to the stock market forever. If we try to explain the choice of some households not to hold stocks in subsequent periods without reference to any participation costs, we are pushed back almost to the same position as before, namely trying to justify zero stockholding in the absence of fixed costs. In fact, the task is even more formidable, since we now have to justify zero stockholding among households that tend to be older, more educated, and richer than those without previous stock market experience.

It is, of course, still possible to justify temporary absences from the stock market even without participation costs. Occasional bad spells of cash on hand may well force some households into a situation of zero asset holding where both short sales constraints are binding (as discussed above). How often households will be pushed to such corners depends on various household characteristics, but mainly on how wealthy they are. In saving and portfolio models, the amount of accumulated wealth is heavily influenced by the degree of impatience characterizing the household (Deaton, 1991; Carroll, 1997). Impatient households, that is, those who discount future utility significantly relative to current utility, tend to accumulate fewer assets and to run into binding borrowing constraints more often.

Some preliminary idea of how often this happens in theory can be obtained from the findings of Haliassos and Michaelides (1999) who calibrate a portfolio model for a household assumed to have an infinite horizon.[12] Highly impatient infinite-horizon households[13] accumulate very little and are predicted to run into binding short sales constraints and zero stockholding 35 per cent of the time. More patient households[14] accumulate more assets and are predicted to have zero stockholding only 5 per cent of the time. There is substantial room both for econometric work to establish the frequency and duration of exits from the stock market for various demographic groups, and for computational models that handle the thorny problem of participation costs contingent on previous stock market experience.

2.4 Participation versus diversification

Households that participate in the stock market do not necessarily hold well-diversified portfolios. It has long been known that household portfolios do not tend to be well diversified (e.g. Blume *et al.*, 1974), and this has stood in direct contrast to the implications of complete portfolios in very standard models in Finance, such as the Capital Asset Pricing

Model (CAPM). Given the above discussion, it should not be difficult to see that entry and participation costs may prove useful for explaining limited diversification as well as limited participation.

Striking examples of limited diversification are the tendencies to hold stocks in the employer firm, in domestic rather than foreign companies, and in newly privatized but not in other companies. Holding stocks in one's employer's firm may be good from the employer's perspective but induces unnecessary positive correlation between labour income and portfolio return. Holding of such stocks, however, is significantly facilitated by the employer who provides them to employees directly, reducing entry costs both in absolute terms and relative to other stocks in the market.

'Home-equity bias' is the tendency of stockholders of a given country to devote most if not all of their stock portfolios to domestic stocks. This tendency has been found difficult to explain with reference to the mean-variance properties of foreign stock returns compared to those of domestic stocks even after adjusting for exchange rate risk, as well as to border restrictions (French and Poterba, 1991; Lewis, 1999). The phenomenon would be much easier to explain if there is an additional fixed cost of entering foreign stock markets, creating a second hurdle for potential stockholders to overcome. This additional cost could arise from more limited familiarity of households with foreign companies relative to those operating at home, higher costs of monitoring foreign companies from abroad, and lack of understanding of foreign policies and institutions. The computational apparatus for a model of a household investing domestically can be adapted to handle this case (Michaelides, 2000).

The case of UK stockholders in privatized utilities who did not spread their investments to other companies is also consistent with an entry-cost explanation. The new stockholders bought public utility stock only after an extensive advertising campaign. There was no similar campaign with regard to other types of stocks, and investors may have been reluctant to acquire them because of lack of familiarity with their properties.

All three examples suggest that, in addition to general stock market entry costs, there may well be significant informational barriers across firms of different types and ownership that discourage portfolio diversification. The required size and empirical relevance of such costs are yet to be determined.

2.5 Portfolio composition puzzles

Portfolio composition puzzles refer to empirical findings based on household portfolio data that cannot be reconciled with existing theoretical models of portfolio behaviour. In principle, such differences can be due either to poor data or to poor theory (or both). In the present context, the quality and detail of available household-level data are such that the ball seems to be in the court of theory. We will see that in some cases theory fails to explain the data because it does not fully capture the economic forces at work. In other cases, theory seems to be pointing in directions that accord with intuition and advice typically given by professionals, but households fail to behave in ways that seem optimal. The former pose a challenge to theory to find the missing mechanisms at work, while the latter probably call for better education of households as to what serves their objectives in the best possible way.

2.5.1 Three portfolio composition puzzles

Comparison of data with existing theoretical models of household portfolios has identified three main puzzles regarding portfolio composition.[15] The first is the 'portfolio specialization puzzle'. Theoretical models imply that it is optimal for small savers and for younger savers to specialize their financial asset holdings completely in the asset that offers an expected-return premium, namely stocks. Only as they get richer and older should they incorporate riskless assets in their portfolios. Indeed, theoretical models suggest that young and small savers should utilize borrowing opportunities to increase not only current consumption but also stockholding above what it would be in the absence of such borrowing opportunities. Yet, household-level data clearly show that small savers and young savers do not confine their financial asset holdings to stocks and, if they do specialize, they tend to hold all their financial wealth in relatively riskless assets.

The second puzzle has to do with how portfolio composition changes as the financial resources of the household change. Household-level data tend to imply positive effects of both household income and financial wealth on the portfolio share of stocks. Yet, existing theoretical models predict exactly the opposite, namely that an improvement in the financial resources of the household should lead to a decrease of the portfolio share invested in stocks among those who do invest in stocks.

The third puzzle refers to the effect of age on portfolio composition. Theory predicts that, as households age, they should reduce the portfolio share of stocks and increase that of the riskless asset for any given level of resources. This is also consistent with the advice typically given to households by financial advisors. Yet, the data seem to suggest either no effect of age on portfolio composition or a slight increase in the portfolio share of stocks as a result of aging. Here the puzzle lies more on the side of justifying actual behaviour rather than of defending theoretical models, since the implications of theory seem to accord with popular intuition.

2.5.2 Why does theory imply portfolio specialization in stocks?

Understanding the forces responsible for the portfolio specialization result in theoretical models is important not only in its own right, but also because it yields insights as to the causes of the other two portfolio composition puzzles. The optimal portfolio share of risky assets turns out to depend crucially on the ratio of current assets to the present value of the stream of labour incomes ('human wealth'). This ratio is usually quite different in static (one-period) models of wealth allocation compared to dynamic intertemporal models of household consumption and portfolio choice.

When current assets are large relative to human wealth (as in static, one-period wealth-allocation models without future labour income), mixed portfolios are optimal. When current assets are limited relative to the size of human wealth, models tend to predict that portfolio specialization in stocks is optimal. Modern intertemporal models of household portfolio choice recognize that households face a stream of future labour incomes. Other things equal, the younger the household and the smaller its current cash on hand, the smaller is the ratio of current wealth to future labour incomes. Thus, the more likely it is that the intertemporal model will imply portfolio specialization in stocks.

What makes the ratio of current assets to human wealth relevant for the predicted portfolio bias towards stocks? The computational literature has uncovered two complementary elements of intuition regarding this bias.[16] The first is the subtle role of human wealth in providing a substitute for holdings of the riskless asset. Despite uncertainty about future earnings, there is always a minimum level below which earnings cannot fall in one's future working life. Possessing the ability to generate this minimum level of earnings is equivalent to holding a safe asset that yields an annual return equal to that same amount. The household can thus be viewed as having surrogate holdings of the safe asset, even when it does not hold any amounts of the regular safe asset. These surrogate holdings reduce the optimal amount of regular riskless asset holdings in the portfolio and create an (apparent) bias towards stocks.

The second point has to do with the ability of stocks to generate future wealth, set against their contribution to the riskiness of future consumption. In view of the equity premium, stockholders expect to earn more on their stock holdings than on an equal amount held in the riskless asset. Young households and those with low current cash on hand plan to finance most of future consumption through future labour income. Thus, by biasing their portfolios towards stocks, they expect to generate more wealth in the future without contributing significantly to the riskiness of future consumption.

Interestingly, short-sales constraints on the two types of assets (safe assets and risky stocks) do not eliminate the portfolio specialization puzzle. When they are binding, short-sales constraints imply zero holdings of both assets. However, the value of relaxing each constraint is not the same to the constrained household.[17] The constrained household would prefer to borrow at the riskless rate, rather than to undertake short sales of stock and face a borrowing rate that is both risky and higher in expected value than the riskless rate. As resources expand, the constrained household ceases to be willing to borrow at the risky rate at some threshold resource level, while it is still willing to borrow at the riskless rate. Thus, immediately past that threshold, its holdings of stocks become positive, while its riskless asset holdings remain constrained at zero.[18]

Portfolio specialization survives even when various assumptions of the model are relaxed. It is obvious that high risk aversion will not reverse the ranking of constraints. The same is true if the household is misinformed about the actual size of the equity premium (as long as it perceives a premium).

An important exception to this list regards households whose earnings tend to move closely together with stock returns. These usually have lower demand for stocks, because stockholding exacerbates their consumption risk (Heaton and Lucas, 1997). Indeed, when faced with short-sales constraints, they may be pushed to a corner with only safe assets. However, as discussed in Section 2.2.4, observed patterns of participation in stockholding among various demographic groups are difficult to reconcile with available empirical evidence on the nature of correlation between stock returns and earnings shocks.[19]

2.5.3 Why do financial resources affect optimal portfolio composition?

The second puzzle arises from the fact that household-level data imply positive effects of income and wealth on the portfolio share of stocks, while existing theoretical models predict that an increase in resources leads to a decrease in the portfolio share invested in stocks. The essence of this theoretical result follows from the discussion of the forces that cause the portfolio specialization puzzle. Starting from asset holding completely specialized in stocks over a range of cash on hand that can be quite substantial, there may be a subsequent range in which the household finds it optimal to include riskless assets in its portfolio and not to rely exclusively on stocks. Effectively, at that point, the ratio of current wealth to human wealth has become sufficiently large to induce an optimal portfolio share of stocks between zero and one.

Utilizing the insights in the previous section, this point occurs when the overall size of financial resources is such that the surrogate holdings of safe assets implied by the lower bounds on future earnings are no longer deemed sufficient in relation to the holdings of stocks. Moreover, at that point the household has accumulated sufficient current resources so as not to be lured by the wealth-generating power of stocks into holding a portfolio specialized in stocks.

2.5.4 Why does age affect optimal portfolio composition?

Theory predicts that, as households age, they should reduce the portfolio share of stocks and increase that of the riskless asset for any given level of resources. This result follows from the effect of aging on the ratio of current assets to human wealth. With aging, the household experiences a reduction in human wealth since the number of remaining working years diminishes. Thus, for a given level of cash on hand, aging generates an increase in the ratio of current cash on hand to human wealth. This creates an incentive to include safe assets in portfolios previously specialized in stocks, so as to replenish some of the surrogate safe assets that were lost because of the reduction in the number of remaining working years. Moreover, since current assets are larger relative to their human wealth, households feel less of a need to rely on the equity premium for generating future financial wealth.

It is not clear that financial advisors have precisely these mechanisms in mind when they recommend to aging households to move out of stocks and into safer assets. However, these factors can rationalize the concern of financial advisors with the reduced length of horizon facing older households.

2.5.5 Prospects for resolving the portfolio composition puzzles

Unlike the puzzle regarding stock market participation, our understanding of the portfolio composition puzzles is quite limited and not much theoretical progress has been made towards resolving them in the brief period since they were uncovered. Consequently, the discussion regarding portfolio composition puzzles can only be tentative and preliminary.

There is some empirical evidence pointing to the conclusion that households pay much more attention to the participation decision than to the choice of portfolio composition. In other words, households appear to care more about investing in the right assets than about choosing an optimal mix of assets, let alone about continually rebalancing their portfolios. The evidence comes in two pieces. First, there is survey evidence, for example, in the United States Survey of Consumer Finances, that households do not rebalance their portfolios often, in particular their stockholdings. Responses in the Survey suggest that most households buy stocks and then refrain from trading stocks for long periods of time.

The second piece of evidence refers to the extent to which households optimize their asset selection and portfolio composition in view of the tax code and changes therein. In this context, James Poterba (2001) observes that households appear more concerned about which assets to hold than about the optimal portfolio mix dictated by the tax system. In some sense, this is even stronger evidence of inertia. Not rebalancing the stock portfolio in response to stock market movements could perhaps be justified by reference to transactions costs that dwarf the return benefits of continual rebalancing and excessive churning. It is more difficult to justify the choice of suboptimal portfolio composition and portfolio inertia when households suffer tax consequences as a result.

The leading explanation for the stockholding participation puzzle is fixed costs of entry and participation in the stock market. Existing research on the minimum cost size that would be sufficient to deter entry assumes that households know about the range of available financial assets, form a perception of participation costs (that need not be objectively accurate), and compare costs to expected benefits of stock market participation. The main finding in this literature is that, if households do know about all available assets, then relatively small costs can deter entry. Recently, survey evidence has emerged (e.g. in the case of Italy) suggesting that a sizeable fraction of households are not even aware of the full range of assets available to them. These information barriers form a more fundamental block to stock market entry, since they prevent households from even contemplating stock investment.

Could fixed costs of entry and participation in the stock market be extended to account for puzzles regarding conditional portfolio shares? Clearly, ignorance of stocks alone cannot account for anything but a zero portfolio share of stocks. However, it is possible that a household has passively acquired stocks, through inheritance or through a company reward scheme, and does not know how to trade this asset or how to figure out its optimal portfolio share given the household's circumstances. In either case, observed portfolio shares of stocks are likely to differ from optimal shares predicted by theory and to be largely insensitive to changes in wealth, income, age, or some other demographics.[20] With detailed household-level data, it should be possible to devise empirical tests of the extent to which changes in portfolio shares are attributable to changes in market valuations of already acquired assets rather than conscious rebalancing on the part of households.

Ignorance and cost perceptions of households are not immutably fixed, but can be influenced by information provided through issuers of stock and financial practitioners. Newly privatized companies or companies that want to widen their stockholder base have clear incentives to disseminate information to potential stockholders. So do mutual fund companies that want to advertise the range of funds they run. Whether such supply-side provision of information will be effective in reducing ignorance and perceived costs of participation and of portfolio rebalancing will crucially depend not only on the amount of disseminated information but also on whether households trust this information. In view of the incentives of firms and of mutual fund companies to oversell their stocks or stock funds, some government supervision may be necessary to ensure factual accuracy and to promote trust on the part of households.

2.6 Some conclusions for practitioners

Perhaps the clearest message from household portfolio theory is that fixed costs faced by potential or actual investors represent the key factor in stock market participation or non-participation of households. Such costs are created not only by the fees charged by brokers and mutual funds for entry and for continuing participation, but also by inertia and ignorance about all or different stockholding opportunities. Inertia and ignorance can normally be overcome through financial education programmes. Such programmes, ranging from mass advertising to tailor-made training workshops, can be instrumental in alerting households to stockholding opportunities and expanding the customer base.

The recent experience in the United States and in the United Kingdom can yield some useful pointers in this context. The successful privatization experience in the United Kingdom suggests that persistent advertising can be quite helpful in encouraging household participation. So does the takeoff in mutual-fund participation in the United States in the 1990s, which took place only after about a decade of aggressive mass mailings and other advertising by US mutual funds. Bayer *et al.* (1996) studied the effects of financial education on getting employees to sign up for new types of retirement accounts in the United States. They found that employer-sponsored seminars, especially frequent ones, have been much more effective than all other ways of disseminating information. They were unable to detect any effects of written materials, such as newsletters and summary plan descriptions, regardless of frequency.

If entry and participation costs are important deterrents, mutual funds and other institutional investors should also strive to simplify investment procedures and maximize the degree of financial guidance, book-keeping and other services offered to their investors. This will induce households not only to participate in the first place, but also to stay with the fund even when the stock market goes through difficult times and choices become more confusing and riskier.

Advertising campaigns or simplified procedures can be significantly reinforced by word of mouth. There is some relevant ongoing research on the influence of a household's 'reference group' on portfolio behaviour (Gollier, 2001c). The idea advanced in this research is that consumption is not only valued on its own, but also in comparison to consumption in the household's reference group. Since portfolio returns are important in influencing consumption, this may induce households to imitate the portfolio behaviour of their peers. They will thus be more likely to invest significant amounts in stocks if other households in their reference group invest in the stock market and make gains. From the point of view of practitioners, targeting peer groups may be effective for promoting not only smoking and alcohol consumption but also other dangerous activities such as stockholding.

References

Arrow, K. (1974) *Essays in the Theory of Risk Bearing*, Amsterdam: North Holland.

Bayer, P. J., B. D. Bernheim and K. J. Scholz (1996) 'The effects of financial education in the workplace: evidence from a survey of employers', NBER Working Paper 5655.

Bertaut, C. C. (1998) 'Stockholding behaviour of US households: evidence from the 1983–1989 survey of consumer finances', *Review of Economics and Statistics*, **80**: 263–75.

Blume, M. E., J. Crockett and I. Friend (1974) 'Stock ownership in the US: characteristics and trends', *Survey of Current Business*, **54**: 16–40.

Campbell, J. Y. and L. M. Viceira (2002) *Strategic Asset Allocation – Portfolio Choice for Long-Term Investors*, Oxford: Oxford University Press.

Carroll, C. D. (1997) 'Buffer stock saving and the life cycle/permanent income hypothesis', *Quarterly Journal of Economics*, CXII, 3–55.

Cocco, J., F. Gomes and P. Maenhout (1999) 'Consumption and portfolio choice over the life-cycle', Mimeo, Harvard University.

Cochrane, J. H. (1997) 'Where is the market going? Uncertain facts and novel theories', NBER Working Paper No. 6207.

Davis, S. J. and P. Willen (2000) 'Occupation-level income shocks and asset returns: their covariance and implications for portfolio choice', CRSP Working Paper No. 523.

Deaton, A. (1991) 'Saving and liquidity constraints', *Econometrica*, **59**: 1221–48.

Donkers, B. (2000) 'Loss aversion, probability weighting and the stock holding puzzle', mimeo.

Epstein, L. G. and S. E. Zin (1990) 'First-order risk aversion and the equity premium puzzle', *Journal of Monetary Economics*, **26**: 387–407.

French, K. and J. Poterba (1991) 'Investor diversification and international equity markets', *American Economic Review*, **81**: 222–6.

Gollier, C. (2001a) *The Economics of Risk and Time*, Cambridge, MA: MIT Press.

Gollier, C. (2001b) 'What does theory have to say about household portfolios?', in Guiso, Haliassos and Jappelli (eds) *Household Portfolios*, Cambridge, MA: MIT Press.

Gollier, C. (2001c) 'Equilibrium portfolios with consumption externalities', mimeo, University of Toulouse.

Guiso, L., M. Haliassos and T. Jappelli (2001) *Household Portfolios*, Cambridge, MA: MIT Press.

Haliassos, M. and C. C. Bertaut (1995) 'Why do so few hold stocks?', *The Economic Journal*, **105**: 1110–29.

Haliassos, M. and C. Hassapis (2001) 'Non-expected utility, saving, and portfolios', *The Economic Journal*, **111**: 69–102.

Haliassos, M. and A. Michaelides (1999) 'Portfolio choice and liquidity constraints', forthcoming in *International Economic Review*.

Haliassos, M. and A. Michaelides (2001) 'Calibration and computation of household portfolio models', in Guiso, Haliassos and Jappelli (eds) *Household Portfolios*, Cambridge, MA: MIT Press.

Heaton, J. and D. Lucas (1997) 'Market frictions, savings behaviour, and portfolio choice', *Macroeconomic Dynamics*, **1**: 76–101.

Heaton, J. and D. Lucas (2000a) 'Portfolio choice in the presence of background risk', *The Economic Journal*, **110**: 1–26.

Heaton, J. and D. Lucas (2000b) 'Asset pricing and portfolio choice: the importance of entrepreneurial risk.' *Journal of Finance*, **55**: 1163–98.

Lewis, K. (1999) 'Trying to explain home bias in equities and consumption', *Journal of Economic Literature*, **38**: 571–608.

Michaelides, A. (2000) 'International portfolio choice and liquidity constraints: can small information costs explain the home-equity bias puzzle?', mimeo, University of Cyprus.

Paiella, M. (2000) 'Transaction costs and limited stock market participation to reconcile asset prices and consumption choices', mimeo.

Polkovnichenko, V. (2000) 'Heterogeneous labour income and preferences: implications for stock market participation', mimeo, University of Minnesota.

Poterba, J. (2001) 'Taxation and portfolio structure: issues and implications', in Guiso, Haliassos and Jappelli (eds) *Household Portfolios*, Cambridge, MA: MIT Press.
Quiggin, J. (1982) 'A theory of anticipated utility', *Journal of Economic Behaviour and Organization*, **3**: 323–43.
Vissing-Jorgensen, A. (2002) 'Towards an explanation of household portfolio choice heterogeneity: non-financial income and participation cost structures', NBER Working Paper No. 8884.
Yaari, M. (1987) 'The dual theory of choice under risk', *Econometrica*, **55**: 95–115.

3

Survey Design and Estimation of Portfolio Models

Raffaele Miniaci and Guglielmo Weber

3.1 Introduction

In this chapter, we explain why household survey data on wealth and portfolio choice should be of interest to the financial community. We argue that there are two major advantages in using household survey data. First, the investigator can distinguish between two potentially different decisions: the decision of whether to hold any stocks and the decision on how much to invest in this type of assets for given financial wealth. Second, the investigator is able to concentrate on demand for stocks by resident households, a well-defined and relatively homogenous group whose behaviour can be related to standard economic theory.

The analysis of household wealth data is interesting if financial markets are incomplete. Under incompleteness, the standard model of expected utility maximization implies that individual households' demand for stocks will vary not only as a function of their risk aversion, but also in response to uninsurable individual risks, such as labour income risk, longevity risk, and risk related to illiquid assets (such as housing).

We first consider various sources of information on household portfolio choice: aggregate flow of funds statistics, financial intermediaries customer data and survey data. We explain the reasons why household behaviour is best investigated using survey data, ideally random samples with an oversample of the wealthy.

We then discuss the techniques that are commonly used to elicit wealth information from respondents who may be unwilling to fully disclose their financial situation or unaware of the exact amounts involved. We also appraise some methods that are commonly employed to gross up the survey wealth data to the published flow of funds statistics.

We also review the contents of the five country surveys (France, Germany, Italy, the Netherlands and the United Kingdom) used in the project, and provide a brief overview of the estimation methods that are employed to study the determinants of the two separate decisions of whether to hold any stocks in the first place and in case of how much to invest in stocks.

The chapter is organized as follows. In Section 3.2 we discuss advantages and disadvantages of different data sources on household wealth. We focus on household survey data, and on the sampling issues and methods to elicit information, which are especially relevant when questions concern sensitive topics, such as wealth and portfolio decisions. In Section 3.3 we illustrate the main characteristics of the household surveys used in the country studies for the present volume. In Section 3.4 we turn to econometric issues and estimation techniques: cross-section techniques for discrete choice and for sample separation problems are illustrated.

3.2 Data sources on household portfolio composition

There are three main data sources available to the researcher to study household portfolio composition: the aggregate 'flows of funds' statistics, produced by central banks or national statistical bureaus; banks' and financial intermediaries' accounts, a by-product of their business activity; and household surveys, either specifically designed to collect data on household wealth and composition or at least with a questionnaire section devoted to the issue.

3.2.1 Flow of funds

Flow of funds statistics are typically collected by either the central bank or the statistical office and record all transactions carried out by one country's banks and financial intermediaries. The great attraction of this type of aggregate statistic is its direct link to national accounts and other economy-wide measures of economic activity (such as the stock exchange market valuation). By definition, they cover the whole domestic market: transactions made by residents and non-residents, households and business sector are all recorded if the bank or financial intermediary is located in the country. By construction, they are meant to capture transactions made by all individuals, throughout the wealth distribution (that is highly skewed), with the exception of direct financial foreign investment.

Flow of funds statistics thus provides a useful benchmark for the analysis. They are unlikely to be directly useful though, as aggregation results in major information loss, particularly when behaviour is so heterogeneous. It is also worth stressing that the benchmark may not be too useful if we are interested in resident households.

3.2.2 Banks and financial intermediaries accounts

Banks and financial intermediaries accounts are potentially rich sources of information on household behaviour, as they give the exact amount of assets held by the customers. They are often used for marketing purposes, for credit scoring and for personal portfolio advice. If the main aim of the researcher is to draw some inference on the behaviour of the whole population and not only on the sub-population of the current customers of a specific bank or financial intermediary, they have important drawbacks:

1. The sub-sample of customers is not representative of the whole population because of the endogenous nature of the sample selection: an individual is recorded in broker house administrative archives just because of his/her portfolio allocation (and intermediary choice). If information on the population at large is available from an external source, corrections for the choice-based sampling design are possible (see Cosslett, 1981, 1993, 1997 and Manski and Lerman, 1977).
2. For those households who split their overall asset positions among financial institutions, single financial institutions accounts provide partial coverage of their portfolios and are likely to produce misleading evidence on their behaviour. This issue might be particularly relevant for the wealthiest households, who are likely to hold assets through more than one institution.
3. Administrative records do not normally contain a great deal of information on economically interesting household characteristics such as family composition, occupation, labour or business income, real estate wealth, and debts. These are key determinants of household portfolio decisions even if the attention is limited to the sub-sample of the customers of a specific financial institution.

Ameriks and Zeldes (2000) give an interesting example of how this kind of data can be used: they use the information contained in the TIAA-CREEF archives to study how individuals (teachers) change the allocation of their pension fund over time. Further examples are found in the consumer credit literature (Gross and Souleles, 2000; Alessie *et al.*, 2001).

3.2.3 Household survey data

In many countries household surveys are specifically designed to collect information on households wealth and its composition. These data sources are preferable to the flow of funds statistics and the financial intermediaries accounts when the main aim is to investigate household behaviour. Questions can be asked on any topic and therefore survey data give a detailed picture of the demographic, income and wealth characteristics that are potentially relevant determinants of household portfolio allocation decision. Sampling schemes are usually such to give samples that are representative of all the population, but the wealthy are sometimes oversampled to capture the right tail of the wealth distribution. Information on all the assets (and debts) is collected independently of the financial intermediary used by the households. Though household survey data are potentially richer than the other data sources, some issues must be considered in order to evaluate the quality of these data and their representativeness.

3.2.4 Sample design

When household surveys are designed, the investigators have to choose among different available sampling schemes.

The choice of the sampling scheme is crucial in order to obtain a household sample which is by construction representative of all the reference population (at least ex-ante) with respect to some variables of interest. If, for instance, the major concern is to have a household sample that is representative of the whole population with respect to the geographical distribution of the households on the national territory and to the distribution of family size, then a two-stage sampling design can be adopted where at the first stage a sample of municipalities is drawn in each area of interest with probability proportional to their dimension, and then, conditional on the municipality drawn, households are drawn with probability proportional to their size. Similar sampling schemes are widely adopted for family expenditure surveys and labour force surveys. But for surveys whose main aim is to collect data on household wealth such a sampling design has a drawback: almost surely, the aggregate wealth measure obtained on the basis of such a survey is lower than the estimate from the flow of funds statistics. The reason for this difference is mainly due to the fact that most of the wealth is held by a few households, that is, the wealth distribution is heavily skewed. This explains why many wealth-specific household surveys oversample the wealthy: by doing so they try to get wealth estimates more consistent with those obtained by aggregate statistics, and they also tend to improve the coverage of all kinds of possible household portfolios. To oversample the wealthy it is necessary to have some external information in order to identify the groups of potentially rich from which to draw a sample. This information may be obtained by geo-marketing companies, tax-files, or financial intermediaries (see Juster *et al.*, 1999).

Measuring wealth is difficult not only because of its skewed distribution, but also because the very poor and the very rich tend to refuse to participate in the survey. This creates an endogenous sample selection problem whose solution is not obvious if no information is available on households refusing to respond.

Sometimes, the survey data is not collected in such a way as to produce a representative sample. This is the case with quota samples, for instance (see Foreman, 1991, for an introduction to sampling principles). In quota samples, new sampling units with similar characteristics replace non-cooperating respondents until their pre-determined quota has been filled. This cuts down on data collection costs but makes the resulting sample hard to use. If these characteristics are either endogenous to the problem (wealth) or omitted from the estimating equation, inference based on quota sample data will be seriously biased. A similar problem occurs if non-response is endogenous, but this affects representative samples, too.

A further issue is the choice of the respondent: once the household has been selected and it has accepted the interview, which member should be interviewed in order to get the highest quality information on household wealth? Should it be the 'head of household' (however defined), the 'financial officer' (the individual who usually takes-care of managing the household portfolio), or each single household component?

3.2.5 Eliciting wealth information

In survey data, the available measure of wealth and assets amount is often inaccurate. Asset and liability questions have a sensitive nature and a high degree of complexity. Survey respondents may refuse to answer direct questions on asset holdings because of their unwillingness to reveal overall wealth, or because they really do not know (an active investor might not know if he/she held a particular asset at the point in time to which the questionnaire refers).

Techniques to deal with sensitive data problems have been devised, such as randomized response, which may be used both for the intensive and extensive margins. The randomized response literature is summarized in Fox and Tracy (1986) and Chaudhuri and Mukerjee (1988). The basic idea is very simple: respondents may be more willing to answer truthfully to embarrassing questions if the interviewer does not know what question they have been asked. The respondent is therefore asked to reply to a randomized question (the sensitive question with probability p, and another specified question with probability $1-p$). As long as the population average of the other question is known, the population average of the sensitive question can be inferred. Extensions of this method to continuous variables exist and could be used for wealth.

In the case in hand, failure to answer the questions are more likely related to the objective difficulties involved in providing exact answers to questions on asset values. The respondent may simply not know the answer to the question, particularly if the answer requires adding several different accounts, placing a value on hard-to-measure assets like a business, evaluating the assets at prices of 5–6 months previous the interview time. In all of these cases, the respondent can either give his/her best estimate, or refuse to respond or say 'don't know'. If we are interested in estimates of wealth for individual households, other techniques have been devised that can cope with refusals and 'don't know' answers. Among the best-known techniques are the range card and unfolding brackets methods, widely employed in the US (particularly in the Health and Retirement Study). Juster and Smith (1997) discuss the relative merits of these techniques: with the former, respondents who cannot or will not provide exact answers to amount questions are shown a range card and asked to place themselves in one of the fixed brackets indicated there; with the latter, respondents are first asked if the amount is less or more than a given threshold, and then again, then another threshold higher or lower than the previous one, depending on their earlier reply. The unfolding brackets technique is deemed superior to the traditional request that respondents look for written financial records and can be used in telephone interviews, unlike the range card technique.

It is worth stressing that with unfolding brackets, respondents who do not know exact amounts are asked if the asset value exceeds a certain amount (normally a round number). If they answer 'yes', a similar question is asked for a larger amount, until the respondent replies in the negative. The sequence of 'yes', 'no' and 'don't know' produced by this list of questions is not invariant to the level of amounts proposed to the interviewed person (anchoring effect, see Hurd 1998 and Alvarez *et al.*, 1999). The resulting data points may suffer from non-standard measurement error, similar in nature to the coarse data problems that can be tackled as in Hejitan and Rubin (1990).

An interesting technique adopted in one of the surveys used in this project (the French Patrimoine 97) provides respondents with a choice among three alternatives: give the exact amount, provide a range for the amount, or select out of a range card given to them by the interviewer.

A different technique is employed in another survey (the Italian SHIW), whereby respondents are first given a range card and then have to state the exact amount within the chosen bracket or at least tell the interviewer whether the amount is closer to the upper or lower bound.

When exact or approximate amounts are not available, estimates for some financial assets can be obtained directly if investment income is known or indirectly, by imputation methods that exploit observable characteristics.

3.2.6 Grossing up survey measures of household wealth

Most representative sample surveys contain population weights, which can be used to gross up survey estimates to the underlying population. These weights are particularly useful when the survey design requires oversampling of population groups of particular interest (such as the wealthy, say). The weights normally scale down observations belonging to over represented groups, and vice versa, but do not correct for non-response.

When population weights are not provided, but information on the population at large is available from an external source, corrections for the special features of sampling design are possible (see Cosslett, 1981, 1993, 1997 and Manski and Lerman, 1977). This type of correction is implemented by Alessie (1999) with the Dutch data used in this project.

3.3 The data sets used in the OEE project

In the project we use survey data for five European countries: France, Germany, Italy, the Netherlands and the United Kingdom. The data sets have some common features but differ in a number of important aspects (see Table 3.1).

The French data are drawn from Patrimoine 97, a large paper and pencil interview (PAPI) survey, run by the central statistical office, which involves over 10 000 households (the response rate is 70 per cent). By design, Patrimoine 97 oversamples wealthy households and collects good quality information on many of the socio-economic variables of interest, both at household and individual level. A potential advantage in using this survey to analyse households portfolio choice is given by the presence of variables related to household credit access, the way households manage their portfolios, intergenerational transfers and a set of questions aimed at evaluating risk aversion. However, it does not contain any information on consumption and health status.

The German data are drawn from the 1998 income and expenditure survey (EVS), a very large quota sample, PAPI survey, run by the central

Table 3.1 Characteristics of the household surveys used in the project

Run by:	**France Patrimoine 97 INSEE**	**Germany EVS 98 FSO**	**Italy SHIW 98 Bank of Italy**	**Netherlands CSS 97 CentER**	**United Kingdom FRS 98 CSO**
Overall survey characteristics					
Data collection	CAPI	PAPI	CAPI	CAPAR	CAPI
Sample unit	Household	Household	Household	Household	Household
Sampling scheme	Stratified sample	Quota sampling	Two stage sampling (municipalities and households)	Four stage sampling (communities, banks of phone numbers, phone numbers, households)	Two stage sampling (post code areas and households)
Sample dimension	10 200	50 000	7 100	2 800	22 900
Response rate	70%	N.A.	43%	18%	66%
Panel component	None	None	~50% of the sample	100% of the sample	None
Repeated cross sections	Every 6 years	Every 5 years	Yes	Annual panel	Every year
Respondent (wealth questions)	Head	Head	Head	Head + Individuals	Head + Individuals
Public use files since	1986	1993	1977	1993	1993
Over sampling of the rich	Yes	No	No	Yes	No
Data quality					
Household income	Good	Excellent	Good	Fair	Excellent
Consumption	None	Good	Fair	Poor	None
Financial wealth	Good	Fair	Good	Good	Fair
Education	Good	Good	Good	Good	Good
Occupation	Good	Good	Good	Good	Fair
Subjective expectations	Good	None	Good	Good	None
Health	Fair	None	Poor	Good	None

Table 3.1 (cont.)

Run by:	France Patrimoine 97 INSEE	Germany EVS 98 FSO	Italy SHIW 98 Bank of Italy	Netherlands CSS 97 CentER	United Kingdom FRS 98 CSO
Methods to elicit wealth information					
Participation	Yes	Yes	Yes	Yes	Yes
Exact amount	Yes	Yes	Yes	Yes	Sub-sample
Self-reported range	Yes	Yes	No	No	No
Pre-assigned brackets	Yes	Yes	Yes	Yes	Yes
Investment income	Yes	Yes	Imputed	No	Yes
Wealth information					
Number of financial assets	27	6	17	44	19
Home	Value	Value	Value	Value	Value
Own business	Value	Value	Value	Value	Value
Other real wealth	Value	Value	Value	Value	Value
Pension wealth	None	None	Replacement rate	None directly	None
Mortgage	Value	Value	Value	Value	Value
Other debts	Value	Value	Value	Value	None

statistical office (Statistiche Bundesamt), involving over 50 000 households. The quota-sampling criterion is based on socio-demographic characteristics that correlate well with income. As explained above, quota samples differ from random (stratified) samples because new sampling units replace non-cooperating respondents with similar characteristics up to the point where their quota is filled. There is evidence that the resulting household income distribution for the EVS sample is too concentrated toward central income classes, which has consequences on ownership rates and on the overall coverage of wealth if compared to the flow-of-funds statistics. Being partially based on bookkeeping, household income data are of excellent quality; expenditure and socio-economic data are of good quality; while portfolio composition can be recovered only at a high level of aggregation. There is no information on health status of household members, or on their subjective expectations or risk attitudes.

The Italian data are drawn from the 1998 survey on household income and wealth (SHIW), a computer assisted personal interview (CAPI) survey run by the Bank of Italy, which involve some 7000 households, half of which have been participating in the same survey in earlier years. The response rate in 1998 was 43 per cent. The quality of data on individual characteristics and income is good, while information on consumption is collected using few recall questions. The financial wealth section of the questionnaire is fairly detailed and it is organized in such a way that respondents are first asked whether they know the existence of the various financial assets. SHIW contains subjective probability questions and it is one of the two surveys (the other is the Dutch CSS) with some information on pension wealth (expected replacement rate and years of contribution to the Social Security System). For the part of the sample that took part in 1995 (over a half) risk aversion can be evaluated.

The Dutch data are drawn from the CentER saving survey (CSS) panel, a computer assisted panel research (CAPAR) survey run by CentER (Tilburg University), involving some 2000 households who were interviewed online (every participating household had been equipped with a PC and modem, see Nyhus (1996)). The response rate is low (18 per cent) but sampling weights have been computed that correct for non-representativeness. CSS is targeted at the structure of individual and household wealth and saving behaviour. Therefore, unlike all the other surveys used in this project, CSS collects detailed information on individual portfolios. Potentially, this gives the most precise picture of household portfolios, but aggregating to household level or to broader asset categories might be a problem if some member of the household refuses to participate to the survey or does not respond to any specific question on some of the 44 asset and debt categories considered. An advantage of the CSS survey is that it includes an oversample of wealthy households, and it devotes particular attention to economic-psychological concepts and health status of the respondents.

The British data are drawn from the 1998 Family Resources Survey (FRS), a large CAPI survey run by the Central Statistical Office and involving some 23 000 households in Great Britain (response rate: 66 per cent). Its two-stage sampling scheme is aimed to improve the representativeness of the sample in terms of income distribution. Information on individual income is of excellent quality, but for most of the households the data on portfolio allocation is limited to ownership information for broad categories of assets and a banded variable on total amount of liquid financial assets. It is only for households who report holdings in the £1500–20 000 range that the exact amount for each asset is collected. For the others, an imputation procedure based on investment income data is the potential solution to the problem.

3.4 Econometric issues and estimation techniques

The econometric analysis of household wealth data is interesting if financial markets are incomplete. Under incompleteness, the dynamic decision of how much wealth to accumulate is related to portfolio choice and is affected by uninsurable individual risks, such as labour income risk, longevity risk, and risk related to illiquid assets (such as housing). The econometric problems that arise in this area are therefore largely common to the analysis of survey data in general. For instance, the household wealth accumulation process is likely to reflect age, time and cohort effects, and many of the key components of wealth probably suffer measurement error. Of particular interest, in this context, is the large number of zeros, which may be due to corner solutions or to other reasons.

The portfolio related questions that have been empirically addressed using household survey data can be broadly typified as follows:

1. How is financial wealth accumulated over the life cycle, and how does it relate to total net worth (including housing wealth, own business, human capital and pension wealth)? Of particular interest is the behaviour of the elderly, whose limited decumulation has been interpreted as evidence against the life-cycle hypothesis: non-trivial

corrections are needed for the effects of differential mortality by wealth before proper inference can be made.

2. How do households decide whether or not to invest in stocks? Here, the key open question is why so many households do not have direct or indirect holdings of stocks. This is known as the stockholding puzzle (Haliassos and Bertaut (1995)) and is the micro analogue of the equity premium puzzle.
3. How do households allocate their (financial or total) wealth across asset categories? Is the stock portfolio share chosen in a manner consistent with the participation decision?

Question 1 has been widely investigated in the empirical literature (see e.g. Poterba, 1994; Sheiner and Weil, 1992; Alessie *et al.*, 1995). Much of the analysis consists of plotting age profiles for some index (mean, median, upper quartile) of total net worth or financial wealth. These profiles can be drawn conditional upon observable characteristics, and in this case regression techniques are used (either OLS or LAD, depending on whether the moment under investigation is the conditional expectation or the conditional median. Quantile regression techniques are reviewed in Buchinsky (1998) and Horowitz (1993)). The most interesting problems in this area are the identification of cohort effects and the correction for non-random attrition (differential mortality by wealth).

As Shorrocks (1975) notes, a cross-sectional wealth–age profile will give a misleading picture of individual age profiles for at least two reasons. First, if earlier generations are lifetime poorer, their wealth holdings will be lower than the wealth holdings of later generations: This may produce false evidence for decumulation. Secondly, if there is differential mortality by wealth (wealthy individuals live longer), the average wealth of survivors may increase with time even if each surviving individual is decumulating. This may, therefore, produce false evidence against decumulation. The first problem can be resolved (in the absence of pure trend-like time effects, as discussed in Deaton and Paxson, 1994) by pooling cross sections over a long time period, and producing wealth–age profiles for year-of-birth cohorts (see Poterba and Samwick (1997) and Attanasio (1998), among others). The second is more complex, and its solution requires assumptions on the relation between mortality and wealth (see for instance Attanasio and Hoynes, 2000).

Question 2 has been addressed in a number of recent papers. For identification we require some theory on why the participation in financial markets for stocks is limited. Informational problems have been cited by King and Leape (1998); liquidity trading has been emphasized by Allen and Gale (1994); others have stressed the combined effect of transaction costs (Vissing-Jørgensen, 2002) and the existence of indivisible risky consumer durable goods, undiversifiable own-business risk, and so on. The very existence of a large number of households that do not invest in any risky assets suggests that econometric analysis must address the issue of data censoring. This is a standard problem in the analysis of labour supply and of consumer demand for a number of goods (tobacco, motor fuel, etc.). The household portfolio literature has so far mostly used parametric techniques such as logit (Haliassos and Bertaut, 1995) and tobit (Guiso *et al.*, 1996; see also Hochguertel *et al.*, 1997, for an application of the two-limit tobit estimator), or probit (King and Leape, 1998). However, censored quantile regressions could be fruitfully used to address this issue without reliance on strong distribution assumptions (Powell, 1984; Fitzenberger, 1997; Buchinsky, 1998).

Question 3 is likely to become one of the most intensely investigated, given the increased stock market participation over the last two decades in the US, UK and many European countries. It is closely related to question 2 if the analysis concentrates on very broad asset categories (risky versus low-risk financial assets, say); if several assets are considered it becomes more complex. A good, recent example where three financial assets are considered and the corresponding complete model of asset demands is estimated on a single cross section taking into account zero holdings is Perraudin and Sørensen (2000).

In what follows, we shall concentrate on the key issue of estimating stock market participation and on how non-random participation affects the equation for investment in stocks. As the only available data are from a single cross section, the participation decision must be assumed to be static. We shall describe methods that can then be applied to estimate both the participation equation and the continuous portfolio choice equation.

3.4.1 Discrete choice models

Assume our aim is to study if households own risky assets and that cross-sectional survey data set is available. We may or may not observe the value of the desired level (or share) of risky assets w_i^* for each household *i*, but we know whether households hold risky assets:

$$w_i = \begin{cases} 1 & \text{if } w_i^* > 0 \\ 0 & \text{if } w_i^* \leq 0 \end{cases}$$

if short sales are not permitted. We assume that the desired level of risky assets w_i^* depends on a set of observable socio-economic characteristics of the household (x_i – a $k \times 1$ vector) and on a set of unobservable characteristics represented by the scalar random variable ε_i

$$w_i^* = \beta' x_i + \varepsilon_i$$

where β is a set of unknown parameters that we want to estimate. Therefore:

$$w_i = \begin{cases} 1 & \text{if } \varepsilon_i > -\beta' x_i \\ 0 & \text{if } \varepsilon_i \leq -\beta' x_i \end{cases}$$

and

$$E(w_i/x_i) = \Pr(w_i = 1/x_i) = \Pr(\varepsilon_i > -\beta' x_i)$$

If investment decisions are independent across households, then the joint probability of $(w_1, \ldots, w_N)$, given the observable characteristics of the households $X = (x_1', \ldots, x_N')'$, is

$$\Pr((w_1, \ldots, w_N)/X) = \prod_{i=1}^{N} \Pr(w_i / x_i)$$

and ownership probabilities can be studied using standard cross section discrete models. The simplest model for discrete dependent variables is the linear probability model which assumes $E(w_i/x_i) = \beta' x_i$ and exploits the regression equation

$$w_i = \beta' x_i + u_i$$

with $E(u_i/x_i) = 0$. Consistent estimates of β can be obtained using Ordinary Least Squares (OLS), though the obvious non-normality of $u_i|x_i$ and its heteroskedasticity make OLS inefficient. But the main problem with the linear probability model is that the predicted probability $\hat{w}_i = \hat{\beta}' x_i$ can lie outside the admissible range (0, 1).

If we are willing to make a distributional assumption on the stochastic term ε_i, we have parametric models that are fully consistent with the idea that what we are estimating is a probability, and therefore its predicted value should lie in the (0, 1) range by construction. Assume that for all the households ε_i has the cumulative distribution function (cdf) F. Then

$$\Pr(w_i/x_i) = \Pr(\varepsilon_i > -\beta' x_i) = 1 - F(-\beta' x_i)$$

and the log-likelihood function is

$$\ln L = \sum_{i=1}^{N} w_i \ln(1 - F(-\beta' x_i)) + (1 - w_i)\ln F(-\beta' x_i)$$

If F is the logistic function, then

$$F(-\beta' x_i) = \frac{1}{1 + \exp(\beta' x_i)}$$

and we have a logit model. When we assume ε_i to be independent $N(0, \sigma_\varepsilon^2)$, then

$$F(-\beta' x_i) = \Phi\left(-\frac{\beta' x_i}{\sigma_\varepsilon}\right) = 1 - \Phi\left(\frac{\beta' x_i}{\sigma_\varepsilon}\right)$$

and the model is a probit model. In this case we identify, and estimate, β/σ_ε, not β and σ_ε separately. It is standard practice to assume that $\sigma_\varepsilon = 1$, but this assumption should be kept in mind when estimation results are interpreted. In both logit and probit models we easily get Maximum Likelihood (ML) estimates of β. These estimates are consistent and fully efficient, if distributional assumptions hold. If heteroskedasticity is present, and/or the assumption of normality fails to hold, then ML estimates of the probit model is not consistent. Distributional assumptions are not required if estimates rely on semi-parametric or non-parametric techniques. More sophisticated models and estimation techniques have been devised to deal with the joint decision to hold different kinds of assets (see Maddala, 1983; Amemiya, 1985 and Pudney, 1989 for further references).

This class of discrete choice model is the simplest way to generate zero holdings of risky assets. An alternative approach is Cragg's (1971) double hurdle model, which allows for zero holdings to be generated either as corner solutions or as a result of other considerations (e.g. lack of information). See also Pudney (1989), pp. 160–2.

3.4.2 Truncation, censoring and sample selection models

Assume that information on the level (or share) of risky assets owned by households is available and that we want to exploit not only the dichotomous participation (or ownership) variable as in the discrete choice models, but also the (continuous) variation of the level of risky assets across households. Given that not all the households hold risky assets, $w_i = w_i^*$ is observed only for participating families. As participation is correlated with the level of risky assets that the household would like to hold, then drawing inferences on the distribution of risky assets, $f(w_i^*)$, requires taking into account that the sample conveys information on the risky asset distribution conditional upon ownership, $f(w_i^*/\text{ownership})$. To understand the consequences of this and to keep the framework as simple as possible, consider the case in which w_i^* is independent across individuals and there exists a minimum amount c that the household has to invest in the risky asset to enter the market (fixed participation costs). Therefore the desired level w_i^* is observed only if $w_i^* > c$ and

$$f(w_i^*/\text{ownership}) = f(w_i^*/w_i^* > c) = \frac{f(w_i^*)}{\Pr(w_i^* > c)}$$

If the data are on owners only (as might be the case if data come from bank accounts), we have truncated models, where the log-likelihood function is

$$\ln L = \sum_{i=1}^{N} w_i[\ln f(w_i^*) - \ln \Pr(w_i = 1)]$$

If data on both owners and non-owners are available, non-owners convey information only on the probability of being below threshold c, which is the case of the censored regression models. In this case the log-likelihood function is

$$\ln L = \sum_{i=1}^{N} w_i[\ln f(w_i^*) - \ln \Pr(w_i = 1)] + (1 - w_i)\ln \Pr(w_i = 0)$$

But assume for instance that non-participation is primarily a problem of lack of information on the availability of the asset. If so, it would be reasonable to model the ownership decision on the basis of a different process from that generating w_i^*. A proper model could be

$$w_i = \begin{cases} w_i^* & \text{if } 1(y_i^* > 0) = 1 \\ \text{not observed} & \text{otherwise} \end{cases}$$

where y_i^* is a continuous latent variable, in general correlated with w_i^*, and $1(\cdot)$ is an indicator function which is equal to 1 if the argument is true, and zero otherwise. Therefore $1(y_i^* > 0) = 1$ only if household i holds risky assets. Models like this are usually referred to as sample selection models, and their log-likelihood function is

$$\ln L = \sum_{i=1}^{N} 1(y_i^* > 0)\ln f(w_i^* / y_i^* > 0) + (1 - 1(y_i^* > 0))\ln \Pr(y_i^* <= 0)$$

It is clear that from a statistical point of view a censored regression model can be considered as a particular type of sample selection model.

In what follows we shall concentrate on censored regression and sample selection models, given that survey data contain useful information on both owners and non-owners. Consider the following censored regression model where $c = 0$

$$w_i^* = \beta' x_i + \varepsilon_i \tag{1}$$

$$w_i = \max(w_i^*, 0) \tag{2}$$

The model is similar to the standard discrete choice model discussed above, with the difference that the real value of the latent variable is observed if it satisfies the criterion (2). Thus, a possible estimation strategy is to extend to this case the estimators adopted for discrete choice models. If we assume $\varepsilon_i \sim iiN(0, \sigma_\varepsilon^2)$ we have a standard Tobit model (Amemiya, 1985). In some cases, a lower and an upper threshold are jointly considered. An example of the application of a two-limit Tobit model to portfolio analysis is given by Hochguertel *et al.* (1997). Parameters estimates can be obtained via ML procedure and their consistency relies on the normality assumption. Such assumption is particularly strong in this framework, as it is well known that assets distribution is skewed.

Consider now the following sample selection model:

$$w_i^* = \beta' x_i + u_i \tag{3}$$

$$y_i^* = \delta' z_i + v_i \tag{4}$$

$$y_i = 1(y_i^* > 0) \tag{5}$$

$$w_i = \begin{cases} w_i^* & \text{if } y_i = 1 \\ 0 & \text{otherwise} \end{cases} \tag{6}$$

where x_i and z_i are exogenous with respect to u_i, v_i. If $\text{Cov}(u_i, v_i) = 0$, as long as β is the full set of relevant parameters, the discrete choice model in (4) and (5) can be neglected and β be estimated on the subsample with positive w's. But to impose $\text{Cov}(u_i, v_i) = 0$ is rarely reasonable, because it is equivalent to assuming that sample selection is exogenous, that is that being an owner or not does not depend on the level of risky assets desired, once allowance is made for the observables.

Different two-step procedures, as in Heckman (1979), have been proposed to correct for sample selection bias when $\text{Cov}(u_i, v_i) \neq 0$: they first compute the appropriate sample selection correction term and then estimate the augmented primary equation. In general, given the sample selection model (3)–(6), the expected quantity (or share) of risky assets for household i is:

$$E(w_i / x_i, z_i, y_i = 1) = \beta' x_i + E(u_i / v_i > -\delta' z_i, x_i, z_i) \tag{7}$$

Equation (7) shows that the simple OLS estimator of β is not consistent. One possible solution is to make assumptions on the form $E(u_i/v_i, x_i, z_i)$ and on the distribution of v_i. Assumptions on the form of the distribution of u_i are not necessary. This is an advantage of two-step estimators, because standard ML estimators rely on the normality assumption of u_i, a hypothesis hardly defensible in household portfolio studies. Furthermore, heteroskedasticity of u_i is allowed. For instance, one could assume

$$v_i \sim iiN(0, 1)$$

$$E(u_i / x_i, z_i, v_i) = E(u_i / v_i) = \rho v_i$$

where ρ is an unknown parameter (see Wooldridge, 1995). Then

$$E(w_i / x_i, z_i, y_i = 1) = \beta' x_i + \rho E(v_i / v_i > -\delta' z_i, x_i)$$

where $E(v_i/v_i > -\delta' z_i, x_i)$ equals the inverse Mills ratio. At the first step, consistent estimates for δ are obtained as explained when discussing the probit model and the corresponding estimated inverse Mills ratio $\hat{\phi}(\cdot)/\hat{\Phi}(\cdot)$ is computed; at the second step the following equation is estimated:

$$w_i = \beta' x_i + \rho \frac{\hat{\phi}_i}{\hat{\Phi}_i} + v \tag{8}$$

on the observations with $y_i = 1$. Equation (8) can be estimated by OLS. Inference must take heteroskedasticity and the presence of a predicted regressor into account. A hypothesis is crucial: the normality of v_i, which is necessary to estimate the probit model at the first stage with a ML estimator. This assumption can be relaxed following Powell's (1987) suggestions.

3.5 Conclusions

In this chapter we have argued why household survey data on wealth and portfolio choice should be of interest to the financial community. In all the surveys used in this project there are useful data to relate demand for stock to age, wealth, occupation and education; some of them have also variables related to health status, pension wealth, risk aversion, saving motivations and expectations. The adopted sampling schemes are such that information on both owners and non-owners are collected, ownership decision can always be observed independently from the decision on how much to invest into a specific asset, and portfolio composition can be fully recovered independently from the number of intermediaries used by the interviewed. Therefore, if the aim is profiling the stockowners, both for marketing or policy issues, survey data on wealth and portfolio choice are the kind of data needed. Banks and financial intermediaries accounts data might be more detailed in terms of portfolio description, but they suffer from at least two important drawbacks: they only cover a self-selected subsample of the whole population, and portfolio description is restricted to those assets owned or traded through the specific intermediary. We show which techniques can be used to improve survey data quality on portfolio composition and how to gross up the survey wealth data to the published flow of funds statistics.

We have also provided a brief overview of the estimation methods that are employed to study the determinants of the two separate decisions of whether to hold any stocks in the first place and in case of how much to invest in stocks. Extensions of these models are developed in the literature to consider two important cases: contemporaneous choices concerning two or more assets and choices repeated over time. The first extension requires implementing complex computer demanding econometric techniques, the second is data demanding. If we want to study how portfolio choice varies with time, we obviously need to observe households across time. In other words, cross-sectional surveys are not enough for questions like: how likely is an individual to exit stock market during a given period?; is retirement related to portfolio reshaping?; how household portfolios react to income or health shocks? To answer these questions, panel data are needed. These are rare data: only two of the five surveys used in this book have at least a panel component. But if a better understanding of household portfolio choice is an issue for central banks, policy makers, academic and financial communities, then European household panel surveys are the data collection projects worth investing in.

References

Alessie, R. (1999) The construction of sample weights for the CentER Saving Survey, mimeo, http://center-ar.kub.nl.

Alessie, R., A. Lusardi and A. Kapteyn (1995) 'Saving and wealth holdings of the elderly', *Ricerche Economiche*, **49**: 293–314.

Alessie, R., S. Hochguertel and G. Weber (2001) 'Consumer credit: evidence from Italian micro-data', CEPR Discussion Paper no. 3071.
Allen, F. and D. Gale (1994) 'Limited market participation and volatility of asset prices', *American Economic Review*, **84**: 933–55.
Alvarez R., B. Melenberg and A. van Soest (1999) 'Nonparametric modeling of the anchoring effect in an unfolding bracket design', CentER W.P. 1999-115.
Amemiya, T. (1985) *Advanced Econometrics*, Oxford: Basil Blackwell.
Ameriks, J. and S. Zeldes (2000) 'How do households portfolio shares vary with age?', TIAA-CREF Working Paper.
Attanasio, O. (1998) 'Cohort analysis of saving behavior by U.S. households', *Journal of Human Resources*, **33**: 575–609.
Attanasio, O. and H. Hoynes (2000) 'Differential mortality and wealth accumulation', *Journal of Human Resources*, **35**(1): 1–29.
Buchinsky, M. (1998) 'Recent advances in quantile regression models: a practical guideline for empirical research', *Journal of Human Resources*, **33**: 88–126.
Chaudhuri, A. and R. Mukerjee (1988) *Randomized Response Theory and Techniques*, New York: Dekker.
Cosslett, S. (1981) 'Maximum likelihood estimators for choice-based samples', *Econometrica*, **49**: 1289–316.
Cosslett, S. (1993) 'Estimation from endogenously stratified samples', in Maddala, Rao and Vinod (eds), *Handbook of Statistics*, Vol. 11, Amsterdam: North-Holland.
Cosslett, S. (1997) 'Nonparametric maximum likelihood methods', in Maddala and Rao (eds), *Handbook of Statistics*, Vol. 15, Amsterdam: North-Holland.
Cragg, J. (1971) 'Some statistical models for limited dependent variables with application to the demand for durable goods', *Econometrica*, **39**: 829–44.
Deaton, A. and C. Paxson (1994) 'Intertemporal choice and inequality', *Journal of Political Economy*, **102**: 437–67.
Fitzenberger, B. (1997) 'A guide to censored quantile regressions', in Maddala and Rao (eds) *Handbook of Statistics*, Vol. 15, Amsterdam: North-Holland.
Foreman, E. K. (1991) *Survey Sampling Principles*, New York: Marcel Dekker.
Fox, J. and P. Tracy (1986) *Randomized Response: A Method for Sensitive Surveys*, London: Sage Publications.
Gross, D. B. and N. S. Souleles (2001) 'Do liquidity constraints and interest rates matter for consumer behavior? Evidence from Credit Card Data', *Quarterly Journal of Economics*, forthcoming.
Guiso L., T. Jappelli and D. Terlizzese (1996) 'Income risk, borrowing constraints and portfolio choice', *American Economic Review*, **86**: 158–71.
Haliassos, M. and C. Bertaut (1995) 'Why so few hold stocks?', *Economic Journal*, **105**: 1110–29.
Heckman, J. (1979) 'Sample selection bias as a specification error', *Econometrica*, **47**: 153–61.
Heitjan, D. F. and D. R. Rubin (1990) 'Inference from coarse data via multiple imputation with application to age heaping', *Journal of the American Statistical Association*, **85**: 304–14, 410.
Hochguertel, S., R. Alessie and A. van Soest (1997) 'Savings accounts versus stocks and bonds in household portfolio allocation', *Scandinavian Journal of Economics*, **99**: 81–97.
Horowitz, J. (1992) 'A smoothed maximum score estimator for the binary response model', *Econometrica*, **60**: 505–31.

Horowitz, J. (1993) 'Semiparametric and nonparametric estimation of quantal response models', in Maddala, Rao and Vinod (eds), *Handbook of Statistics*, Vol. 11, Amsterdam: North-Holland.

Hurd, M. (1998) 'Anchoring effects in the HRS: experimental and nonexperimental evidence', NBER WP T0219.

Juster, F. and J. Smith (1997) 'Improving the quality of economic data: lessons from HRS and AHEAD', *Journal of American Statistical Association*, **92**: 1268–78.

Juster, F., J. Smith and F. Stafford (1999) 'The measurement and structure of household wealth', *Labour Economics*, **6**: 253–75.

King, M. and J. Leape (1998) 'Wealth and portfolio composition: theory and evidence', *Journal of Public Economics*, **69**: 155–93.

Maddala, G. (1983) *Limited Dependent and Qualitative Variables in Econometrics*, New York: Cambridge University Press.

Manski, C. and S. Lerman (1977) 'The estimation of choice probabilities from choice-based samples', *Econometrica*, **45**: 1977–98.

McCullagh, P. and J. Nelder (1983) 'Quasi-likelihood functions', *Annals of Statistics*, **11**: 59–67.

Newey, W. (1990) 'Efficient instrumental variables estimation of nonlinear models', *Econometrica*, **59**: 809–37.

Nyhus, E. (1996) 'The VSB – CentER saving project: data collection methods, questionnaires and sampling procedures', VSB – CentER Progress Report no. 42.

Orsi, R. and S. Pastorello (1999) 'La composizione del portafoglio delle famiglie italiane: un modello a fattori per variabili qualitative', in *Ricerche quantitative per la politica economica – 1997*, Roma: Banca d'Italia.

Perraudin, W. and B. Sørensen (2000) 'The demand for risky assets: sample selection and household portfolios', *Journal of Econometrics*, **97**: 117–44.

Poterba, J. (1994) *International Comparisons of Household Saving*, Chicago: NBER University of Chicago Press.

Poterba, J. and A. Samwick (1997) 'Household portfolio allocation over the life-cycle', NBER Working Paper No. 6185.

Powell, J. (1984) 'Least absolute deviation estimation for the censored regression model', *Journal of Econometrics*, **25**: 303–25.

Powell, J. (1987) 'Semiparametric estimation of bivariate latent variable models', Working Paper No. 8704, Social Systems Research Institute, University of Wisconsin – Madison.

Pudney, S. (1989) *Modelling Individual Choice: The Econometrics of Corners, Kinks and Holes*, Oxford: Basil Blackwell.

Shorrocks, A. (1975) 'The age-wealth relationship: a cross-section and cohort analysis', *The Review of Economics and Statistics*, **57**: 155–63.

Sheiner, L. and N. Weil (1992) 'The housing wealth of aged', NBER Working Paper No. 4115.

Vella, F. (1998) 'Estimating models with sample selection bias: a survey', *The Journal of Human Resources*, **33**: 127–69.

Vissing-Jørgensen, A. (2002) 'Towards an explanation of household portfolio choice heterogeneity: non-financial income and participation cost structures', NBER Working Paper No. 8884.

Wedderburn, R. (1974) 'Quasi-likelihood functions, generalized linear models, and the Gauss-Newton method', *Biometrika*, **61**: 439–47.

Wooldridge, J. (1995) 'Selection correction for panel data models under conditional mean independence assumptions', *Journal of Econometrics*, **68**: 115–32.

Part II

Stockholding in European Countries

4
Stockholding in France*

Luc Arrondel and André Masson

4.1 Introduction

In France, like in other European countries, the past fifteen years has been a time of drastic financial market developments due mainly to greater international integration and coordination (in response to European Union directives), financial liberalization (in particular the privatization of public services), and product innovation (especially the rise of retirement accounts – PEP – and life insurance). One of the most striking results has been the quick adjustment of households' behaviours to this new financial context, especially through the increasing share of stocks in portfolios and the diffusion of retirement accounts. In the middle of the eighties, only some 7 per cent of French households owned stocks compared with around 17 per cent in 2000.[1] For life insurance and retirement accounts, the rate of ownership has gone up, over the same period, from around 30 per cent to around 47 per cent of households.

In this chapter, we study portfolio choice decisions of French households concerning stockholding. The chapter is organized as follows: in Section 4.2, we provide a brief analysis of household portfolio composition and its evolution during the last decade (from national accounts). Section 4.3 presents the main feature of the data and describes stockholding in France. The empirical analysis uses the 1997 INSEE Survey on Wealth ('Patrimoine 97') with a sample of 10 207 French households. In Section 4.4, we examine the respective characteristics of stockholders and non-stockholders. Section 4.5 presents briefly the theory of portfolio choice and its recent developments, in order to justify the econometric specifications used for assets demands. Results for stockownership

* The authors thank H. Calvo for his comments.

and investment are shown in Section 4.6. Section 4.7 summarizes the main conclusions.

4.2 The household portfolio in France

The last decade witnessed significant developments in the composition of French households. The most significant changes have been the increased share of financial assets in total gross wealth (from 44 per cent in 1990 to 53 per cent in 1997), a share which is now greater than the one of real assets. Beyond potential changes in households' portfolio choice behaviours, this trend is due mainly to the evolution of asset prices during this period. First, the speculative bubble on Parisian housing market during the eighties deflated: all in all, national housing prices were constant during the nineties. Second, at the same time, the Stock Exchange index (CAC 40) increased by about 100 per cent. On the other hand, taxes on capital gains on financial assets have been much more important since 1992.

If we look at savings data rather than wealth data, we note that the French gross saving rate was about 12.5 per cent in 1990 and about 16 per cent in 1997. This tendency continued in 2000 and 2001, with a saving rate also around 16 per cent. But, during the same period, the financial saving rate increased from about 3 per cent to around 6.6 per cent in 2000 and about 7.7 per cent in 2001.

Table 4.1 reports the aggregate shares of financial assets in total financial wealth from 1990 to 1997.[2] These aggregate statistics give us an insight into some of the key changes that occurred in financial wealth holdings in France. The table reveals that the composition of households' financial assets changed significantly over the sample period. The proportion of financial wealth held in currency and bank deposit (transaction and saving accounts) decreased from 39.3 per cent in 1990 to 32.6 per cent in 1997. The proportion of financial wealth held in stocks rose markedly, from 26.2 per cent to 32.4 per cent, whereas that of mutual funds and managed investment accounts (including money market funds) fell from 13.7 per cent to 7.5 per cent. The proportion of financial wealth held in bonds was quite limited and rather constant over the sample period (between 2.5 per cent and 4 per cent). But the main change in the composition of financial wealth concerns the share of life insurance in portfolios: it more than doubled over the sample period, increasing from 9.6 per cent to 19.4 per cent.

These trends can be explained by a number of factors.

The first ones deal essentially with the evolution of relative market prices of transferable securities. As we have seen before, the market

Table 4.1 Composition of household financial wealth: aggregate financial accounts

Financial assets	Asset shares	
	1990	1997
Currency, transaction and savings accounts	39.32	32.63
Government bonds	3.88	2.72
Other bonds		
Stocks	26.19	32.44
Mutual funds and managed investment accounts*	13.70	7.46
Defined-contribution pension funds	—	—
Cash value of life insurance	9.56	19.39
Other financial assets	7.35	5.35
Total financial assets (in billion of French Francs)	9,145	15,898
Total financial assets (in billion of Euro)	1,394	2,424
Memo: Stocks, mutual funds and defined contribution pension funds	39.89	39.90
Average financial assets per household (in French Francs)	426,360	669,996
Total number of households	21 449,000	23 728,500

Note
* Including money market funds.

Source: National accounts INSEE.

value of stocks increased drastically during the 1990s (the CAC 40 stock exchange index has doubled). Moreover, the relative distribution of (pre-tax) rates of return on financial assets changed substantially: the annual real rate of return on stocks rose from 0.4 per cent over the period 1990–94 to 15.3 per cent over the period 1995–98; the one on mutual funds also increased from 2.5 per cent (during 1990–94) to 5 per cent (during 1994–97), but the rate of return on money market funds fell from 6.2 per cent to 2.7 per cent over the same sample time periods; the rate of return on bonds (from the private sector) increased from 7.1 per cent during 1990–94 to 9 per cent during 1994–97; lastly, the rates of return on non-taxable savings accounts (still in real terms) remained approximately constant, around 2 per cent. Moreover, the privatization of State-owned companies[3] since 1993 have been very popular and could have been responsible for a larger diffusion of an 'equity culture'.[4] All in all, these changes in relative prices and cultural factors help to understand the sizeable increase of the fraction of households holding stocks, from 9.1 per cent in 1992 to 14.5 per cent in 1997.

On the other hand, capital gains of transferable securities are more heavily taxed than they were before 1992. But, in any case, capital gains on French stocks remain tax exempted if households hold their shares for at least five years on a managed investment account (PEA: 'Plan Epargne en Actions'): in 1997, 7.3 per cent of French households held such accounts and more than 14 per cent in 2000.[5]

The second group of factors concerns the development of life insurance markets. New long-term saving assets appeared at the end of the 1980s and new products were created (PEP: 'Plan Epargne Populaire'). The eventuality of a reform of the social security system and the expectations of diminishing pension benefits prompted households to rely increasingly on their own saving retirement. These assets have some fiscal allowances, concerning especially their transmission to other individuals: like 'pure' life insurance contract. Households can bequeath these assets freely and with total exemption of inheritance taxes. Long-term saving assets concern 46 per cent of the French households in 1997 (39.5 per cent in 1992).

4.3 Data on stockownership in France

Periodically, the French National Institute for Statistics and Economic Studies (INSEE) carries out households' surveys in order to evaluate the total amount and the composition of their wealth (1986, 1992, 1998). The last one 'Patrimoine 97', used in this chapter, was made in 1997–98 on a sample of 10 207 households. This survey is an abridged version of the questionnaire from the earlier survey on 'Actifs financiers 1992' (Arrondel, 1996).

4.3.1 The 'Patrimoine 1997' survey: brief description

The basic survey unit is the 'household' which is defined as a group of individuals sharing the same dwelling. The sample is taken from the data of the previous census of population (1990). It is carried out on an initial representative sample of 14 800 households. To have significant information on non-wage-earners' households and on the rich, the latter are over-represented in the sample. Hence, the proportion of farmers, self-employed and professionals was initially three times their proportion in the census and the proportion of executives was initially multiplied by 1.5. The response rate was around 70 per cent, non-responding families including families who refuse to respond and families who had moved.

In particular, the 'Patrimoine 97' survey provides:

1. Detailed information on the socio-economic and demographic situation of the members of the household (diplomas, occupational

group, marital status, information about children...), as well as on the biographical and professional paths of each spouse (youth, career, unemployment spells or other interruptions of professional activity);

2. Detailed data on the household's income, on the amount and the composition of its wealth (including liabilities and professional assets); moreover, some questions aim at measuring their ability of access to the credit market; as far as stocks are concerned, we know also the financial institution in which the households own their stocks, how they manage their portfolio (no management, own management, management with financial advisor, management only by financial advisor) and if they had owned stocks one year before;
3. Brief information on the inter-generational transfers received and given (financial helping out, gifts and inheritance) and more generally on the 'history of its wealth'; some questions concern also parents' socio-economic characteristics and wealth composition. Table 4.2 reports summary statistics of the households' characteristics from the survey.

In addition, a complementary questionnaire gives a general idea of the individuals' degree of exposure and aversion to risk, as subjectively perceived and assessed by them (cf. appendix). It consists of a 'recto–verso' questionnaire, which was distributed to the interviewees at the end of the first interview. Submitted to the whole sample of 10 207 households, this page had to be filled in individually by the interviewee and his/her spouse (if applicable) and to be returned by post to INSEE. Only 4633 individuals answered this questionnaire (corresponding to 2954 households). The content is slightly different for employed persons than for unemployed or non-working persons. More specifically, the former are asked to assess their short- and long-term risks of unemployment, as well as the likely change in their future income over the next 5 years. In addition, a small game on lotteries enables, in two steps, to divide the individuals into four groups according to their degree of relative risk aversion – a method initially introduced by Barsky *et al.* (1995).[6]

4.3.2 The quality of amounts

In order to avoid refusals or evasive answers to questions concerning the value of assets, different solutions have been tried out. In the case of financial assets (especially stocks), households have three possibilities: they can give the exact amount; or else, they can give a self-assessed

Table 4.2 Summary statistics

Variable	Sample mean	Standard deviation
Age	51.10	17.72
Education		
less than high school	0.70	0.46
high school	0.13	0.33
college	0.17	0.38
Married	0.53	0.50
Male	0.75	0.43
Singles	0.30	0.46
Between 2 and 4 household members	0.62	0.49
More than 4 household members	0.08	0.27
One-income recipient	0.47	0.50
Two-income recipients	0.44	0.50
More than two-income recipients	0.05	0.23
Unemployed	0.06	0.24
Wage earner	0.71	0.45
Self-employed	0.14	0.35
Pension recipient	0.30	0.46
Income*	22 122	17 204
Total financial assets*	32 171	114 281
Participation		
Proportion investing in stocks	0.15	0.36
Proportion investing in mutual funds	0.13	0.34
Proportion investing in stocks or mutual funds	0.23	0.42
Amount invested		
In stocks, among stockholders*	25 116	90 822
In mutual funds, among those who invest have mutual funds*	21 358	71 971
In stocks, mutual funds and pension funds, among those who invest in these assets*	28 828	106 547
Number of observations	10 207	10 207

Note
* In Euro.

Source: Patrimoine 97 INSEE survey.

bracket, that is, a minimum and a maximum value; or else again, they can choose among fixed value brackets of amounts. For stocks, we know also the method used by households to evaluate amounts: according to bank statements, buying value, minimum anticipated value, and market value. To appraise real estate and other capital assets, households give a bracket, that is, a minimum and a maximum value. Finally, to evaluate total gross wealth, which includes assets declared in the survey but also those not declared (such as gold, durable goods…), fixed value brackets were given to households. When amount of assets are given in brackets, the 'simulated residual' method (Gouriéroux *et al.*, 1987) is used to obtain a single value (Arrondel, 1996).

The greatest disparities between the figures of National Wealth Account and the 'Patrimoine 97' survey estimates concern (in varying degrees) financial assets, investment in real estate, and some professional assets. Gaps may be due to differences in the scope chosen or in the method of valuation used, but also to the limited reliability of answers in households' surveys. The 'Patrimoine 97' survey has the advantage of offering a comprehensive coverage of assets. Yet, it is impossible to avoid errors and biases resulting from omissions, lack of knowledge, deliberate concealment of facts, or a subjective definition of wealth different from the survey's conventional definition (with discount for risk, depreciation of inherited property without usufruct, etc.).

In 1992, Arrondel *et al.* (1996) estimated from the previous wealth survey ('Actifs financiers 92') that the total amount of listed shares measured in the survey represented some 50–60 per cent of the total amount of listed share evaluated in national accounts. Total financial assets represented 40 per cent of the same assets evaluated in national accounts and total gross wealth, 70 per cent. With the 'Patrimoine 1997' survey, results appear to be similar (Talon, 1999). Moreover, it seemed that rates of ownership in the survey were more accurate than data on stockholding amounts: one reason is that information on asset ownership resulted from two parts of the questionnaire (the first part consisting simply of the list of assets that have to be fulfilled by interviewees). On the other hand, there are also several flaws in the national accounts figures, concerning in particular the valuation of the stocks of unlisted shares.

The big difference in the amounts invested in stocks between Tables 4.1 and 4.3 comes from all these problems of evaluation.[7]

4.3.3 Data on stockownership

Table 4.3 looks at the ownership of various forms of stocks as well as at the amounts invested in 1997. The fraction of households with direct stockholding is about 15 per cent. More precisely, around 12 per cent of households have listed shares, 1.4 per cent have non-listed shares and 3.1 per cent own employers' shares. The proportion of households with indirect stockholding – mainly through mutual funds – is around 13.5 per cent. It follows that the upper bound of (direct or indirect)

Table 4.3 Data on direct and indirect stockholding

	Detail on survey questions		
	Ownership (%)	Amount (in FF)	Amount (in Euro)
Direct stockholding			
Stocks	*15.0*	*25 044*	*3 818*
Listed stocks	11.9	20 252	3 087
Unlisted stocks	1.4	3 857	588
Employers' stocks	3.1	934	142
Indirect stockholding			
Mutual funds (excluding money market funds) and other managed accounts	13.5	18 900	2 881

Source: Patrimoine 97 INSEE survey.

stockownership in France can be estimated to be around 23 per cent of the population. The average amount invested in (direct) stocks is about 3800€ (25 000€ among direct stockholders) and households invest on average 6700€ in stocks or in mutual funds (29 000€ among owners).[8]

4.4 Descriptive statistics on stockownership

We describe first the population of stockholders. Then, we analyse briefly the amount invested in stocks among households who invest in these assets.

4.4.1 Who holds stocks?

Table 4.4 shows that both the ownership of direct stockholding and indirect stockholding displays a hump-shaped age profile, at least in a cross-section. The proportion of households holding direct stockholding rises from 8.5 per cent at young age to a peak of almost 20 per cent at ages 50–60, before falling to 13.5 per cent after one is 70 years old. This hump-shaped age profile, albeit less pronounced, is also found for indirect stockholding: around 17 per cent of people aged 50–59 own mutual funds but only 14 per cent after the age of 70. This decline at old age could result either from the selling of stocks for life cycle purposes, that is, consumption smoothing during retirement (Arrondel and Masson, 1990), or simply from a cohort effect in a cross-section: owing to economic growth, older households come from poorer generations. The increase in stockholding during the first part of the life cycle could

Table 4.4 Direct and indirect stockholding by age (in %)

	<30	30–39	40–49	50–59	60–69	≥70	Total
Direct stockholding	8.5	14.5	16.7	19.3	16.4	13.4	15.0
Indirect stockholding	7.5	13.5	14.7	16.7	12.2	14.1	13.5
Direct plus indirect stockholding	14.3	23.6	25.1	28.0	23.6	21.3	23.1
Sample proportion	11.8	19.1	20.3	15.9	13.4	19.5	100.0

Source: Patrimoine 97 INSEE survey.

Table 4.5 Direct and indirect stockholding by education

	Less than high school	High school	College	Average
Direct stockholding	10.9	23.8	25.8	15.0
Indirect stockholding	10.6	19.7	20.9	13.5
Direct plus indirect stockholding	18.1	33.3	36.0	23.1
Sample proportion	70.3	12.5	17.2	100.0

Source: Patrimoine 97 INSEE survey.

be explained by the progressive accumulation of financial information (King and Leape, 1987).

Table 4.5 reports the ownership of stocks according to the level of education. It shows that education is an important explanatory factor of direct (respectively indirect) stockholding: only 11 per cent of households (respectively 10.5 per cent) with less than high school education hold stocks to compare with almost 26 per cent (respectively 21 per cent) of households with college education. The fact that the management of a portfolio needs specific information on stock exchange could explain this effect, at least in part (King and Leape, 1987); but the latter could also represent the influence of labour supply flexibility on risky assets demand (Bodie *et al.*, 1992), if we assume that labour supply flexibility increases with the level of education.[9]

The first four columns of Table 4.6 report stockholding by financial wealth quartiles; the last two columns focus on households in the top 5 per cent and in the top 1 per cent of the financial wealth distribution. As expected, stockholding increases sharply with the level of financial wealth. Less than 2 per cent of households in the first quartile own

Table 4.6 Proportion of households investing in stocks, by financial asset quartiles

	Quartile I	Quartile II	Quartile III	Quartile IV	Top 5%	Top 1%	Average
Direct stockholding	1.8	7.3	13.9	37.2	66.7	82.9	15.0
Indirect stockholding	1.7	6.0	13.3	33.0	55.1	59.5	13.5
Direct plus indirect stockholding	3.5	12.5	23.9	52.5	80.3	84.9	23.1

Source: Patrimoine 97 INSEE survey.

direct stockholding in contrast to 37 per cent of households in the fourth quartile. This proportion is almost 67 per cent in the top 5 per cent of the financial wealth distribution and almost 83 per cent in the top 1 per cent. The rate of ownership of mutual funds rises also with the level of financial wealth, but at a smaller pace: 'only' 60 per cent of households in the top 1 per cent of the financial wealth distribution have indirect stockholding.[10]

Standard portfolio choice theory (see Section 5.1) with perfect capital market (no transaction costs, no taxes, no information costs, possibility of short sales of assets allowed...) predicts that all investors own each risky asset in a proportion of wealth that depends on the characteristics of assets and on individual's risk aversion (Merton, 1971). Fixed transaction costs, holding costs, and imperfect and costly information can explain why portfolios are not perfectly diversified (King and Leape, 1998). So, the effect of household's resources on stocks demand could reflect both the presence of such costs and the fact that risk aversion is decreasing with wealth.

Table 4.7 reports demographic characteristics of stockholders and non-stockholders. First, the effect concerning age, education and resources confirms previous results in Tables 4.4–4.6: stockholders are younger, better educated and wealthier than non-stockholders. One sees that male-headed households own stocks more often than female-headed households. Heterogeneity in tastes could explain this effect.[11] This heterogeneity in risk attitudes could also explain why self-employed (heads of) households and wage-earners employed in the private sector hold more stocks, if we assume that occupational choice is endogenous and depends on risk aversion. On the other hand, households with

Table 4.7 Demographic characteristics of stockholders and non-stockholders

Variable	Direct stock-holders	Indirect stock-holders	Direct plus indirect stockholders	Non stock-holders
Age	51.9	52.6	51.7	50.9
Less than high school	0.51	0.55	0.55	0.75
High school	0.20	0.18	0.18	0.11
College	0.29	0.27	0.27	0.14
Gross financial wealth*	105 600	97 400	84 400	16 700
Current income*	33 125	32 350	31 600	19 250
Married	0.62	0.64	0.62	0.50
Male	0.83	0.83	0.83	0.73
Singles	0.24	0.22	0.23	0.32
Between 2 and 4 household members	0.69	0.72	0.70	0.60
More than 4 household members	0.06	0.05	0.06	0.08
One-income recipient	0.43	0.41	0.42	0.54
Two-income recipients	0.52	0.53	0.53	0.41
More than two-income recipients	0.05	0.06	0.06	0.05
Wage earner	0.75	0.79	0.77	0.70
Self-employed	0.18	0.15	0.16	0.13
Unemployed	0.03	0.03	0.03	0.07
Pension recipient	0.31	0.31	0.31	0.30
Work in private sector	0.49	0.53	0.51	0.44
Work in public sector	0.16	0.13	0.15	0.15
Inheritance and gift received	0.54	0.54	0.52	0.33
Inter vivos transfers	0.36	0.37	0.35	0.25
Past illness (short periods)	0.30	0.30	0.32	0.37
Past illness (long periods)	0.02	0.02	0.02	0.05
Urban resident	0.65	0.64	0.63	0.58
Parents own risky assets	0.21	0.19	0.19	0.08
Number of observations	1 702	1 492	2 556	7 651

Note
* In Euro.

Source: Patrimoine 97 INSEE survey.

two-income recipients invest more in stocks, and households whose head is unemployed invest less in stocks: these two effects are consistent with Kimball's (1992) portfolio choice model in which a household exposed to a higher (exogenous) risk in future income or to strong liquidity constraints reduces its investments in risky assets and increases its insurance coverage or its share of liquid savings. Likewise, increased risk on health seems also to explain less risky portfolio. However, all these gross effects will have to be confirmed in the econometric analysis (*ceteris paribus*).

Moreover, households whose parents own(ed) risky assets have a greater probability for stockownership. This effect could represent some heterogeneity of information about capital market or also an effect of inheritance expectations. This imperfection concerning information could also explain the effect of education: heads that have college education hold stocks more often.

4.4.2 Asset share invested in stocks

Tables 4.8–4.10 display average individual shares of financial wealth invested in stocks and mutual funds, according to age, education, and financial asset quartiles, for those who have invested in these assets. Globally, the average share invested in stocks is around 21 per cent of financial wealth for direct stocks and around 28 per cent for direct and indirect stocks together.

There is not a very pronounced age pattern for the share of financial wealth invested in stocks. Old people seem, however, to invest more in

Table 4.8 Asset share invested in stocks, mutual funds (for stockholders) by age

	<30	30–39	40–49	50–59	60–69	≥70	Total
Direct stockholding	20.4	23.1	21.8	19.4	22.2	22.5	21.7
Indirect stockholding	21.6	23.7	24.1	22.7	24.3	26.4	24.1
Direct plus indirect stockholding	23.4	27.7	28.6	27.0	28.0	31.5	28.2

Source: Patrimoine 97 INSEE survey.

Table 4.9 Asset share invested in stocks, mutual funds (for stockholders) by education

	Less than high school	High school	College	Total
Direct stockholding	21.8	24.3	19.6	21.7
Indirect stockholding	25.4	22.6	22.4	24.1
Direct plus indirect stockholding	27.9	30.7	27.0	28.2

Source: Patrimoine 97 INSEE survey.

Table 4.10 Asset share invested in stocks, mutual funds (for stockholders) by financial asset quartiles

	Quartile I	Quartile II	Quartile III	Quartile IV	Top 5%	Top 1%	Total
Direct stockholding	44.7	27.5	21.3	19.6	23.0	30.4	21.7
Indirect stockholding	44.5	32.8	27.6	20.0	20.6	23.0	24.1
Direct plus indirect stockholding	45.0	31.7	27.7	26.4	33.3	45.8	28.2

Source: Patrimoine 97 INSEE survey.

these assets (22 per cent and 31 per cent respectively for direct stocks and direct plus indirect stocks). Households headed by high school graduates hold a higher share of financial wealth in stocks (23.8 per cent and 30.3 per cent respectively). Lastly, there is rather a decreasing relationship between the share of stocks and the level of financial assets for the bottom 95 per cent of households, but the relation is reversed among the top (financial) wealth holders.

4.5 Theoretical framework and econometric specification

In this section, we present first the inter-temporal portfolio choice model and then underline its recent developments. Finally, we outline the econometric method.

4.5.1 The inter-temporal portfolio choice model under complete markets

Merton (1969) and Samuelson (1969) have generalized the portfolio choice model of Arrow (1965), integrating it into a life cycle model. At each period, the consumer determines simultaneously her optimal consumption level and wealth composition. She maximizes a Von Neuman-Morgenstern inter-temporal expected-utility function depending on consumption and on all the possible combinations of assets that exist on the market. The capital market is perfect (no taxes, no transaction costs), the path of future incomes and lifetime are known with certainty, all the assets are perfectly divisible and transactions can be made continuously over time. If the consumer's utility function is additively separable over time and if returns on assets are independently distributed over time, then portfolio choices are independent of consumption decisions (*first theorem of separation*). In addition, if instantaneous utilities are iso-elastic (constant relative risk aversion, CRRA), the fraction of wealth invested in each asset is independent of wealth and even of the investor's age if the distribution of returns on assets is stationary.[12] The portfolio choice depends thus only on instantaneous utility and on returns on assets in the current period.[13] Contrary to consumption decisions, portfolio choices can be described as myopic behaviour, being independent of time considerations.[14] In other words, myopia is optimal.

Merton (1971) has also shown that portfolio choices come to an allocation process between two 'mutual funds' that depend only on the technical characteristics of the assets. If there is a riskless asset, the first mutual fund contains only this safe asset, while the second one is a linear combination of the risky assets. In that case, portfolio choices consist only in determining the risky fraction of wealth (*second theorem of separation*). Hence, if all investors have homogeneous price expectations, they own the 'market portfolio' and their risky part of wealth has a common composition (Merton, 1973). Being perfectly diversified, their portfolios differ only in the fraction of their wealth invested in risky assets which depends on the inverse of their relative risk aversion. So, the demand for risky asset, A, is given by (index t omitted):

$$\frac{A}{W} = \frac{\alpha - r}{\sigma^2 \gamma} \tag{1}$$

where W denotes the net wealth of the consumer, γ his relative risk-aversion coefficient, α and σ^2 are respectively, the expected return and the variance on risky asset, r the return on the safe asset.

4.5.2 Recent developments in the theory of portfolio choice

In recent theoretical developments, portfolio choice models include *transaction costs* and reconsider the hypothesis of an *exogenous and certain labour income*. They also study the influence on risky portfolio of other investment decisions like *housing*.

King and Leape (1998 and 1987) have shown that it is possible to generate incomplete portfolios if we introduce some market imperfections: transaction and holding costs (in time and money), costly information, no short sales on assets. As a result, the second theorem of separation, allowing the investor to decide only between the riskless asset and the risky 'mutual fund', is no longer valid. Her portfolio may now be incomplete (Mayshar, 1979). Proportional costs and taxes alone cannot lead to incomplete portfolios, because they can be integrated into the net returns on assets; however, they explain already the fact that trade on the market cannot be carried out continuously, but is rather spaced out over time (Constandinides, 1986). More generally, the equivalence with the static portfolio choice model of Tobin-Markowitz no longer holds.[15] However, King and Leape (1998) have shown that, *conditional* on the combination of assets held, the assets demands are the same as in Merton's mean-variance model – relation (1).

Bodie *et al.* (1992) have studied the influence of labour supply flexibility on risky investments. Very briefly, the main prediction of the model is that the more flexible their labour supply, the more risky their investments because households could increase their income if they make *ex post* bad investments.

Recent theoretical saving models and portfolio choice have also placed greater emphasis on prudent behaviour in the face of an uncertain future income, and have emphasized the influences of multiple risks and borrowing constraints on portfolio choices.[16]

Pratt and Zeckhauser (1987) establish a set of conditions on preferences – 'proper' risk aversion – that guarantee that an additional independent undesirable risk (i.e. decreasing expected utility) increases the sensitivity to other undesirable risks. Kimball (1993) and Gollier and Pratt (1996), building on this notion of proper risk aversion, provide a general framework to study the interaction between background risk (uninsurable and unavoidable risk) and other undesirable risks.

Kimball (1993) defines as *'standardness'* the property for a utility function that guarantees that an additional independent undesirable risk increases the sensitivity to other loss-aggravating ones (i.e. when an independent risk is added to the initial loss). He introduces the concept of *temperance* (measured by the ratio $\theta = -u''''/u'''$) which describes the desire to reduce total exposure to risk, that is, to moderate an endogenous risk in response to an increase in another unavoidable risk. He indeed shows that for an additional independent undesirable risk, the 'demand' for another endogenous risk decreases if and only if absolute risk aversion *and* absolute prudence are decreasing functions. This condition is satisfied for CRRA utility function. Under this assumption of 'standardness', temperance is greater than *prudence* ($p = -u'''/u''$, Kimball, 1990), which is itself greater than absolute risk aversion a ($\theta > p > a$), and the magnitude of reduction in endogenous risk is a positive function of the difference between temperance and prudence ($\theta - p$). Gollier and Pratt (1996) define a weaker concept, 'risk vulnerability' (or weak proper risk aversion), whereby preferences with this property are such that adding a non-positive mean (unfair) background risk is equivalent for the consumer to an increase in aversion to any other independent risk.[17]

So, within this static framework, an increase in income risk makes households less willing to bear a rate of return risk, thus reducing their demand for risky securities,[18] even when the two risks are independent. In other words, the two risks are *substitutes*. These results also hold in a multi-period portfolio model (Elmendorf and Kimball, 2000; Viceira, 1999; Campbell and Viceira, 2002).

Income risk also affects the relation between borrowing constraints and the composition of the household's portfolio. Koo (1995) has shown that the possibility that consumers will be subject to a liquidity constraint in the future makes them less willing to bear risk today (i.e. it is *as if* their risk aversion raised). Then, constrained households hold less risky assets than others do. More precisely, 'liquidity constraints reduce willingness to take risk if absolute risk tolerance is increasing and convex' (Gollier, 2001). In short, the effect of (expected) borrowing constraints reinforces the negative effect of income risk on portfolio choice.

Hence, the main prediction of these theoretical models is that when consumers face several risks simultaneously (of which one is unavoidable and uninsurable), they reduce the optimal investment in risky securities (they reduce endogenous risk). This effect is reinforced if consumers expect to be liquidity constrained in the future. These predictions are, however, not easy to test, the main problem in the empirical analysis being to find appropriate measures of income risk and liquidity constraints (cf. *infra*).

Other investment decisions could also influence risky portfolio allocation. Flavin and Yamashita (1998) assume that preferential tax treatment of owner-occupied housing and transaction costs create frictions large enough to constrain households to take into account, in their portfolio choice, the level of housing consistent with their consumption demand for housing. So, home ownership influences greatly portfolio allocations, and consumption and investment decisions are no longer separable. For instance, if the ratio of housing to net worth declines as the household accumulates wealth, the housing constraint induces an age-pattern in financial portfolios: young households will have a strong incentive to reduce portfolio risk (if risk aversion is decreasing in financial wealth), whereas older households will invest more in risky assets.

4.5.3 Econometric specification

I posit the following relation for the share of risky assets in financial wealth:

$$A/F = g(X\beta) + \varepsilon \qquad (2)$$

with $A \geq 0$ is demand for risky assets and F is total financial wealth. X is a vector of variables that influence the demand for risky investments. ε is an error term.

The set of explanatory variables X has been chosen according to the theoretical model. In portfolio choice models where capital markets are imperfect (transaction costs, holding cost, imperfect information) portfolios are incomplete (King and Leape, 1998). So portfolio choice depends on household's income and wealth (to finance transaction and information costs) and on the stock of financial information (proxied by age, education, parents' wealth composition).

We take into account different sources of future exogenous risk. For risk on *health*, we use current and past health problems. For *family* risks, we control by marital status and number of people in the household. Two sets of explanatory variables are used to take account of *income* risk depending on the sample used in the estimation: the total sample of households (10 207 observations), or only the restricted sample of households (2954 observations) who have replied to the complementary questionnaire on risk attitudes (cf. *supra*):

1. When using the total sample, we introduce the sector of professional activity of the household – public vs. private – and, for those working in the private sector, the existence of past or present unemployment period; we add the nature of professional activity (employee vs. self-employed), professional status (retired vs. active), and the number of income recipients in the household, which may also convey some information on future income riskiness.
2. When we regressed stock demand on the restricted sample of respondents to the complementary questionnaire on risk attitudes, we used direct measures of risk aversion (in four brackets) and of subjective income risk (cf. appendix). We added also a proxy variable for individual liquidity constraint (cf. appendix).

Among the X-variables, the effect of age can be given different interpretations (Arrondel and Masson, 1996). Bodie *et al.* (1992) show that the young enjoy greater labour flexibility than the old and may therefore be more inclined to hold risky assets; Gollier and Zeckhauser (1997) show that young households take on relatively more portfolio risk than more mature households if (and only if) absolute risk tolerance is convex with wealth. On the other hand, King and Leape (1987) claim that financial information is acquired progressively over the life cycle, which means that the young should have a less diversified portfolio than the old. Life cycle effect could be justified by the fact that if households need liquidity to finance consumption during old age, they will hold less risky portfolios (Arrondel and Masson, 1990). Lastly, if young people want to be homeowners (due to favourable fiscal treatments, for example), they will invest less in stocks because they hold less financial wealth (Flavin and Yamashita, 1998).

A simple OLS regression of (2) leads to inconsistent estimates due to the fact that a lot of households do not own risky assets.[19] In the same way, OLS regressions of (2) on the subsample of investors who hold risky assets is subject to selection bias (Heckman, 1976). So, we model the demand for risky assets as a two-stage decision process (King and Leape, 1998), where the first step is a probit model for the probability of ownership and the second step estimates conditional demands for risky assets, while introducing the opposite of the Mill's ratio in the set of regressors to correct selectivity bias. In other words, households choose first whether or not to hold such risky assets, and then, conditional on the combination on assets chosen, decide how to allocate total financial wealth between safe and risky securities.[20] We use different sets of explanatory variables to explain the 'discrete' and 'continuous' choices. Assuming that information costs mainly explain the decision to hold or not risky assets (Arrondel and Masson, 1990), we introduce education and the presence of risky assets in parents' wealth only in the probit model. Moreover, this hypothesis guarantees that the opposite of Mill's ratio is not co-linear with the determinants of the continuous choice.[21]

4.6 Econometric analysis for demand of stocks

In this section, we first study participation on the stock market. Then, we analyse the continuous choice of investment in stocks for households who hold these assets.

4.6.1 Probit regressions for stockownership

Tables 4.11 and 4.11bis display results of the econometric analysis concerning, respectively, the total sample and the restricted sample of respondents to the complementary questionnaire on risk attitudes.

4.6.1.1 Econometric estimates of age

In the probit regression for the participation in stocks, we use a third order age-polynomial (not reported in the tables). Econometric estimates of the effect of age on Figures 4.1–4.3 corroborate the hump-shaped age profile obtained in the descriptive analysis for direct stockholding: everything being equal, participation in stocks is maximum

Table 4.11 Probit regressions for participation in stocks and mutual funds

Variable	Stocks		Mutual funds		Stocks and mutual funds	
	Coefficient	Asymptotic *t* stat.	Coefficient	Asymptotic *t* stat.	Coefficient	Asymptotic *t* stat.
Age						
30–39	0.017	1.189	0.013	0.950	0.021	1.140
40–49	0.017	1.165	0.006	0.410	0.003	0.180
50–59	0.020	1.237	0.001	0.100	−0.001	−0.070
60–69	0.009	0.406	−0.012	−0.630	−0.016	−0.600
>70	−0.009	−0.439	0.005	0.270	−0.026	−0.970
High school	0.058	5.514	0.023	2.450	0.060	4.470
College	0.048	4.966	0.014	1.590	0.049	3.960
Second financial wealth bracket	0.124	7.355	0.090	5.830	0.170	9.110
Third financial wealth bracket	0.212	11.896	0.198	11.800	0.310	16.080
Fourth financial wealth bracket	0.398	20.530	0.357	19.310	0.527	26.420
Second income bracket	0.050	3.846	0.009	0.830	0.049	3.150
Third income bracket	0.071	5.077	0.047	3.740	0.106	6.140
Fourth income bracket	0.132	8.225	0.090	6.250	0.186	9.420
Married	0.002	0.196	0.001	0.060	−0.001	−0.040
Male	0.025	2.331	0.003	0.320	0.023	1.610
Between 2 and 4 household members	0.031	−2.420	−0.001	−0.110	−0.026	−1.640
More than 4 household members	−0.019	−1.215	−0.023	−1.600	−0.033	−1.610
Two-income recipients	0.013	−1.444	−0.015	−1.810	−0.023	−1.970
More than two-income recipients	0.048	−3.516	−0.032	−2.510	−0.067	−3.580
Self-employed	0.006	−0.732	−0.039	−5.300	−0.044	−3.950
Private sector, no unemployment period	0.039	3.915	0.086	8.500	0.107	7.980

Table 4.11 (cont.)

Variable	Stocks		Mutual funds		Stocks and mutual funds	
	Coefficient	Asymptotic *t* stat.	Coefficient	Asymptotic *t* stat.	Coefficient	Asymptotic *t* stat.
Private sector, unemployment period in the past	0.025	1.330	0.082	4.180	0.094	3.860
Private sector, currently unemployed	0.050	2.309	0.062	2.910	0.072	2.640
Retired or no activity	0.031	1.677	0.048	2.690	0.071	2.900
Never active	0.031	1.418	0.003	0.140	0.020	0.740
Inheritance and gift received	0.023	3.326	0.028	4.330	0.044	4.790
Inter vivos transfers	0.011	1.365	0.012	1.720	0.026	2.490
Past illness (short periods)	0.004	0.502	−0.001	−0.090	0.008	0.870
Past illness (long periods)	0.008	−0.406	−0.021	−1.180	−0.030	−1.210
Urban area (>20 000 habitants)	0.024	3.564	0.012	1.940	0.029	3.300
Parents own risky assets	0.064	6.076	0.031	3.340	0.072	5.180
Number of observations	10 207		10 207		10 207	
Number of households holding the asset	1 702		1 492		2 556	
Chi^2 (31 d.l.)	1 935.08		1 615.64		2 611.85	

Note: The coefficients are the change in the the probability of ownership.
Reference groups are

- Less than high school
- First financial wealth bracket
- First income bracket
- Single
- One-income recipient
- Public sector.

Source: Patrimoine 97 INSEE survey.

Table 4.11bis Probit regressions for participation in stocks and mutual funds

Variable	**Stocks**		**Mutual funds**		**Stocks and mutual funds**	
	Coefficient	**Asymptotic *t* stat.**	**Coefficient**	**Asymptotic *t* stat.**	**Coefficient**	**Asymptotic *t* stat.**
Age (10E-1)	0.135	3.240	0.069	1.880	0.119	2.420
Age^2 (10E-2)	−0.013	−3.380	−0.008	−2.400	−0.014	−2.950
High school	0.007	0.270	0.018	0.770	0.028	0.900
College	0.028	1.180	0.006	0.300	0.014	0.470
Financial wealth (10E-7)	2.760	12.050	1.910	9.600	4.590	13.790
Financial $wealth^2$ (10E-14)	−1.680	−10.490	−1.100	−7.750	−2.740	−12.310
Income (Log.)	0.060	3.010	0.043	2.380	0.094	3.870
Income risk (standard error of future income 10E-5)	0.140	2.190	0.120	2.060	0.236	2.840
Married	0.060	2.190	0.016	0.660	0.053	1.640
Male	0.055	1.970	0.040	1.550	0.062	1.820
Between 2 and 4 household members	−0.134	−3.670	−0.013	−0.420	−0.105	−2.580
More than 4 household members	−0.117	−3.130	−0.072	−1.920	−0.147	−2.940
Two-income recipients	0.003	0.110	−0.036	−1.740	−0.044	−1.550
More than two-income recipients	−0.083	−2.300	−0.067	−2.030	−0.111	−2.400
Self-employed	−0.042	−1.840	−0.041	−1.960	−0.064	−2.210
Inheritance and gift received	0.058	3.230	0.055	3.300	0.082	3.720
Inter vivos transfers	−0.003	−0.150	0.009	0.500	0.034	1.340
Past illness (short periods)	0.013	0.670	0.004	0.260	0.018	0.780
Past illness (long periods)	−0.039	−0.830	−0.060	−1.330	−0.063	−1.080
Urban area ($>$20 000 habitants)	0.026	1.460	0.008	0.520	0.014	0.660
Parents own risky assets	0.115	4.370	0.007	0.340	0.097	3.110
Borrowing constraint	−0.352	−2.230	−0.540	−3.650	−0.667	−3.550

Table 4.11bis (cont.)

Variable	**Stocks**		**Mutual funds**		**Stocks and mutual funds**	
	Coefficient	**Asymptotic *t* stat.**	**Coefficient**	**Asymptotic *t* stat.**	**Coefficient**	**Asymptotic *t* stat.**
No answer	0.069	2.380	0.000	0.000	0.072	2.120
$2 \leq$ CRRA < 3.76	0.052	2.530	0.014	0.750	0.052	2.100
$1 \leq$ CRRA < 2	0.037	1.180	−0.018	−0.660	−0.003	−0.090
CRRA < 1	0.077	1.860	0.015	0.410	0.059	1.220
Number of observations	2 387		2 387		2 387	
Number of households holding the asset	516		445		750	
Chi^2 (26 d.l.)	529.4		354.1		651.8	

Note: The coefficients are the change in the probability of ownership.
Reference groups are

- Less than high school
- Single
- One income recipient
- CRRA ≥ 3.76.

Source: Patrimoine 97 INSEE survey.

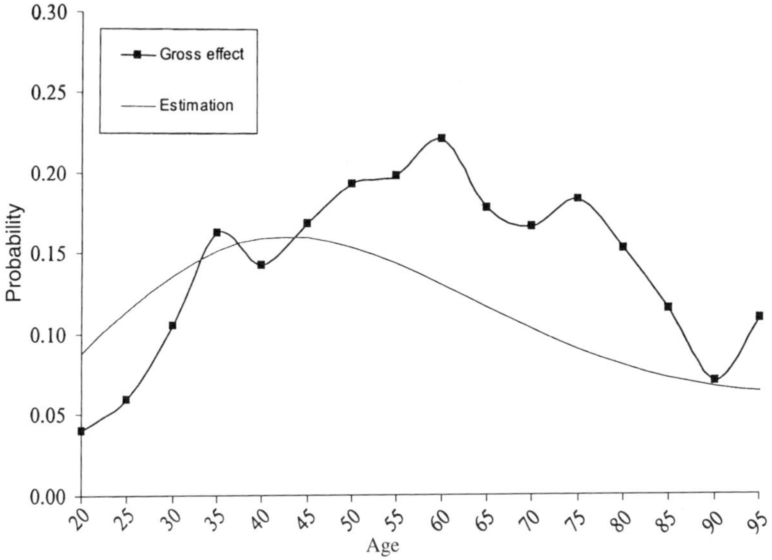

Figure 4.1 Direct stockholding by age (probability)

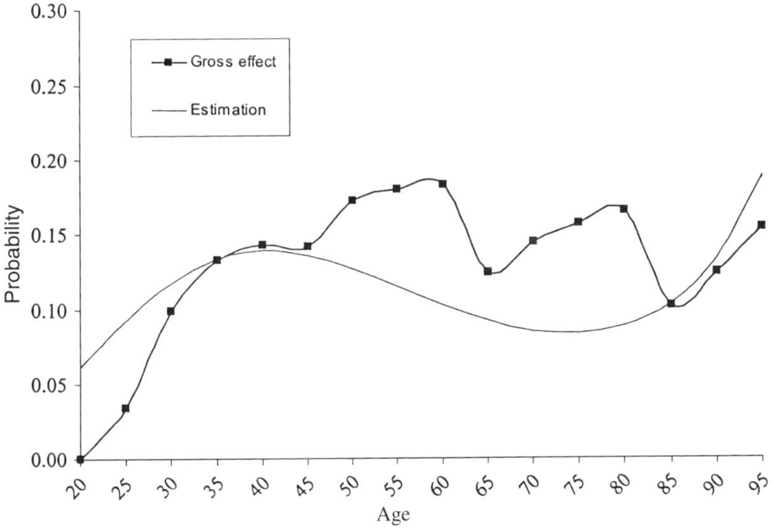

Figure 4.2 Indirect stockholding by age (probability)

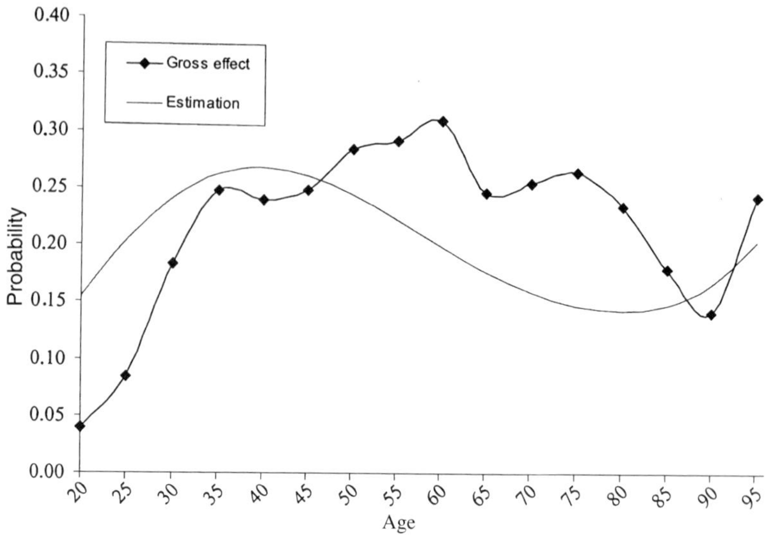

Figure 4.3 Direct and indirect stockholding by age (probability)

around 40 years old. For mutual funds, we note an increased relationship after 75 years (observed also in the descriptive analysis).

Estimated on cross-section data, this effect of age could reflect, at least in part, cohort effects. Figure 4.4 plots the average ownership rates of stocks and shares (including direct and indirect stockholding) derived from the Eurostat panel for the period 1994–2000 (Lollivier, 2001). Generally, in cohort graphs, the age effect is interpreted as the 'common shape' of the different cohort lines with respect to age; the horizontal distance between the different cohort profiles measures cohort effects; and fluctuations over time, assumed to affect in a similar way all cohort profiles, are period effects. Figure 4.4 reveals that stockownership follows a hump-shaped age profile with a peak around 60.[22] So, this result confirms a life cycle pattern for the demand for stocks and shares.

4.6.1.2 Other effects

The effects of financial wealth (and inheritance) and income are positive and consistent with the presence of fixed transaction costs (see Table 4.11). The stock of information inherited from parents – proxied by the ownership of the same assets in parents' wealth – also increases the probability of ownership of risky assets. These variables could also proxy an effect of inheritance expectations. The level of education of

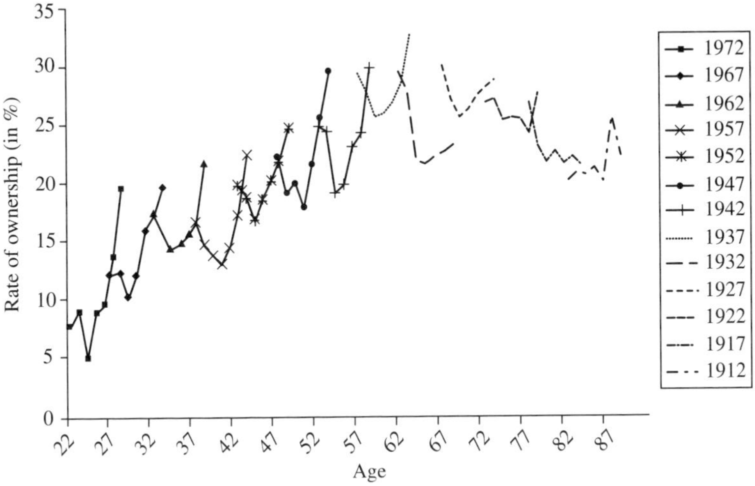

Figure 4.4 Proportion of stockholders (in %)

the household's head has also a positive effect. Workers in the private sector (being less risk averse?) take more risks in their portfolio by holding more stocks. Households with more than one-income recipients have a lower probability of stockownership. These two last effects do not support the assumption of a 'temperant' behaviour between different sources of risk (cf. *supra*). Gift or inheritance received have a positive effect (with wealth given) on stockholding: perhaps households keep stocks inherited from their parents. Finally, living in town is a favourable factor to hold stocks.[23]

Some effects are specific to the definition of stocks. For direct stockholding, results support previous findings that female-headed household have a more risk-averse behaviour (see note 11). Inversely, single households have a more risky portfolio of direct stocks. For indirect stockholding, we obtain a negative effect of being self-employed.

Probit regressions for stockownership on the restricted sample of respondents to the questionnaire on risk attitudes exhibit similar results for the previous variables (cf. Table 4.11bis).[24] The coefficient of the proxy for liquidity constraints is negative: households expecting to be liquidity constrained in the future invest less in risky assets. The effect of the individual measure of risk aversion has the expected sign for direct stockownership: less risk-averse households invest more often in risky assets. The coefficient of the expected variance of income is significantly different from zero but it has the opposite sign as expected by new theories of risk management:[25] households whose future income is more risky are also those who invest more in risky assets.[26] In other words, income risk and endogenous risk do not appear to be substitutes.[27]

4.6.2 Conditional shares of stocks

Like it was found in previous findings, there are few variables that are statistically significant in the conditional asset demand equation (Tables 4.12 and 4.12bis).

For direct stockholding, the conditional asset share depends positively on 'big gains' at the Stock Exchange. Managing portfolio personally or entrusting it to financial advisors for managing it increases the share of stocks in financial wealth.[28] Total demand for stocks (direct or indirect)[29] show an increasing share with age. We obtain also the same effect of big gains at the Stock Exchange and of the mode of management than for direct stockholding.[30]

So, it appears that conditional demand for stocks are mainly explained by the variables which proxy price fluctuations on the capital market. These results, combined with the previous ones concerning participation in the stock market, seem to confirm, at least in part, the model of King and Leape (1998), where transaction costs are one of the main explanatory factors of portfolios incompleteness. In this model, assets demands, conditional upon ownership, depend mainly on technical characteristics of assets and on the degree of risk aversion of individuals.

4.7 Conclusions

Let us sum up the main conclusions. In 1997, around 15 per cent of French households owned stocks directly and around 23 per cent directly or indirectly (through mutual funds). Stockholding exhibited a hump-shaped pattern according to age, with a peak of 28 per cent in the 50–59 age bracket, and increased very sharply with the level of (financial) wealth, concerning 85 per cent of the households in the top centile. Stockholders are better educated, more often self-employed or employees in the private sector. Moreover, the frequency of stockownership is higher for male-headed or two-income recipients households, and also when parents themselves own(ed) stocks.

The econometric analysis confirms most of these descriptive results and shows the relevance of explanatory factors behind the classic

Table 4.12 Regressions for the asset share invested in stocks and mutual funds

Variable	Stocks		Mutual funds		Stocks and mutual funds	
	Coefficient	Asymptotic *t* stat.	Coefficient	Asymptotic *t* stat.	Coefficient	Asymptotic *t* stat.
Age						
30–39	0.435	0.652	0.106	0.155	0.405	0.930
40–49	0.477	0.718	0.454	0.642	0.692	1.537
50–59	0.511	0.735	0.551	0.727	0.779	1.616
60–69	0.827	0.929	0.947	0.975	1.159	1.823
>70	0.785	0.837	0.944	0.980	1.250	1.887
Second financial wealth bracket	−1.153	−0.500	−0.456	−0.225	−1.102	−0.842
Third financial wealth bracket	−1.795	−0.789	−0.839	−0.388	−1.686	−1.253
Fourth financial wealth bracket	−2.278	−0.962	−1.349	−0.518	−2.248	−1.471
Second income bracket	−0.371	−0.503	0.035	0.051	−0.155	−0.326
Third income bracket	−0.289	−0.431	−0.083	−0.123	−0.306	−0.680
Fourth income bracket	−0.399	−0.601	−0.128	−0.157	−0.383	−0.760
Married	0.137	0.379	0.173	0.473	0.152	0.616
Male	0.164	0.340	−0.098	−0.205	0.053	0.164
Between 2 and 4 household members	−0.315	−0.623	0.071	0.136	−0.083	−0.238
More than 4 household members	−0.574	−0.904	0.014	0.020	−0.303	−0.663
Two-income recipients	−0.066	−0.231	−0.050	−0.163	−0.056	−0.275
More than two-income recipients	−0.236	−0.389	−0.216	−0.357	−0.256	−0.615
Self-employed	0.075	0.268	−0.193	−0.479	−0.077	−0.344
Private sector, no unemployment period	0.155	0.429	0.186	0.291	0.200	0.645
Private sector, unemployment period in the past	0.288	0.378	0.227	0.261	0.248	0.479
Private sector, currently unemployed	0.278	0.301	−0.351	−0.336	0.099	0.139
Retired or no activity	0.170	0.291	−0.071	−0.101	−0.064	−0.142
Never active	0.094	0.090	0.235	0.158	0.558	0.656

Table 4.12 (cont.)

Variable	Stocks		Mutual funds		Stocks and mutual funds	
	Coefficient	Asymptotic *t* stat.	Coefficient	Asymptotic *t* stat.	Coefficient	Asymptotic *t* stat.
Inheritance and gift received	−0.119	−0.484	0.092	0.285	−0.068	−0.364
Inter vivos transfers	−0.133	−0.532	−0.047	−0.185	−0.192	−1.068
Past illness (short periods)	−0.132	−0.519	0.070	0.280	−0.093	−0.538
Past illness (long periods)	−0.187	−0.184	−0.240	−0.194	−0.208	−0.273
Urban area (> 20 000 habitants)	0.010	0.039	0.145	0.549	0.064	0.359
Gains at stock exchange	0.842	2.892	−0.047	−0.143	0.946	3.691
Loss at stock exchange	0.140	0.280	0.217	0.313	0.240	0.586
Manage portfolio individually	0.568	3.860	0.166	0.743	0.606	4.836
Follow their financial advisor	0.343	2.085	0.036	0.198	0.324	2.805
Financial advisor manager	0.673	3.658	0.119	0.561	0.555	4.197
No indication about managing	0.829	1.017	0.255	0.484	0.451	1.155
Constant	0.041	0.013	−1.601	−0.340	0.255	0.114
Mill's ratio	−0.418	−0.517	0.192	0.114	−0.634	−0.753
Number of households holding the asset	1 702		1 492		2 556	
R^2	0.10		0.09		0.07	

Note: The dependent variable is the logistic transformation of asset share in financial assets.
Reference groups are:

- Less than high school
- First financial wealth bracket
- First income bracket
- Single
- One-income recipient
- Public sector
- No specific management.

Source: Patrimoine 97 INSEE survey.

Table 4.12bis Regressions for the asset share invested in stocks and mutual funds

Variable	Stocks		Mutual funds		Stocks and mutual funds	
	Coefficient	Asymptotic t stat.	Coefficient	Asymptotic t stat.	Coefficient	Asymptotic t stat.
Age (10E-1)	−0.232	−0.230	1.064	0.724	0.454	0.637
Age^2 (10E-2)	0.023	0.245	−0.086	−0.678	−0.039	−0.614
Financial wealth (10E-7)	2.490	0.518	−4.520	−0.064	3.440	0.986
Financial $wealth^2$ (10E-14)	−1.170	−0.365	0.085	0.020	−1.990	−0.816
Income (Log.)	−0.052	−0.092	−0.075	−0.089	−0.035	−0.081
Income risk (standard error of future income 10E-5)	−0.272	−0.252	0.407	0.295	0.120	0.151
Married	0.219	0.312	0.260	0.385	0.256	0.613
Male	0.225	0.322	0.408	0.418	0.372	0.777
Between 2 and 4 household members	−0.399	−0.463	0.002	0.002	−0.175	−0.322
More than 4 household members	−0.386	−0.336	−0.479	−0.330	−0.545	−0.708
Two-income recipients	0.003	0.007	−0.121	−0.229	−0.076	−0.250
More than two-income recipients	−0.051	−0.050	0.007	0.006	−0.215	−0.351
Self-employed	−0.127	−0.294	−0.512	−0.802	−0.378	−1.105
Inheritance and gift received	−0.112	−0.291	−0.076	−0.139	−0.084	−0.301
Inter vivos transfers	0.175	0.437	−0.069	−0.135	−0.009	−0.030
Past illness (short periods)	−0.085	−0.221	−0.162	−0.338	−0.188	−0.693
Past illness (long periods)	0.268	0.164	0.138	0.055	0.052	0.048
Urban area (>20 000 habitants)	0.232	0.550	0.215	0.433	0.276	0.987
Borrowing constraint	0.691	0.104	0.280	0.029	0.861	0.170
No answer	0.360	0.643	0.309	0.401	0.320	0.802
$2 \leq CRRA < 3.76$	0.277	0.692	−0.056	−0.118	0.183	0.653

Table 4.12bis (cont.)

Variable	Stocks		Mutual funds		Stocks and mutual funds	
	Coefficient	Asymptotic *t* stat.	Coefficient	Asymptotic *t* stat.	Coefficient	Asymptotic *t* stat.
$1 \leq CRRA < 2$	0.306	0.552	−0.042	−0.056	0.359	0.847
$CRRA < 1$	0.188	0.263	0.146	0.174	0.311	0.621
Gains at stock exchange	1.496	2.590	−0.018	−0.028	0.906	1.862
Loss at stock exchange	−0.697	−0.798	0.235	0.274	−0.154	−0.231
Manage portfolio individually	0.492	2.075	−0.146	−0.346	0.472	2.263
Follow their financial advisor	0.383	1.512	−0.042	−0.122	0.368	1.877
Financial advisor manager	1.049	3.192	0.013	0.033	0.886	3.689
No indication about managing	0.806	0.428	0.373	0.372	0.519	0.786
Constant	−2.258	−0.292	−5.169	−0.407	−3.851	−0.656
Mill's ratio	0.451	0.467	0.671	0.352	0.503	0.676
Number of households holding the asset	516		445		750	
R^2	0.12		0.12		0.08	

Note: The dependent variable is the logistic transformation of asset share in financial assets.
Reference groups are:

- Single
- One-income recipient
- $CRRA \geq 3.76$
- No specific management.

Source: Patrimoine 97 INSEE survey.

portfolio choices based on transaction and agency costs, and heterogeneous information. It emphasizes also the negative effect of (proxies for) liquidity constraints (as new theoretical models predict) and risk aversion but, more surprisingly, the positive effect of future income risk. Contrary to the predictions of new risk theory, income risk and portfolio risk do not appear to be substitutes: households whose income is more risky are those who invest more often in stocks. These conclusions need however further qualifications and more investigations concerning, notably, the (presumably negative) correlation between income risk and capital risk.

This study should also allow for a better understanding of the equity premium puzzle in France. In the long run (during the twentieth century), the real average annual return on equity was between 5 and 8 per cent higher than the return on risk free asset (Allais and Nalpas, 1999). To account for this equity premium (which is still lower than in the US), the standard portfolio choice model predicts that the optimal share of wealth invested in risky assets should equal 160 per cent and 40 per cent, respectively, for a relative risk aversion of 1 and 4. The presence of (transaction and information) costs and credit constraint could in part explain this puzzle.

Appendix: the definition of relative risk aversion, earnings uncertainty and borrowing constraints

Relative risk aversion

Suppose that you have a job which guarantees for life your household's current income – R. Other companies offer you various contracts which have one chance out of two (50 per cent) to provide you with a higher income and one chance out of two (50 per cent) to provide you with a lower income.

Are you prepared to accept Contract A which has 50 per cent chance of doubling your income R and 50 per cent chance that your income will be reduced by one third?

For those who answer YES: Contract A is no longer available. You are offered Contract B instead which has a 50 per cent chance of doubling your income R and 50 per cent chance that it will be reduced by one half. Are you prepared to accept?

For those who answer NO: you have refused Contract A, you are offered Contract C, which has a 50 per cent chance of doubling your income R and 50 per cent chance that it will be reduced by 20 per cent. Are you prepared to accept?

Earnings uncertainty

Within the next 5 years, your total household revenue (the rise in prices excluded):

- will have increased by more than 25 per cent
- will have increased by 10–25 per cent
- will have increased by less than 10 per cent

- will be constant
- will have decreased by less than 10 per cent
- will have decreased by 10–25 per cent
- will have decreased by more than 25 per cent
- will have marked ups and downs (indicate the minimum and maximum annual income).

You dispose of 100 points to be distributed among the 8 items, according to the degree to which you agree or you disagree with the relative statement.

The probability of being liquidity constrained

In 'Patrimoine 97' survey, households are asked two questions aimed at measuring their ability to access the credit market. These questions are similar to that of the SHIW Italian survey (Guiso *et al.*, 1996). We classify consumers as liquidity constrained if they respond positively to at least one of the two following questions. The first indicates whether a consumer is a 'discouraged borrower' and the second whether he is a 'turned down applicant':

- Did you renounce to finance expenditures on durable goods (main residence, cars ...) or did you renounce to restore your home because you expected that bank or other financial intermediaries will refuse the loan or the mortgage?
- Did you renounce to finance expenditures on durable goods (main residence, cars ...) or did you renounce to restore your home because bank or other financial intermediaries refused the loan or the mortgage?

There are 11.7 per cent of households who are liquidity constrained in the total sample and 9.8 per cent in the sample of respondents at the recto–verso questionnaire.

We estimate first the probability of being liquidity-constrained controlling individuals' characteristics and we use the predicted measure as proxy for the existence of future borrowing constraints in asset–demand equation. The instruments of borrowing constraints are the following: global income, age, dummy for retirement, occupation dummies, education, household's composition, social status of parents, wealth of parents, dummies for unemployment (present and past), dummies for health problems (severe or minor), dummies for professional status and regional localization.

References

Alessie, R., S. Hochguertel and A. van Soest (2001) 'Household portfolios in The Netherlands', in L. Guiso, M. Haliassos and T. Jappelli (eds), *Household Portfolios*, Cambridge, MA: MIT Press.

Allais, O. and N. Nalpas (1999) 'The equity premium puzzle: an evaluation of the french case', *mimeo*, University of Paris I.

Arrondel, L. (1996) 'Patrimoine des ménages : toujours le logement, mais aussi les actifs de précaution', *Economie et Statistique*, **296–7**: 33–62.

Arrondel, L. (2000) 'Risk management, liquidity constraints, and the demand for risky assets in France', Paris, DELTA Doc. 00-20.

Arrondel, L, and A. Masson (1990) 'Hypothèse du cycle de vie, diversification et composition du patrimoine', *Annales d'Economie et de Statistique*, **17**: 1–45.

Arrondel, L. and A. Masson (1996) 'Gestion du risque et comportements patrimoniaux', *Economie et Statistique*, **296–7**: 63–89.

Arrondel, L., F. Guillaumat-Tailliet and D. Verger (1996) 'Montants du patrimoine et des actifs: qualité et représentativité des déclarations des ménages', *Economie et Statistique*, **296–7**: 145–64.

Arrow, K. J. (1965) *Aspect of the Theory of Risk Bearing*, Yrjö Johnson Lectures, Helsinki.

Barsky, R. B., M. S. Kimball, F. T. Juster and M. D. Shapiro (1995) 'Preference parameters and behavioural heterogeneity: an experimental approach in the health and retirement survey', *Quarterly Journal of Economics*, CXII, **2**: 537–80.

Bodie, Z., R. C. Merton and W. F. Samuelson (1992) 'Labour supply flexibility and portfolio choice in a life-cycle model', *Journal of Economic Dynamics and Control*, **16**: 427–49.

Bottazzi, L., P. Pesenti and E. van Wincoop (1996) 'Wages, profits and the international portfolio puzzle', *European Economic Review*, **40**: 219–54.

Campbell, J. Y. and L. M. Viceira (2002) *Strategic Asset Allocation: Portfolio Choice for Long-Term Investors*, Lectures in Economics, Clarendon: Oxford University Press.

Constantinides, G. M. (1986) 'Capital market equilibrium with transaction costs', *Journal of Political Economy*, **94**: 842–62.

Drèze, J. and F. Modigliani (1972) 'Consumption decisions under uncertainty', *Journal of Economic Theory*, **5**: 308–35.

Dumontier, F., C. Martinez, C. Roineau, C. Rougerie and A. Tanay (2001) 'Patrimoine des ménages en 2000: une épargne plus risquée', *Insee Première*, no. 756.

Eeckhoudt, L. and M. Kimball (1992) 'Background risk, prudence, and the demand for insurance', in G. Dionne (ed.), *Contributions to Insurance Economics*, London: Kluwer Academic Press.

Eeckhoudt, L., Ch. Gollier and H. Schlesinger (1996) 'Changes in background risk and risk taking behaviour', *Econometrica*, **64**(3): 683–9.

Elmendorf, D. W. and M. S. Kimball (2000) 'Taxation of labour income and the demand for risky assets', *International Economic Review*, **41**: 801–32.

Flavin, M. and T. Yamashita (1998) 'Owner-occupied housing and the composition of the household portfolio over the life-cycle', NBER Working Paper No. W6389.

Gollier, Ch. (2001) *The Economics of Risk and Time*, Cambridge, AM: MIT Press.

Gollier, Ch. and J. W. Pratt (1996) 'Weak proper risk aversion and the tempering effect of background risk', *Econometrica*, **64**: 1109–23.

Gollier, Ch. and R. Zeckhauser (1997) Horizon length and portfolio risk, NBER, Technical Working Paper 216.

Gouriéroux, C., A. Monfort, A. Renault and A. Trognon (1987), 'Simulated residuals', *Journal of Econometrics*, **34**: 201–52.

Guiso, L. and T. Jappelli (1998) 'Background uncertainty and the demand for insurance against insurable risk', *The Geneva Papers on Risk and Insurance Theory*, **23**: 7–27.

Guiso, L., T. Jappelli and D. Terlizzese (1996) 'Income risk, borrowing constraints and portfolio choice', *American Economic Review*, **86**: 158–72.

Haliassos, M. (2002) 'Stockholding: recent lessons from theory and computations', chapter 2, this volume.

Heaton, J. and D. Lucas (2000) 'Portfolio choice in the presence of background risk', *Economic Journal*, **110**: 1–26.
Heckman, J. (1976) 'The common structure of statistical models of truncation, sample selection and limited dependent variables and a simple estimator for such models', *Annals of Economic and Social Measurement*, **5**: 475–92.
Hochguertel, S. (1998) 'Households' portfolio choices', Tilburg, CentER Dissertation Series, no. 38.
Jianakoplos, N. and A. Bernasek (1998) 'Are women more risk- averse?', *Economic Inquiry*, **36**: 620–30.
Kimball, M. S. (1990) 'Precautionary saving in the small and in the large', *Econometrica*, **58**: 53–73.
Kimball, M. S. (1992) 'Precautionary motives for holding assets', in J. Eatwell, M. Milgate and P. Newman (eds), *The New Palgrave Dictionary of Money and Finance*, London: Macmillan.
Kimball, M. S. (1993) 'Standard risk aversion', *Econometrica*, **61**: 589–611.
King, M. A. and J. I. Leape (1987) 'Asset accumulation, information, and the life cycle', N.B.E.R. WP2392.
King, M. A. and J. I. Leape (1998) 'Wealth and portfolio composition: theory and evidence', *Journal of Public Economy*, **69**: 155–93.
Koo, H. K. (1991) 'Consumption and portfolio choice with uninsurable income risk', Princeton University, mimeo.
Lollivier, S. (2001) 'Dynamique des patrimoines individuels', *mimeo* Crest, Paris.
Mayshar, J. (1979) 'Transaction costs in a model of capital equilibrium', *Journal of Political Economy*, **87**: 673–700.
Merton, R. C. (1969) 'Lifetime portfolio selection under uncertainty: the continuous time case', *Review of Economic Studies*, **51**: 247–57.
Merton, R. C. (1971) 'Optimal consumption and portfolio rules in a continuous time model', *Journal of Economic Theory*, **3**: 373–413.
Merton, R. C. (1973) 'An intertemporal capital asset pricing model', *Econometrica*, **41**: 867–87.
Miniaci, R. and G. Weber (2001) 'Econometric issues in the estimation of household portfolio models', in L. Guiso, M. Haliassos and T. Jappelli (eds), *Household Portfolios*, Cambridge, MA: MIT Press.
Mossin, J. (1968) 'Optimal multiperiod portfolio policies', *Journal of Business*, **41**: 215–29.
Pratt, J. and R. Zeckhauser (1987) 'Proper risk aversion', *Econometrica*, **55**: 143–54.
Robin, J. M. (2000) 'Modèles structurels et variables explicatives endogènes', Doc. Méthodologie statistique no. 2002, INSEE, Paris.
Samuelson, P. A. (1969) 'Lifetime portfolio selection by dynamic stochastic programming', *The Review of Economic Studies*, **51**: 239–46.
Schubert, R., M. Brown, M. Gysler and H. W. Brachinger (1999) 'Financial decision-making: are women really more risk-averse?, *American Economic Review*, **89**: 381–5.
Szpiro, D. (1995) 'La diffusion des produits financiers auprès des ménages en France', *Economie et Statistique*, **281**: 41–60.
Sundén, A. and B. J. Surette (1998) 'Gender differences in the allocation of assets in retirement savings plans,' *American Economic Review Papers and Proceedings*, **88**: 207–11.

Talon, G. (1999) 'Structure et disparités du patrimoine des ménages', *Synthèses*, no. 28, Insee, Paris.
Viceira, L. M. (1999) 'Optimal Portfolio choice for long-horizon investors with non-tradable labour income', N.B.E.R. WP7409.
Vissing-Jorgensen, A. (1999) 'Towards an explanation of household portfolio choice heterogeneity: non-financial income and participation cost structures', mimeo, University of Chicago.

5

Stockholding in Germany

*Axel Börsch-Supan and Lothar Essig**

5.1 Introduction

Germany is not a country of stockholders. Financial portfolios are still dominated by relatively safe assets, notably checking and savings accounts and domestic bonds, and by illiquid assets, mainly life insurance policies.[1] In 1993, only 12 per cent of West Germans directly held stocks while almost two-thirds of West German households owned a whole life insurance policy and about one-third held domestic bonds. Private pension funds are still uncommon.

There are, however, signs for change. Table 5.1 shows financial shares derived from aggregate financial accounts compiled by the Deutsche Bundesbank. This table indicates that conventional saving products decrease in significance (first two rows), while more sophisticated financial products (second two rows) have increased their portfolio share from about 40 per cent to more than 60 per cent between 1975 and 1992.

Table 5.1 gives only a very coarse picture. This chapter will shed more light on who holds stocks in Germany, how stockholding evolves during the life cycle and how it is related to wealth, education, and other demographic characteristics. Moreover, the chapter may help to give some answers why stockholding – either directly or indirectly through mutual funds and other managed investment accounts – is still underdeveloped in Germany and why it may change in the future.

* We thank Michael Haliassos and Tullio Jappelli for their helpful comments and their excellent template text which we followed closely. We gladly acknowledge financial support by the Observatoire de l'Epargne Européenne, the Deutsche Forschungsgemeinschaft (via SFB 504), and the European Commission (via TMR 'Savings, Pensions and Portfolio Choice'). This work builds on work by Angelika Eymann who deceased much too young during the course of this project.

Table 5.1 Financial asset shares (aggregate financial accounts), 1975–92

	West Germany: households and non-profit organizations				
	1975	**1980**	**1985**	**1990**	**1992**
Checking, deposit, and savings accounts	51.6	46.7	39.6	37.1	35.4
Building society savings contracts	7.8	7.3	5.5	4.1	3.7
Stocks, bonds, mutual funds on stocks and bonds and other financial assets	27.4	31.7	38.5	40.4	42.5
Insurance and pension wealth	13.2	14.5	16.3	18.6	18.6
Total financial assets	100%	100%	100%	100%	100%

Source: Deutsche Bundesbank (1994b), Deutsche Bundesbank (1999b) and own computations.

The saving and portfolio choice behaviour of German households has attracted the interest of a number of researchers[2] since a combination of three features distinguish the saving patterns of Germans from those in other industrialized countries: First, financial saving rates have been fairly high by international standards, notwithstanding a very generous social security system. Second, home ownership rates are exceptionally low and have risen only very slightly during the last two decades. Third, consumer credit is rare compared to the Anglo-Saxon countries; debt financing of real estate increased to roughly two-thirds of the sales value of housing only in the course of the nineties.

In spite of this general interest, there are only a few empirical studies of the determinants of German households' portfolio choices. Most of these studies focus exclusively on the impact of socioeconomic characteristics on West German households' behaviour.[3] The lack of a panel survey of financial behaviour in Germany and the very restricted access to earlier waves of the Income and Expenditure Survey (EVS) have inhibited empirical researchers interested in the determinants of portfolio composition, direct and indirect stockholding, and their changes over time.

Eymann and Börsch-Supan (2001) provide a more thorough and econometric analysis of East and West German households' portfolios. They analyse how they can be traced back to financial institutions and socio-demographic characteristics, using both macro- and micro-data. While they present stylized facts and recent trends in the households' general portfolio composition, this chapter focuses specifically on stockholding, either directly or indirectly through mutual funds and other managed investment accounts. In order to overcome the most severe data deficiencies, we combine several data sets, most important among them the German EVS. We will rely on two waves of this data set: The 1998 survey gives us the most recent picture, but we also need the 1993 survey because much of the 1998 data turns out to be too coarse for the questions asked in this chapter.

The chapter is structured as follows. The following section presents stylized facts about macroeconomic trends and major policy changes in Germany during the past decade. Section 5.3 describes our main data sources. Section 5.4 is devoted to participation. It investigates in detail who holds stocks, analysing differences in stockholding by socioeconomic characteristics and total financial wealth. Section 5.5 turns to portfolio shares of stocks, that is, the amount of wealth invested in stocks. This analysis is more complicated than participation since it requires very detailed financial data that German households provide only reluctantly. Section 5.6 explores the reasons why so few German households hold stocks. It discusses policy issues specific to Germany, such as taxes, savings subsidies, and pension policy, and it indicates how stockholding may change in the future. Section 5.7 concludes.

5.2 Macroeconomic trends and policy environment

This section briefly presents the recent macroeconomic trends in Germany as well as changes in the regulatory and general policy environment that may have affected stockownership in Germany.

5.2.1 Macroeconomic trends

Unlike in the other countries in Europe and in the United States, the early 1990s were dominated by the post-unification boom in Germany, see Figure 5.1. Slower growth eventually also hit Germany, but later and then much deeper. In the year 1993, at the trough of the downturn, GDP fell by 1.1 per cent (Figure 5.1). A period of slow stabilization followed until the recent recession in early summer 2001 began to hit all industrial countries including Germany (not shown in Figure 5.1).

The year 1998 brought a new government under social-democratic leadership and first-time participation of the green party after 16 years of the conservative Kohl government. The first year of the new government was characterized by a great deal of uncertainty which only stabilized after the sudden resignation of the secretary of finance.

The stock market in Germany shared the run up elsewhere. Figure 5.2 shows the German stock index (DAX) relative to two common indexes in the United States.

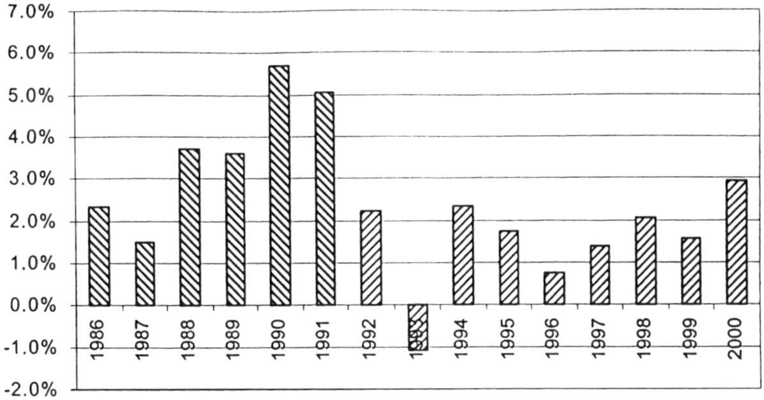

Figure 5.1 Growth rates of GDP, 1985–2000

Source: Statistisches Jahrbuch (2001). 1986–91: West Germany, 1992–2000: Germany.

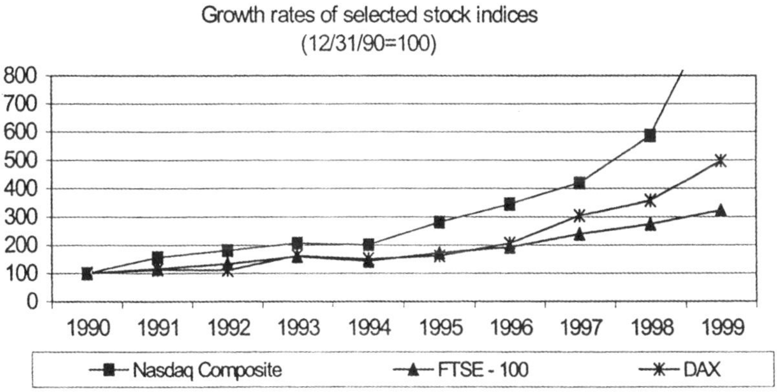

Figure 5.2 Growth rates of selected stock indices

Source: Deutsche Börse (1999).

The decade of the 1990s also brought a few but incisive structural changes that will impact on stockholding. A main change was the privatization of a few but very large state-owned firms, most notably Deutsche Telekom and Deutsche Post. The privatization of Deutsche Telekom is particularly important for this chapter as it marked the start of a 'Volksaktie', a popular stock, that was bought by many medium-income households who had not previously participated in stockholding.

In 1992, a small reform of the public pay-as-you-go social security system was put in place. This reform substantially reduced future benefits by linking benefits to net rather than gross wages, thereby introducing a mechanism that reduces benefits when contributions increase (sharing of the burden between young and old generation). The reform also increased future retirement ages (phased in until 2004) but left most early retirement incentives in place (see Börsch-Supan, 2000 for a discussion). The diminished expectation of pension benefits could potentially increase the demand for private pensions and thus also indirect stockholding; this will be discussed in Section 5.6.

The 1992 pension reform quickly proved to be insufficient, and a new pension reform was decided on in 1998 shortly before the federal elections. The new government in 1998 first revoked this reform, but then changed this policy in order to follow the path of benefit cuts. Moreover, and important for this study, the so-called 'Riester-Reform' introduced a new funded pillar that is effective since January 2002. Section 5.6 will discuss the implications of this new pillar on stockholding in Germany.

Finally, the 1990s were characterized by some spectacular mergers among banks and between insurance companies and banks, preparing the way for new pension instruments that combine financial and insurance products in the wake of the Riester-Reform. The most significant merger was between Allianz, the largest German insurance company, and Dresdener Bank, the third largest German bank, potentially easing the current institutional restrictions on indirect stockholding.

5.2.2 Policy environment

Financial regulations were revised frequently in the eighties and nineties, leading to changes in the real returns on assets both before and after taxes. In the following sections, we summarize the effects of financial market deregulation, privatization, and German reunification on the German stock market. We then briefly visit the main substitute markets and look at related developments in the German bonds and money markets.

5.2.2.1 Stock markets

Until recently, German stock markets were thin, decentralized, and comparatively 'neglected'. In 1990, stock market capitalization amounted to just 23 per cent as compared with 42 per cent in the Netherlands, 87 per cent in the United Kingdom, and 55 per cent in the United States.[4] Moreover, Wenger and Kaserer (1997) report that cross-holdings account for at least 27 per cent of the gross capitalization; 46.8 per cent of the stocks are held by banks and non-financial companies. Hence, only 11.4 per cent of common stocks are held by private and institutional investors. Even after the soaring stock prices of the late nineties (Figure 5.2), capitalization has risen to only 39.4 per cent of GDP in Germany as compared to 130 per cent in the Netherlands, 155 per cent in the United Kingdom, and 144 per cent in the United States.

The deregulation of the German stock markets began only in 1989. It was initiated by the need to transpose European Union (EU) directives into German law in order to comply with the regulations of the single market in services. Unlike that of bond markets, stock market deregulation was initiated by foreign rather than domestic interest groups. At first, German authorities were not at all quick in transposing EU directives into law.[5] The process only gained speed when the regionally separated stock markets in Germany were centralized (1993) and the Frankfurt stock exchange was reorganized and expanded (1990, 1991 and 1997). The Stock market gathered momentum with the privatization of some public sector industries, notably the initial public offering of Deutsche Telekom shares in November 1996 mentioned earlier. We expect that the process will accelerate further when Germany's ailing pay-as-you-go social security system is reformed by adding a new funded pillar to the pension system and further reducing the generosity of public health insurance.[6]

Major advances in stock markets deregulation, whose purpose was to make the German market more attractive to domestic and foreign institutional investors, to private investors with modest wealth, and to smaller companies willing to issue stocks, were made in 1990, 1994 and 1998. These legal changes substantially lowered transaction costs (1990). Access for international and domestic institutional investors (especially mutual funds) was widened (1990, 1994 and 1998). Entry barriers for small corporations (discriminatory accounting and codetermination rules) and for private investors (minimal stock values) were reduced in 1994. In the end, stock market surveillance was tightened substantially (1994 and 1998). To foster widespread ownership, the corporate income tax code was revised in December 1999. This controversial change will eventually make capital gains tax-free if they derive from sales of corporate reserves, which consist mainly in corporate cross-holdings valued at cost. Anticipation of the reform led to an 18 per cent spurt in the DAX performance index in just a month (December 1999).

For a person subject to the top marginal tax rate of 56 per cent, Stehle (1999) shows that the average annual after-tax yield from German stocks was 4.6 per cent from January 1969 to December 1997. From January 1988 to December 1998, however, it was 11.5 per cent. The difference between the after-tax yield of government bonds and stocks, averaged 4.8 per cent, for the whole period, was 11.1 per cent in the latter decade.[7]

The German stock market appears to have gained in attractiveness only in the wake of the third wave of the deregulation. We have four pieces of evidence: First, the number of initial public offerings started to increase in 1997 and then rocketed, in 1999, to roughly ten times the previous average level.[8] Second, turnover on the stock market increased by roughly 30 per cent in 1996, 1997, and 1998 and exceeded the growth rate of the DAX performance index in 1996 and 1998.[9] Third, the DAX performance index accelerated only recently, as evident in Figure 5.2. Fourth, Table 5.2 shows that the share of stocks in household portfolios held largely stable during the first half of the nineties and started to rise only after 1995.

Table 5.2 Financial asset shares according to aggregate financial accounts

	Unified Germany: households excluding non-profit organizations			
	1990	**1993**	**1995**	**1997**
Checking, deposit, and savings accounts	37.8	38.0	35.7	33.6
Bonds	20.0	18.0	18.9	17.1
Stocks	5.5	5.8	5.5	8.3
Mutual funds and managed investment accounts	3.9	6.2	7.6	8.6
Building society savings contracts	4.1	3.7	3.4	3.4
Insurance and pension wealth	20.9	20.9	21.8	22.5
Other financial assets	7.8	7.4	6.9	6.6
Total financial assets	*37.5*	*39.2*	*40.4*	*42.8*
Real estate wealth	83.0	82.4	82.7	81.9
Stock of durable goods	17.0	17.6	17.3	18.1
Total non-financial assets	*62.5*	*60.8*	*59.6*	*57.2*
Mortgage loans	76.6	75.8	78.1	79.6
Consumer credit	23.4	24.2	21.9	20.4
Total debt	*13.1*	*13.4*	*14.2*	*14.8*

Source: Deutsche Bundesbank (1994b), Deutsche Bundesbank (1999b) and own computations.

5.2.2.2 Bond markets

The small size of the German stock market may be even more of a surprise since its main competitors, the bonds and money markets, are also small in Germany. During the eighties, the government and the universal banks in Germany typically relied on the domestic bond market to finance the budget deficit and refinance loans. Thus, bond issues by non-bank companies were nearly negligible until the late nineties. Capital export restrictions hindering foreigners' purchase of domestic bonds were abolished in the mid-eighties. Bond market deregulation sought to widen the range of possible purchasers of domestic bonds, which consisted more or less exclusively of government and bank bonds. Deregulation was also supported by the Bundesbank, because it secured the role of the central bank's minimum reserve policy as a major instrument of monetary control. In hindsight, the deregulation process came just in time to permit German banks and several government agencies to attract international capital to issue bonds in order to finance the rebuilding of East Germany after reunification. The share of rebuilding financed by issuing new stock was minimal.

5.2.2.3 Money markets

Money market mutual funds appear to have been an important avenue facilitating stockholding by a broad audience in the United States, mainly during the early 1980s. This 'facilitating device' has been lacking in Germany. Unlike the deregulation process of the bond market which had occurred earlier than in other European countries, the process of deregulating the German money market started only in 1989. As of 1985, the Deutsche Bundesbank used the money market as the primary means to control monetary growth. The Deutsche Bundesbank therefore opposed the deregulation of the money market throughout the late eighties and only gradually gave in to the introduction of commercial papers (1989, 1991) and of money market mutual funds (1994). Their share is still small but growing, as Table 5.2 has shown.

The Bundesbank estimates do not allow disentangling stock- and bond-based mutual funds. Deutsche Bundesbank (1994c) reports that the increase in mutual fund units in the early nineties was accounted for almost exclusively by bond-based mutual funds. Presumably, the increase in the late nineties is due to stock-based funds, both in absolute and relative terms. The example of mutual funds shows that we cannot unambiguously assign a causal link for these changes. The data deficiencies both in the financial accounts and in the survey data mean that it remains unclear whether it was the gradual loosening of the regulations for mutual funds, beginning in 1990, or the increased yields on both bonds and stocks that boosted the attractiveness of the funds. More can be learned from micro data to which we now turn.

5.3 Data: the German income and expenditure survey (EVS)

Our main data set is the German income and expenditure survey ('Einkommens-und Verbrauchsstichprobe', EVS). Since 1962/63 the EVS has been carried out by the Federal Statistical Office every 5 years. The idea behind the EVS is to provide a comprehensive examination of the economic and social situation of private households (Euler, 1992). Data on income, expenditures, home ownership, wealth and debt is collected.[10] The data has been confidential until recently. The EVS 1993 was the first wave released as *'scientific use file'* which is accessible to all researchers for a nominal fee. The *'scientific use file'* of the EVS 1998 has just been released. It is accessible to all researchers in principle but the fee is very high and often prohibitive except for research institutes. The EVS 1993 included for the first time the new states and foreigner households. The EVS 1993 includes the main socioeconomic characteristics of all household members, while earlier surveys carry information only about the head of the household. The EVS 1993 is the newest data set with a reliable data base for stockholding and the portfolio share of stocks, and we have to base much of our analysis on these data.

The EVS 1998 returned to a more restrictive set of variables and bunched assets which were reported separately in 1993, again in broad categories. Most significantly, for this chapter, indirect stockholding cannot properly be identified in the 1998 survey. To make matters worse, the general category 'funds' includes not only stock- and bond-based mutual funds, but also funds based on real estate. Hence, using the category 'funds' as an upper limit of stockholding is essentially meaningless, and we therefore do not provide such numbers for the EVS 1998.

Parts of the EVS 1998 have been evaluated in tabular form (see Hahlen, 1998). A general analysis of saving behaviour using the EVS 1998 can be found in Börsch-Supan and Reil-Held (2002). Details about sample properties such as coverage and representativeness of the EVS micro data have been relegated to an appendix. Here, we just summarize the four most important points:

- *Accuracy*: The EVS requires very careful record keeping by the interviewed household and thus is likely to generate high-quality data.

During the survey period each household keeps a monthly diary in which all income sources and expenditures for the most important areas are recorded. In addition, for one month in the year, a detailed recording of all expenditures is done in detail.

- *Representativeness*: Although the EVS is claimed to be a representative sample of Germany's private households, it does not include persons living in institutions and – most significantly for this study – households with very high incomes. In the EVS 1993, the monthly net household income was limited to 35,000 DM. Since the highest income bracket of the micro-census is 7,500 DM or more, the weights are not guaranteed to represent the upper income segment (Laue, 1995). There is also doubt about how representative is the bottom income segment (Börsch-Supan *et al.*, 1998). Comparisons of the EVS with other data sources indicate too much weight given to middle-income brackets. Overall, the EVS is likely to underestimate stockholding, and it is important to keep this in mind especially when we look at the distribution of stockownership by wealth in Section 5.4.3.
- *Coverage*: The coverage of wealth reported in the EVS can be checked against data from the national flow-of-funds statistics constructed by the German Bundesbank, see Börsch-Supan *et al.* (2000). This confirms our suspicion about underestimating stockholding insofar as the coverage of financial wealth of private households is only around 56 per cent of the wealth reported in the aggregate (Guttmann, 1995). The two main reasons for this severe underreporting is that the Bundesbank data includes financial wealth owned by private non-profit organizations while the EVS only includes private households, and that the EVS excludes households with very high incomes as mentioned earlier.
- *Comparability*: There are serious deficiencies in the EVS 1998, compared with the EVS 1993, since variables crucially necessary to analyse stockholding are missing. As a compromise between accuracy and timeliness we always use a combination of the 1993 and the 1998 data.

5.4 Who holds stocks?

With these restrictions in mind, this section begins the analysis of our micro data by describing the stock market participation of German households. It relies on two definitions of stockownership. The first and narrow definition refers to direct stockholding only. Since many households hold stocks through mutual funds, this is an underestimate of total stockholding. The second definition is broader, and includes direct and indirect stockholding. The latter includes also mutual funds and other managed investment accounts (to the extent that these funds invest at least part of their portfolio in stocks). Due to data limitation we cannot distinguish the exact share of these funds that is invested in stocks. Thus, direct and indirect stockholding is an upper bound for total stockholding. In aggregate data – as we have seen in Tables 5.1 and 5.2 – and in the EVS 1998 – as described in the previous section – we cannot compute this upper bound since these data do not distinguish mutual funds by base asset at all.

Table 5.3 reports summary statistics for the 1998 sample. Characteristics refer to the head of the household.

Table 5.3 Summary statistics of sample, EVS 1993 and 1998

	1993		1998	
	Mean	**Std. D.**	**Mean**	**Std. D.**
Age	51.1	16.6	51.2	16.6
Education: less than high school	71.3%	45.2%	n.a.	
Education: high school	11.2%	31.6%	n.a.	
Education: college	17.6%	38.1%	21.2%	40.8%
Married	56.8%	49.5%	52.8%	49.9%
Male	67.8%	46.7%	65.7%	47.5%
Singles	34.1%	47.4%	36.0%	48.0%
Between 2 and 4 household members	60.7%	48.8%	59.5%	49.1%
More than 4 household members	5.3%	22.4%	4.5%	20.6%
One-income recipient	40.7%	49.1%	42.1%	49.4%
Two-income recipients	20.1%	40.1%	18.2%	38.6%
More than two-income recipients	2.5%	15.7%	1.7%	13.1%
Wage earner	52.1%	50.0%	53.3%	49.9%
Self-employed	6.0%	23.8%	6.4%	24.5%
Unemployed	4.3%	20.3%	4.6%	21.0%
Pension recipient	31.7%	46.5%	30.4%	46.0%
Income	27,527	17,998	29,139	19,179
Financial assets	33,026	54,030	35,350	63,236
Real assets	110,823	168,924	115,222	188,585
Credits	17,923	49,711	21,472	60,291
Direct stockownership	12.0%	32.5%	17.6%	38.0%
Indirect stockownership	10.3%	30.4%		
Total stockownership	19.8%	39.8%		
Asset values for those who hold these assets				
Stocks	13,266	45,907	17,500	53,731
Funds	10,920	19,056		
Stocks and funds	13,745	40,022		

Source: EVS 1993 and 1998, all financial values in €.

The average age is 51 years, some 55 per cent are married and about two-third of the household heads are male. More than two-thirds of the 1993 sample has compulsory education. The remaining third has either high school degrees (11.2 per cent in 1993) or college degrees (17.6 per cent in 1993, increasing to 21.2 per cent in 1998). The majority of households (about 60 per cent) has between 2 and 4 members; the proportion of single-earner (40 per cent) is about twice as high as that of two-earners (20 per cent). About 30 per cent of our households are pension recipients, while some 53 per cent are wage earners. Self-employed are relatively rare in Germany (6 per cent, slightly increasing). Four per cent of our households report that they are unemployed.[11]

The proportion of households that hold stock directly was 12.0 per cent in 1993 and increased to 17.6 per cent in 1998. The fraction holding stock indirectly is a bit smaller and amounts to 10.3 per cent of the 1993 sample. The latter figure is obtained on the assumption that at least part of the mutual funds or investment accounts are invested in equity. Since there is some overlap in these categories, total stockownership is not the sum of the two, but a bit lower: 19.8 per cent in 1993, an upper bound of stockholding (direct or indirect) in 1993. As mentioned earlier, the latter data was not available in 1998.

Hence, stock market participation has increased considerably, but it is still low relative to the Anglo-Saxon countries. It is significantly higher, however, than for instance in Italy. There are at least two reasons for the higher participation in Germany compared to Italy, and the lower participation than in the Anglo-Saxon countries. First, entry and management costs have been traditionally high in Italy while they are much lower in Germany, although not as low as in the Anglo-Saxon countries. Germany still has significant minimum investment requirements which prevent participation for many, especially low-wealth households. Second, the German stock market was less volatile than in Italy, where the standard deviation of the real growth rate of stock prices was 35 per cent during the last four decades, almost twice as large as in Germany. Stock prices may also explain part of the difference between Germany and the Anglo-Saxon countries. While their volatility was comparable, their levels were lower in Germany (see Börsch-Supan, 1998) and the recent stock market run-up slower (see Figure 5.2).

We now turn to examine some of these characteristics in detail.

5.4.1 Age and stockownership

We begin with age, see Table 5.4 and Figures 5.3 and 5.4. The age profile of participation is clearly hump-shaped. It peaks around age 47 in

Table 5.4 Direct and indirect stockholding by age (in per cent)

Age	<30	30–39	40–49	50–59	60–69	>70	Total
1993							
Direct stockholding	9.8	13.3	14.2	14.0	12.2	7.4	12.0
Indirect stockholding	12.6	12.0	10.5	11.0	8.9	7.3	10.3
Direct plus indirect stockholding	19.9	22.4	22.2	22.0	18.4	13.2	19.8
Sample proportion	10.3	20.5	16.8	18.4	16.4	17.5	100
1998							
Direct stockholding	16.5	18.9	18.3	21.4	18.7	11.1	17.6
Sample proportion	8.6	22.1	18.5	17.4	14.9	18.3	100

Source: EVS 1993 and 1998.

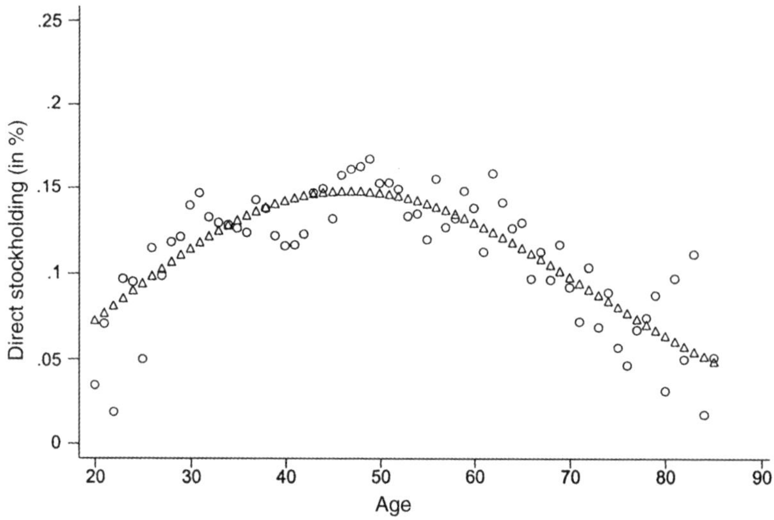

Figure 5.3 Direct stockholding by age, 1993

The figure shows actual means (circles) and fitted values of a third-order polynomial (triangles).

Source: EVS 1993.

1993, and around age 51 in 1998. At this peak, direct stockholding in 1993 is 14.8 per cent (i.e. 3 percentage points above average), and total stockholding 23.2 per cent (again 3 percentage points above average).

We should be careful in interpreting these age patterns since they compound age and cohort effects. Figures 5.3 and 5.4 do not represent the effect of age during the life cycle only; they also include the differences in

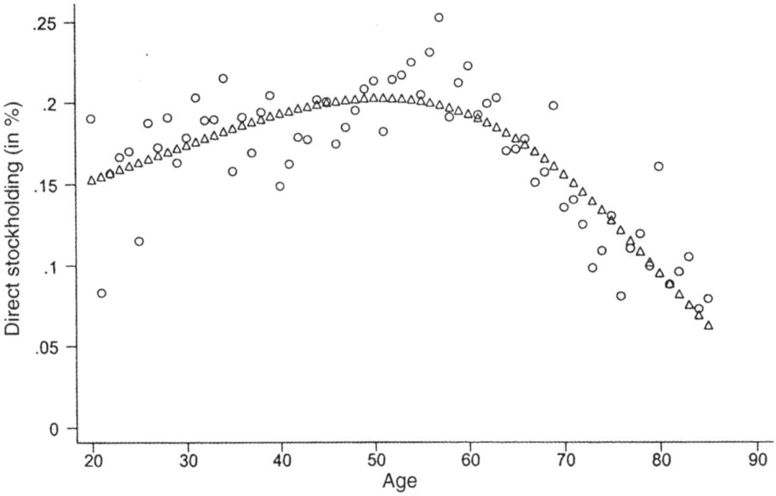

Figure 5.4 Direct stockholding by age, 1998

The figure shows actual means (circles) and fitted values of a third-order polynomial (triangles).

Source: EVS 1998.

attitudes towards stockholding between persons born earlier and born later (so called 'cohort effects'). It would be wrong to infer from Figures 5.3 and 5.4 that households sell their stocks when they age; rather, these are different households who may have started with much lower stock market participation in their life cycles. Similarly, households aged 60–69 years in the future might exhibit a much higher stock market participation because they have grown up in times with higher stockholding.

5.4.2 Education and stockownership

We expect a positive correlation between education and stockholding. Education is correlated with a person's permanent income and wealth, thus, education affects stockholding indirectly through this channel. Education also has a direct effect since it is correlated with an investor's ability to acquire and process information, and with financial sophistication in general.

This positive correlation is indeed what we find in Table 5.5. We classify education into three groups: compulsory education (corresponding to 10 years of schooling in Germany), high school degree (three additional years of schooling, mainly 'Abitur' in Germany) and college degree or higher. The first two categories are bundled in the EVS 1998.

Table 5.5 Direct and indirect stockholding by education (in per cent)

	Less than high school	High school	College	Average
1993				
Direct stockholding	9.8	12.8	20.5	12.0
Indirect stockholding	8.4	12.4	16.6	10.3
Direct plus indirect stockholding	16.6	21.8	31.3	19.8
Sample proportion	71.3	11.3	17.6	—
	No college	**College**	**Average**	
1998				
Direct stockholding	14.7	28.1	17.6	
Sample proportion	78.8	21.2	—	

Source: EVS 1993 and 1998.

Table 5.5 indicates that in the group with college degree participation is almost twice the average. In the group with compulsory education it is less than on average. The effect of education on indirect stockholding is quite similar to that on direct stockholding.

5.4.3 Wealth and stockownership

Gollier (2001) summarizes conditions under which wealth should correlate positively with the ownership and the portfolio share of risky assets such as stocks. In addition to the indirect correlation with education mentioned in the preceding subsection, fixed participation costs in the stock market due to information costs, participation fees, or other types of entry costs imply that investment in stocks is optimal once the investor's wealth exceeds a given threshold. Minimum thresholds for purchasing listed stocks also act as a barrier to entry and lead to a positive correlation between wealth and stockholding even in the absence of fixed participation costs. Indeed, several studies have found wealth to be the major determinant of households' willingness to hold risky assets.[12]

We find the same pattern in Table 5.6 which shows the proportion of direct and indirect stockholders by financial assets quartile and for the top 5 and 1 per cent of the financial wealth distribution. Direct investment in stocks is very rare in the first quartile (3 per cent have stock) but increases quickly in the second quartile (9.4 to 13.3 per cent in 1993 and 1998, respectively). Indirect stockholding features about the same

Table 5.6 Proportion of households investing in stocks, by financial asset quartiles (in per cent)

	Quartile I	Quartile II	Quartile III	Quartile IV	Top 5%	Top 1%	Average
1993							
Direct stockholding	2.9	8.3	14.0	27.8	43.3	56.0	12.0
Indirect stockholding	2.5	6.5	13.4	23.3	33.8	34.9	10.3
Direct plus indirect stockholding	5.1	14.1	25.1	42.5	59.0	69.8	19.8
1998							
Direct stockholding	1.7	14.1	24.4	42.2	59.3	78.9	17.6

Source: EVS 1993 and 1998.

percentages. Hence, even after subtracting the double counting, total stockholding is substantially higher than just direct stockholding among those households who have below median financial wealth.

The effect of wealth on stockownership is rather steep. In the third quartile of the wealth distribution, almost a quarter of the households held stocks in 1993, both directly and indirectly. In 1998, the proportion of households holding stocks only directly had already reached that level. Direct stock market participation in the fourth quartile reached 28 per cent in 1993 and dramatically increased to 42 per cent in 1998. In the top 5 and 1 per cent of the wealth distribution, direct stock holding was 40 per cent and almost 50 per cent in 1993 (increasing to 58 and 77 per cent in 1998).

Still, the main surprise is that direct stockholding remains substantially below the 95 per cent mark even among the very wealthy where one might expect that everybody will hold at least some stocks, particularly after the stock market run up between 1993 and 1998. A quarter of all households in the top 1 per cent wealth distribution, which is even higher in the income distribution, do not hold stocks directly. This is hard to explain with the presence of fixed costs alone and suggests that features other than monetary participation costs are relevant in explaining stockownership. One potential explanation is that the richer households have directly invested in business assets, for example, to have a tighter control over this business than through the stock market. We have little information on business assets (it was not ascertained in the EVS 1998 at all, and unreliably in the EVS 1993) to check this hypothesis, but it may have particular relevance for owners of small enterprises, while large companies are typically held in complicated crossholding schemes involving financial institutions (see Köke, 2001).

It is noteworthy that these qualitative features are similar in Germany and in Italy. However, German households with below median wealth invest in stocks to a much higher extent than Italian households. Thus, the distribution is more 'even' than in Italy.

5.4.4 Characteristics of stockholders and non-stockholders

The descriptive evidence shown thus far suggests that the typical stockholder is middle-aged, with relatively high level of financial assets and possibly a high level of education. In this subsection, we look at the typical stockholders and non-stockholders in more detail. We still focus on correlations between two variables at a time, keeping in mind that the direct effect of the variable at hand on stockholding may be smaller or larger, depending on the magnitudes and directions of indirect effects exerted by third variables through the variable at hand on stockholding. Section 5.4.5 will report multivariate analyses focussing on the direct effects only.

Table 5.7 displays sample means of demographic and economic characteristics for households who invest in stocks (a) directly, (b) indirectly through mutual funds and similar instruments, (c) directly and indirectly together, and (d) who do not own stocks at all. The information for (b) and (c) are not available in 1998, as explained earlier.

Compared to non-stockholders, stockholders are more likely to be married (especially for direct holding), male and have households of between two and four members with more than two-income earners. Earning wages rather than receiving transfers increases the likelihood to buy stocks. The self-employed are substantially more likely to invest in stocks. One explanation for this finding, which is common to other countries as well, is that the self-employed hold a larger fraction of their wealth in their business and invest in stocks in order to diversify their portfolio. In addition, the self-employed are less risk averse and risk aversion increases the propensity to invest in stocks (Guiso and Paiella, 2001). These effects, however, are counteracted by the fact that the self-employed are more exposed to risk, which should discourage them from further investing in risky assets. Needless to say, the unemployed and pension recipients are less likely to invest in stocks, reflecting their low wealth as well as their age.

5.4.5 Econometric estimates

It is important to check these findings in a multivariate analysis in order to distinguish between direct effects of each variable and indirect effects caused by third variables. Hence, we end this section on stock market

Table 5.7 Demographic characteristics of stockholders and non-stockholders

	1993				1998	
	Direct stock-holders	Indirect stock-holders	Total stock-holders	Non stock-holders	Direct stock-holders	Non stock-holders
Married (%)	70.2	63.5	66.7	54.4	64.2	50.3
Male (%)	80.3	74.7	77.2	65.6	78.0	63.1
Singles (%)	21.5	26.6	24.2	36.5	26.2	38.1
Between 2 and 4 household members (%)	73.0	67.8	70.2	58.3	68.7	57.5
More than 4 household members (%)	5.5	5.7	5.7	5.2	5.0	4.3
One-income recipient (%)	43.8	44.4	44.2	39.8	46.9	41.0
Two-income recipients (%)	29.4	27.7	28.4	18.1	24.5	16.8
More than two-income recipients (%)	3.1	3.4	3.3	2.3	2.7	1.6
Wage earner (%)	61.9	63.0	62.6	49.5	61.7	51.6
Self-employed (%)	8.0	6.9	7.3	5.7	9.4	5.8
Unemployed (%)	2.5	1.7	2.2	4.8	2.4	5.1
Pension recipient (%)	23.7	25.2	24.3	33.5	23.2	31.9
Households	4454	3855	7275	24499	8785	30608

Source: EVS 1993 and 1998.

participation ('who holds stocks?') with a multivariate regression analysis, using the probit regression technique. Our dependent variable is whether a household holds stocks, and the independent variables are the socio-economic characteristics mentioned in the previous subsection. While Table 5.7 combines direct and indirect effects on stockholding, Table 5.8 isolates the direct effects which each variable exerts on stockholding.

The numbers in Table 5.8 represent the percentage change if a continuous variable changes by 1 per cent of its value, and the percentage change if a dummy variable is changed from 0 to 1, respectively.

The age pattern is quite pronounced, and is particularly strong for total stockholding in the 1993 sample. Thus, the multivariate analysis confirms what we have seen before. Married households, however, hold stocks less frequently once all other socio-economic characteristics are

Table 5.8 Probit regressions for direct and indirect stockholding

	1993			1998
	Direct stockholding	Indirect stockholding	Total stockholding	Direct stockholding
Age between 36 and 50	−2.9% (0.00)	−4.7% (0.00)	−7.0% (0.00)	−5.2% (0.00)
Age between 51 and 65	−3.1% (0.00)	−5.5% (0.00)	−8.0% (0.00)	−5.9% (0.00)
Over 65 years old	−3.4% (0.00)	−5.1% (0.00)	−7.9% (0.00)	−7.4% (0.00)
High school	2.3% (0.00)	2.4% (0.00)	3.7% (0.00)	n.a.
College	1.1% (0.01)	1.5% (0.00)	0.2% (0.00)	3.8% (0.00)
Married	−2.0% (0.00)	−3.1% (0.00)	−5.1% (0.00)	−1.0% (0.13)
Male	2.1% (0.00)	0.2% (0.587)	2.1% (0.00)	3.4% (0.00)
Between 2 and 4 household members	−0.9% (0.16)	−1.1% (0.06)	−1.5% (0.07)	−4.2% (0.00)
More than 4 household members	−3.7% (0.00)	−2.2% (0.00)	−4.5% (0.00)	−6.4% (0.00)
Two-income recipients	−1.5% (0.00)	−0.5% (0.20)	−1.7% (0.00)	−2.4% (0.00)
More than two-income recipients	−4.2% (0.00)	0.8% (0.361)	−4.5% (0.00)	−2.9% (0.01)
Self-employed	−3.9% (0.00)	−3.2% (0.00)	−7.0% (0.00)	−2.9% (0.00)
Pension recipient	−0.4% (0.55)	0.1% (0.08)	0.2% (0.80)	−1.2% (0.08)
Second income bracket	4.1% (0.00)	5.3% (0.00)	8.6% (0.00)	3.4% (0.00)
Third income bracket	9.1% (0.00)	8.5% (0.00)	15.1% (0.00)	7.1% (0.00)
Fourth income bracket	17.1% (0.00)	12.0% (0.00)	24.4% (0.00)	14.2% (0.00)
Second wealth bracket	9.1% (0.00)	7.5% (0.00)	14.4% (0.00)	17.1% (0.00)
Third wealth bracket	12.9% (0.00)	13.9% (0.00)	23.0% (0.00)	29.3% (0.00)
Fourth wealth bracket	24.7% (0.00)	22.6% (0.00)	37.2% (0.00)	46.1% (0.00)
Households	31,774	31,774	31,774	39,393
Log likelihood	−10128.96	−9407.37	−13562.51	−15072.75
Pseudo R^2	0.1310	0.1082	0.1416	0.1767

DPROBIT estimates using STATA. *z*-values in parenthesis

Source: EVS 1993 and 1998.

accounted for. Here, the multivariate analysis discloses a direct effect which is of opposite sign to the indirect effects generated by other socio-economic characteristics correlated with the marital status.

Single member households, holding all other socio-economic characteristics constant, are most likely to hold stocks. This is visible in Table 5.8 since all other household sizes have negative coefficients.

Income and wealth exhibit the strong gradient that we have seen before. Households in the top quartile of the financial wealth distribution have a nearly 40 per cent higher likelihood to own stocks (directly and indirectly) in 1993 than households with less wealth, all other characteristics equal. This effect is even more pronounced in 1998, although we cannot measure indirect stockholding.

5.5 The amount invested in stocks

So far, we have investigated participation in the stock market. In this section, we look at the intensity of participation, measured as the share of total financial wealth that is invested in stocks. Portfolio shares are much harder to measure since the respondents have to do more than simply say 'yes' or 'no' to the question whether they hold assets. Rather, they have to state the exact amount invested in stocks and the exact amount invested in all other financial assets. Often, households refuse to state these exact amounts, increasing the likelihood that those who remain in the sample are respondents which are not representative. Moreover, reporting errors are much more likely which may bias the reported figures. The results in this section should therefore be taken cautiously. Börsch-Supan and Essig (2002) provide an extensive discussion of the methodological issues which arise in the collection of wealth data. They also report non-response rates and the representativity of numerical answers by various survey methods.

Tables 5.9 and 5.10 show the portfolio shares of stocks by age and education. The complicated pattern in Table 5.9 is likely due to the combination of age and cohort effects. On the one hand, households

Table 5.9 Portfolio share of stocks by age, conditional on stockholding (in per cent)

Age	<30	30–39	40–49	50–59	60–69	>70	All
1993							
Stocks	29.7	18.3	28.5	14.9	20.4	31.1	19.9
Mutual funds	18.6	23.2	17.5	17.3	24.2	29.8	21.5
Stocks and mutual funds	30.3	23.7	26.0	18.8	25.4	35.0	24.0
1998							
Stocks	29.9	24.6	18.9	18.7	22.3	30.1	22.9

Source: EVS 1993 and 1998.

Table 5.10 Conditional portfolio share of stocks by education (in per cent)

	Less than high school	High school	College	All
1993				
Stocks	18.8	24.8	19.8	19.9
Funds	23.1	20.9	18.5	21.5
Stocks or funds	23.1	29.2	23.6	24.0
1998				
Stocks	22.4		23.9	22.9

Source: EVS 1993 and 1998.

Table 5.11 Conditional asset share of stocks by financial asset quartiles (in per cent)

	Quartile I	Quartile II	Quartile III	Quartile IV	Top 5%	Top 1%	Average
Stocks	44.9	27.5	20.2	19.1	23.5	28.0	22.8
	(441)	(1447)	(2569)	(4328)	(1175)	(287)	(8785)

Number of observations in parenthesis.

Source: EVS 1998.

born later are more open to stockholding, creating the high portfolio shares of the young (cohort effect). On the other hand, wealth increases by age, resulting in an increasing portfolio share that peaks in old age (age effect). Only panel data – not existing in Germany (and most other countries) – can tell us which effects dominate in each age range.

The picture is less clear with respect to education and financial wealth, see Tables 5.10 and 5.11.

On first sight, it might seem surprising that richer households allocate a smaller share to stocks than poorer ones. Considering the number of observations in each wealth group, this result is less puzzling: Only a small share of households in the poorer wealth groups invest in shares at all, but if they do so, their share is then rather high, so that these households are less diversified than richer ones.

5.6 Issues specific to Germany

Germany has a tradition of promoting the formation of household wealth. It rests on two pillars – favourable tax treatment of asset holdings and direct savings subsidies. Both pillars have strong implications for stockholding.

Starting in the fifties, German tax and subsidy policies were initially set up to foster the formation of industrial capital and housing in the early post-war years. In the sixties and seventies, the focus was gradually shifted to low- and medium-income earners with children. In the wake of reunification, subsidies and tax exemptions were temporarily expanded to promote industry, infrastructure, and housing construction in East Germany, much in the spirit of the policies of the early fifties. It is in spite of this generous tax treatment that German households hold so little of their portfolio in stocks.

5.6.1 Savings subsidies

Three different systems of subsidies for long-term saving plans were introduced in the late fifties and sixties: Subsidies to undedicated long-term saving contracts (Sparprämie), subsidies to contributions to building society saving contracts (Wohnungsbauprämie), and subsidies to employer-sponsored saving plans (Arbeitnehmer-Sparzulage). Subsidy rates varied over time and were generally higher for dedicated saving plans. In the early years of the Federal Republic, this channeled funds away from stocks, also indirectly, because most employer-sponsored saving plans and occupational pensions were direct investments, not investments funneled through the stock market.

The inflation of the seventies seriously eroded the accessibility of the subsidies because income limits and contribution caps remained unadjusted. In the eighties and nineties, the scope of assets was narrowed to building society saving contracts and loans to the employer, but also included stocks and stock-based mutual funds. Germany may soon see yet another shift in the use of dedicated saving subsidies: It is now planned to funnel most saving subsidies to mutual funds dedicated to retirement income as an individual or company-sponsored supplement to the public pension system. This is likely to increase indirect stock-ownership already in the near future, see Section 5.6.3.

Savings subsidies were available to lower-middle-income households and amounted to less than 200 DM per year during the eighties and nineties.[13] Successive policy changes have left their traces on households' portfolio choice. The decrease in long-term saving contracts in the eighties (Table 5.1) is most likely due to the decrease in real after-tax yields of long-term saving contracts compared with bonds. Table 5.1 suggests that a growing number of eligible households took out building society saving contracts during the nineties, but held their investment to roughly 1000 DM per year, the ceiling for the subsidies. This may have left more room for investment in stocks during the nineties.

5.6.2 Taxation

Stocks and mutual funds were substantially tax-favoured because capital gains were not taxed if assets were held beyond the 'speculation period' which was six months, until recently. However, these periods were lengthened to two years in 2000, significantly reducing this incentive. Moreover, this advantage has to be seen in comparison to tax relief given to other investments. The favourable tax treatment of rented and, to a lesser degree, owner-occupied housing[14] as well as of life insurance contracts form the strongest pillars of German saving policy. Like the subsidies described above, tax exemptions generally favour low- and medium-income employee households with children.[15]

Several changes in the German tax code in the late eighties and nineties are likely to shift the balance slightly more to a leveled playing field. The two most important developments were:

- In 1991, a ruling by the German Supreme Court (*Bundesverfassungsgericht*) forced the government to end tax discrimination between labour and capital income and to introduce a withholding tax on interest income which previously (essentially) escaped taxation. The planned income tax reform in 2000 aims to further reduce loopholes in the personal income tax code and to reduce tax exemptions for interest income by 50 per cent.[16]
- In 1995, another Supreme Court ruling targeted the discriminatory tax treatment of housing against financial assets in 1995. As a consequence, the wealth tax was abolished which had favoured housing and penalized stocks.

5.6.3 Public pensions, pension reform and pension funds

The most important institutional change for future stockholding, however, is most likely the recent pension reform. Our assessment of importance stems from the observation that it does not appear to be a pure coincidence that countries with large and generous pay-as-you-go pension systems have small stock markets, and vice versa (Börsch-Supan and Winter 2001, Triangle). Germany takes an extreme point in this respect: it has an almost pure pay-as-you-go pension system for the current generation of pensioners, and a very small stock market as well. If the observed cross-national correlation is indeed causal, as Börsch-Supan and Winter (2001) claim, then the recent reform will also increase stockholding. This section pursues this argument in more detail.

Currently, the German public pension system ('Gesetzliche Rentenversicherung', GRV) covers about 85 per cent of the German workforce and provides about 85 per cent of their retirement income. For the average current retiree, occupational pension does not play a major role, nor do individual retirement accounts. While there are important exceptions from this general picture, the German system is, broadly speaking, a monolith that makes private retirement investment in stocks largely unnecessary.[17] The omnipresence of the public pension system is also the most plausible cause for the virtual absence of pension funds in Germany. What there is in terms of private pensions is mainly funneled through whole life insurance, while occupational pensions are largely invested in reserve accounts.

Moreover, since benefits are strictly work-related and are computed on a life-time basis in proportion to earnings, public pension benefits are roughly proportional to life-time earnings and exhibit relatively little redistribution. Hence, the need for additional (and often stock-based) investment is proportional to income and not as much a necessity for the richer households as in the UK and the US. Hence, percentages of stockholding and portfolio shares of stocks are not only small, but also rather evenly distributed in Germany, as we have seen in Table 5.11, except for the noticeable decreasing portfolio shares of stocks for richer households. This can also be seen in Table 5.12. While the probability of stockholding increases with wealth, the portfolio share of stocks decreases with wealth. These parameters are two step estimates corrected for sample selection. An explication for this result might lie in the fact that richer households do diversify their investments more carefully.

In the future, however, this pattern is likely to change fundamentally. During the period of this analysis, there have been two major pension reforms, 1992 and 2001, and many smaller adjustments in between. The main changes in the 1992 reform were to anchor benefits to net rather than to gross wages. This mechanism is particularly important when population aging will speed up and thus increase taxes and social security contributions, and it is likely to increase (indirect) stockholding through own retirement savings as a response to lower pension benefits.

The 2001 reform is intended to change the monolithic German system of old-age provision to a genuine multi-pillar system. Benefits will gradually be reduced by about 10 per cent, lowering the replacement rate with respect to the average net earnings from 72 per cent in 1997

Table 5.12 Heckman regression model with sample selection

	Stocks
Regression stage (Portfolio share of stocks)	
Age between 36 and 50	−0.0269 (0.01)
Age between 51 and 65	−0.024 (0.02)
Over 65 years old	0.053 (0.00)
College	0.024 (0.00)
Married	−0.061 (0.00)
Male	0.012 (0.24)
Second wealth bracket	−0.167 (0.00)
Third wealth bracket	−0.231 (0.00)
Fourth wealth bracket	−0.237 (0.00)
Constant	0.465 (0.00)
Selection stage (Stockownership)	
Age between 36 and 50	−0.246 (0.00)
Age between 51 and 65	−0.286 (0.00)
Over 65 years old	−0.430 (0.00)
College	0.269 (0.00)
Married	−0.107 (0.00)
Male	0.185 (0.00)
Second wealth bracket	0.722 (0.00)
Third wealth bracket	1.120 (0.00)
Fourth wealth bracket	1.640 (0.00)
Constant	−1.734 (0.00)
Rho	−0.012
Sigma	0.217
Lambda	−0.003
Log likelihood	−111 000 000
Households: 39 393; Censored households: 30 608; Uncensored households: 8 785	

z-values in parenthesis.

Source: EVS 1998.

to 64 per cent in 2030. The effective benefit cuts are even larger since the credit of earnings points for education and training will be greatly restricted. The resulting 'pension gap' of slightly less than 20 per cent of the current retirement income is supposed to be filled with occupational and individual pensions. This new pillar is not mandatory, but the required private savings will be subsidized or tax privileged.

While it is speculative at this point to project how much savings will be accumulated in response to the 2001 reform, and how much of this will enter the stock market, we have some guidance. Börsch-Supan and Brugiavini (2001) present projections resting on a sophisticated macroeconomic simulation model. In the long run (year 2050), the projected new savings amount to about 10 per cent of current gross fixed capital, and about 16 per cent of gross fixed capital in the production sector. Most of this will be indirect stockholding.

Moreover, their simulations indicate that there will be no sudden decline in the accumulated stock around the year 2030 when the baby boomers retire. Hence, rates of return are likely to remain relatively stable in spite of the demographic changes.[18] This long-run stability of macroeconomic rates of return appears to be an important prerequisite for future stockholding in a country as conservative and risk averse as Germany.

5.7 Conclusions

Stockholding is not very common in Germany but the proportion has been quickly changing between 1993 and 1998 which is the time range which our data covers. The main traits of the German stockholders are similar to those in other countries. They are individuals in their middle ages with high financial wealth and high income. They are also better educated but this effect almost vanishes once one corrects for income and wealth – the *direct* effect of education is probably small. German stockholders are more frequently single and male. Surprisingly, stockholding is less frequent among German households who receive two incomes while recipients of self-employment income – not surprisingly – are more often stockholders than recipients of wage income.

There are many reasons to expect significant portfolio changes in the future. Germany is likely to experience more privatization, and the capital market reforms have just begun. The same holds for social security reform where another reform step is expected after the 2002 Federal elections. The tax treatment of financial wealth, in particular pensions, is under review by the German Supreme Court. The increase in own provision for retirement income – via private and occupational pensions – is likely to be the main reason for future increases in the stock market size, similar to the developments in the Netherlands, the UK and the US since the mid-1980s.

It will be interesting to observe these changes and learn from them, not the least by comparing Germany with countries where private pensions already have more weight – and to compare the German development with countries who reform their capital markets and pension systems at an even slower speed. However, this will require new and better data. It is just astounding how weak the data base for assets and portfolios is in a country which is as wealthy as Germany, and how hard it is to reliably measure stockholdings and the portfolio share of stocks.

Appendix: details on EVS micro data

Representativity

The EVS is claimed to be a representative sample of Germany's private households. Since taking part in the EVS is voluntary for the interviewed households, the Federal Statistical Office applied quota sampling to reach proper representation. This stratified sampling of households is carried out on the basis of the EVS micro-census of the preceding year. The social position of the head of household (unemployed persons are also classified according to age and marital status of the head of household even though the head earns no income), household size and household income are taken into account. The stratified sample is used for the calculation of a target number of interviews and to compute the final (Pöschl, 1993).

The EVS does not include segments of the population living in institutions and households with very high incomes. In the EVS 1993, the monthly net household income was limited to 35,000 DM. Since the highest income bracket of the micro-census is 7,500 DM or more, the weights are not guaranteed to represent the upper income segment (Laue, 1995). There is also doubt about how representative in the bottom income segment (Börsch-Supan *et al.*, 1998). Comparisons of the EVS with other data sources indicate too much weight given to middle income brackets, see section 5.2.3 as well as the discussion on ownership rates in section 5.3.2.[19]

Method of data acquisition

During the survey period each household keeps a monthly diary in which all income sources and expenditures for the most important areas are recorded. Around 70 per cent of total expenditures are accounted for, without encumbering households with too much detailed bookkeeping (Lang, 1998). In addition, for one month in the year, a detailed recording of all expenditures helps account for the remaining 30 per cent.[20] The records in the household-diaries are complemented by two interviews. In the 'basic interview' the composition of the household, socioeconomic characteristics, as well as equipment with durable goods, and living conditions are recorded. Changes during the survey period are noted in the monthly reports. The survey ends with the 'final interview', during which the household is asked for its financial circumstances and public transfer payments. This interview also permits checking the information given during the sample period.

Coverage

The coverage of the wealth reported in the EVS has been checked by using data from the national flow-of-funds statistics constructed by the German Bundesbank, see Börsch-Supan *et al.* (2000). This comparison points to severe undercoverage. Total financial wealth of private households has a coverage of around 56 per cent (Guttmann, 1995). The two main reasons for this severe underreporting is that the Bundesbank data includes financial wealth owned by private non-profit organizations while the EVS only includes private households, and that the EVS excludes households with very high incomes as mentioned earlier. It is important to keep the latter restriction in mind especially when we look at the distribution of stockownership by wealth in Section 5.4.3.

Scientific use files

While earlier surveys are confidential, an extract of the 1993 and 1998 surveys has been 'factually anonymized' and is supplied to researchers. With 40 230 households in 1993 these scientific use files contain nearly 80 per cent of the original sample. The basic and the final interview as well as the summarized diaries for the surveyed period are included. Selected information on income, wealth and expenditure from the upper and bottom decile were aggregated in coarser categories than originally surveyed.[21] Further, selected discrete characteristics were summarized in a sophisticated manner so that no univariate distribution consists of less than 5000 cases. These 'factually anonymized' scientific use files are the basis of the analysis in this chapter.

Coding changes

The Federal Statistical Office carries out several checks for plausibility of the EVS. Obvious coding errors are corrected. Information about wealth is estimated to correct for missing or implausible information. For example, if households offer only information about the sum of their equity wealth, this sum is distributed equally across the different kinds of equities, not a breakdown by type (Lang, 1998 and Euler, 1985). Unfortunately, an external user cannot distinguish between the original information and the changes undertaken by the Federal Statistical Office.

Construction of longitudinal data

Each wave of the EVS represents a separate cross section. Even if a household has participated in two or more surveys, its identification is not possible. This makes the analysis of a major task of this chapter – why has stockholding changed in the recent decade – much harder since we can only compare aggregates in a synthetic panel of the EVS waves 1993 and 1998. Households of each survey are divided into as many homogenous household types ('cells') as possible. We then identify these cells across time. At this point, no panel data on savings and assets is available in Germany, a major obstacle to research on issues like the change in stockholding.

The task is made even more difficult by differences between EVS surveys. The EVS 1993 contains much more detailed information than earlier surveys, but also more information than the EVS 1998. Many variable definitions have changed from survey to survey. In order to obtain consistent variable definitions across cross sections, we often had to restrict ourselves to the smallest common denominator with considerable loss of information. As mentioned earlier, a main victim of this reduction in detail is indirect stockholding. All mutual funds, independent of their financial base (stocks, bonds, and/or real estate) are summarized in one category in the EVS 1998.

References

Bodie, Z., R. C. Merton and W. F. Samuelson (1992) 'Labour supply flexibility and portfolio choice in a life cycle model', *Journal of Economic Dynamics and Control*, **16**: 427–49.

Börsch-Supan, A. (1994a) 'Savings in Germany – Part I: Incentives', in J. M. Poterba (ed.), *Public Policies and Household Saving*, Chicago: University of Chicago Press, 81–104.

Börsch-Supan, A. (1994b) 'Savings in Germany – Part II: Behaviour', in I. M. Poterba (ed.), *International Comparisons of Household Saving*, Chicago: University of Chicago Press, 207–36.

Börsch-Supan, A. (1994c) 'Housing market regulations and housing market performance in the United States, Germany, and Japan', in R. M. Blank (ed.), *Social Protection versus Economic Flexibility*, Chicago: University of Chicago Press, 119–56.

Börsch-Supan, A. (1999) 'Capital productivity and the nature of competition', *Brookings Papers on Economic Activity, Microeconomics 1998*, 205–44.

Börsch-Supan, A. and A. Brugiavini (2001) 'Savings: the policy debate in Europe', *Oxford Review of Economic Policy*, **17**(1): 116–43.

Börsch-Supan, A. and L. Essig (2002) *Sparen in Deutschland. Ergebnisse der ersten SAVE-Studie*. Köln: Deutsches Institut für Altersvorsorge.

Börsch-Supan, A., R. Euwals and A. Eymann (1999) 'Portfolio choice with behavioural decision mechanisms', *Discussion Paper No. 1999–37*, Sonderforschungsbereich 504, University of Mannheim.

Börsch-Supan, A., A. Ludwig and J. Winter (2001) 'Aging and international capital flows', in A. Auerbach und H. Hermann (eds.), *Aging, Financial Markets and Monetary Policy*, Heidelberg: Springer, S. 56–83.

Börsch-Supan, A., A. Reil-Held, R. Rodepeter, R. Schnabel and J. Winter (1999) 'Ersparnisbildung in Deutschland: Meßkonzepte und Ergebnisse auf Basis der EVS', *Allgemeines Statistisches Archiv*, **83**, 385–415. The English version of this paper is available as a Discussion Paper (No. 99-02, Sonderforschungsbereich 504, University of Mannheim).

Börsch-Supan, A., A. Reil-Held, R. Rodepeter, R. Schnabel, and J. Winter (2001) 'The German savings puzzle', *Research in Economics*, **55**(1): 15–38.

Börsch-Supan, A., A. Reil-Held and R. Schnabel (2001) 'Pension provision in Germany', in R. Disney and P. Johnson (eds), *Pension Systems and Retirement Incomes across OECD Countries*, Cheltenham, S: Edward Elgar, 160–96.

Börsch-Supan, A., A. Reil-Held, and R. Schnabel (2002) 'Household saving in Germany', in A. Börsch-Supan (ed.), *Life-Cycle Savings and Public Policy: A Cross-National Study in Six Countries*, Academic Press. Forthcoming.

Börsch-Supan, A. and K. Stahl (1991) 'Do savings programs dedicated to homeownership increase personal savings? An Analysis of the West German Bausparkassensystem', *Journal of Public Economics*, **44**: 265–97.

Börsch-Supan, A. and J. Winter (1999) 'Pension reform, savings behaviour and corporate governance', *Discussion Paper No. 99-48*, Sonderforschungsbereich 504, University of Mannheim.

Börsch-Supan, A. and J. Winter (2001) 'Population aging, savings behaviour and capital markets', *NBER Working Paper 8561*, October 2001.

Brunsbach, S. and O. Lang (1998) 'Steuervorteile und die Rendite des Lebensversicherungs-sparens', *Jahrbücher für Nationalökonomie und Statistik*, **217**: 185–213.

Deutsche Börse (1999) *Deutsche Börse Information Products: Fact Book 1999*.

Deutsche Bundesbank (1988) 'Investmentsparen im Aufwind – Zur Entwicklung des Investmentsparens in den achtziger Jahren', *Monthly Reports*, October, 32–9.

Deutsche Bundesbank (1992) 'Die Entwicklung des Geld- und Sachvermögens westdeutscher privater Haushalte in den letzten zwanzig Jahren', *Monthly Reports*, April, 14–20.

Deutsche Bundesbank (1993a) 'Die Entwicklung des deutschen Auslandsvermögens und der Kapitalerträge', *Monthly Reports*, January, 43–66.

Deutsche Bundesbank (1993b) 'Zur Vermögenssituation der privaten Haushalte in Deutschland', *Monthly Reports*, October, 19–32.

Deutsche Bundesbank (1994a) 'Entwicklung und Bedeutung der Geldanlage in Investment-zertifikaten', *Monthly Reports*, October, 49–70.

Deutsche Bundesbank (1994b) 'Ergebnisse der gesamtwirtschaftlichen Finanzierungsrechnung für Westdeutschland 1960 bis 1992'.

Deutsche Bundesbank (1994c) 'Aufkommen und ökonomische Auswirkungen des steuerlichen Zinsabschlags', *Monthly Reports*, January, 45–57.

Deutsche Bundesbank (1999a) 'Ergebnisse der gesamtwirtschaftlichen Finanzierungsrechnung für Deutschland 1990 bis 1998'.

Deutsche Bundesbank (1999b) 'Zur Entwicklung der privaten Vermögenssituation seit Beginn der Neunziger Jahre', *Monthly Reports*, January, 33–50.

Euler, M. (1985) 'Geldvermögen privater Haushalte Ende 1983', *Wirtschaft und Statistik*, **5**: 408–18.

Euler, M. (1990) 'Geldvermögen und Schulden privater Haushalte Ende 1988', *Wirtschaft und Statistik*, **11**: 798–808.

Euler, M. (1992) 'Einkommens- und Verbrauchsstichprobe 1993', *Wirtschaft und Statistik*, **7**: 463–9.

Eymann, A. and A. Börsch-Supan (2001) 'Household portfolio choice in Germany', in M. Haliassos, L. Guiso and T. Jappelli (eds), *Household Portfolio Choice*, Cambridge, MA: MIT Press.

Gollier, C. (1991) 'Unemployment insurance: Risk-sharing versus efficiency', *The Geneva Papers on Risk and Insurance Theory*, **16**(1): 59–74.

Grimm, M. (1998) 'Die Verteilung von Geld- und Grundvermögen auf sozioökonomische Gruppen im Jahr 1988 und Vergleich mit früheren Ergebnissen', *Discussion Paper No. 14*, University of Frankfurt (Main).

Guiso, L., T. Jappelli and D. Terlizzese (1996) 'Income risk, borrowing constraints and portfolio choice', *American Economic Review*, **86**: 158–72.

Guiso, L. and M. Paiella (2001) 'Risk aversion, wealth and background risk', *CEPR Discussion Paper*, DP 2728.

Guttmann, E. (1995) 'Geldvermögen und Schulden privater Haushalte Ende 1993', *Wirtschaft und Statistik*, **5**: 391–9.

Helmcke, T. and P. Knoche (1992) 'Zur faktischen Anonymität von Mikrodaten', *Wirtschaft und Statistik*, **3**: 139–44.

Hahlen, J. (1998) *Erste Ergebnisse aus der Einkommens- und Verbrauchsstichprobe 1998*. Wiesbaden: Statistisches Bundesamt.

Himmelreicher, R. K. (1999) 'Westdeutsche Haushalte und ihr Vermögen. Eine Längsschnitt-Kohortenanalyse auf Basis des SOEP (1985–1996)', *Manuscript*, University of Bremen.

Hochgürtel, S., R. Alessie and A. van Soest (1997) 'Saving accounts versus stocks and bonds in household portfolio allocation', *Scandinavian Journal of Economics*, **99**: 81–97.

Kim, S. (1992) *Sozialversicherungskapital und das Sparen der privaten Haushalte in der Bundesrepublik Deutschland von 1961 bis 1988*, Hamburg: Verlag Dr. Kovač.

Köke, J. (2001) 'An empirical investigation of corporate governance in Germany', Ph.D. Dissertation, Mannheim University.

Lang, O. (1998) *Steueranreize und Geldanlage im Lebenszyklus*, Baden-Baden: Nomos.

Lang, O., K. H. Nöhrbaß and K. Stahl (1997) 'On income tax avoidance: the case of Germany', *Journal of Public Economics*, **66**: 327–47.

Laue, E. (1995) 'Grundvermögen privater Haushalte Ende 1993', *Wirtschaft und Statistik*, **6**: 488–97.

Pöschl, H. (1993) 'Werbung und Beteiligung der Haushalte an der Einkommens- und Verbrauchsstichprobe 1993', *Wirtschaft und Statistik*, **6**: 385–90.

Schlomann, H. (1992) *Vermögensverteilung und private Altersvorsorge*, Frankfurt (Main): Campus.

Schnabel, R. (1999) 'Vermögen und Ersparnis im Lebenszyklus in Westdeutschland', *Discussion Paper No. 99-43*, Sonderforschungsbereich 504, University of Mannheim.

Schönig, W. (1996) *Ersparnisbildung und Vermögensanlage privater Haushalte*, Frankfurt am Main: Peter Lang.

Stehle, R. (1999) 'Renditevergleich von Aktien und festverzinslichen Wertpapieren auf Basis des DAX und des REXP', *Discussion Paper*, Humboldt-University Berlin, April.

Vissing-Jørgensen, A. (1999) 'Towards an explanation of household portfolio choice heterogeneity: nonfinancial income and participation cost structures', *Manuscript*, March.

Walliser, J. and J. Winter (1999) 'Tax incentives, bequest motives and the demand for life insurance: evidence from Germany', *Discussion Paper No. 99-28*, Sonderforschungs-bereich 504, University of Mannheim.

Wenger, E. and C. Kaserer (1997) 'The German system of corporate governance – a model which should not be imitated', *Working Paper No. 14, American Institute for Contemporary German Studies.*

6
Stockholding in Italy

Luigi Guiso and Tullio Jappelli

6.1 Introduction

Historically, stockownership in Italy – as in other European countries – has not been widespread. Recently, however, there have been important developments in the composition of the portfolio of Italian households. The most significant changes are the increased participation in the equity market, the sharp increase in the share of stocks in the portfolio (held either directly or through mutual funds), and the parallel decline of transaction accounts and government bonds.

In the eighties, direct stockholding accounted for about only 15 per cent of households' financial assets. Indirect holding through mutual funds was virtually absent. The thinness of the Italian stock market and consequently its volatility discouraged equity holding, even after the introduction of mutual funds in 1984. Capital controls, in place until 1989, prevented households from achieving international diversification. The high level of government debt and the high interest rates necessary to finance it, made stocks relatively unattractive.

By 1998, direct stockholding accounted for about 30 per cent of household financial wealth; mutual funds and other managed investment represented another 16 per cent. Stockownership became more widespread and households are now much more used to invest in stocks and mutual funds than in the past.

In this chapter, we provide a thorough analysis of the trends in the portfolio of Italian households and of their propensity to invest in stocks. We study the determinants of the decision to invest in the stock market and of the share of equities in total financial wealth, and identify the main variables that explain household heterogeneity in the propensity to invest in stocks. The main source of data is the Survey of

Household Income and Wealth (SHIW), a biannual survey run by the Bank of Italy with the specific purpose of providing information on household saving, income, and wealth. The survey is particularly well suited for the purpose at hand because it collects detailed information on the composition of household financial wealth and on demographic variables. It is also repeated over time, allowing interesting comparisons in trends in the composition of the household portfolios.

In Section 6.2, we document the main trends in household portfolios that took place in the last decade drawing from the aggregate financial accounts. We also refer to institutional changes and financial reforms that are likely to have contributed to the increase in the share of risky assets in household portfolios and to the development of an equity culture. In Section 6.3, we present household-level data on stockownership in Italy. In Section 6.4, we identify critical variables that are associated with stockownership. The analysis considers variables that economic theory predicts should be relevant to explain the decision to invest in stocks: investor's age (as an indicator of planning horizon), wealth and education (as an indicator of financial information). We then summarize the data with regression analysis. The regressions allow us to explore the relation between the decision to invest in stocks and relevant explanatory variables controlling for other determinants of stockholding. In Section 6.5, we explain the determinants of the share of stocks in total financial wealth among households that have chosen to invest in stocks. We characterize the relation between portfolio shares (conditional on participation) and age, wealth, education and other demographic characteristics. In Section 6.6, we explore further the role of financial information and of transaction costs in shaping the portfolio of Italian households. Section 6.7 summarizes the main patterns of stockholding in Italy.

6.2 Macroeconomic trends in household portfolios

Before turning to a thorough analysis of stockholding with household-level data, we describe the trends of the financial portfolio and of stockholding drawing from the national financial accounts of the household sector. Table 6.1 reports aggregate shares of financial assets in total financial wealth in 1990 and 1998. The table immediately reveals that the composition of household financial assets has changed dramatically during the past decade. Currency and deposits (checking and saving accounts) declined sharply, from 36.8 per cent in 1990 to 22.7 per cent in 1998. The share of government bonds has more than halved, while bonds issued by private corporations have significantly increased.

Table 6.1 Composition of household financial wealth: aggregate financial accounts

The table reports the composition of household financial wealth from the aggregate financial accounts. Transaction accounts include certificate of deposits. Other bonds include bonds issued by private enterprises, Special Credit Institutions and foreign bonds. Cash value of life insurance includes assets held by domestic and foreign insurance companies as a counterpart to life insurance policies sold to residents. The household sector includes also non-profit organizations and unincorporated business.

Financial assets	**Asset shares**	
	1990	**1998**
Currency, transaction and savings accounts	36.80	22.69
Government bonds	27.42	10.35
Other bonds	3.16	9.53
Stocks	20.87	30.53
Mutual funds and managed investment accounts	2.30	16.42
Defined-contribution pension funds	5.93	4.54
Cash value of life insurance	3.09	5.92
Other financial assets	0.43	0.02
Total financial assets	100.00	100.00
Stocks, mutual funds and defined contribution pension funds	29.10	51.49
Total financial asset (billion euro, 1998 prices)	2021	2221
Number of households (million)	18.80	19.70
Financial assets per household (thousand euro)	107	113

The most significant change, however, is the increase in the share of stocks, mutual funds and other managed investment accounts. The combined share has risen from about 23 per cent of financial wealth in 1990 to 47 per cent in 1998. By the end of the millennium direct stockholding accounted for about a third of households financial wealth and mutual funds by 16 per cent. Although part of the increment reflects the increased market valuation that has taken place in the second half of the past decade, this is not the whole story.

The change in portfolio composition towards more stocks reflects a deep change in household portfolio strategies. The importance of foreign assets has also increased steadily over the 1990s. Almost absent in 1990, they now account for more than 6 per cent of financial wealth. Of these, 40 per cent are stocks, 10 per cent mutual funds and 50 per cent long-term bonds, suggesting that foreign assets are offering better opportunities to diversify risk. While home-country bias is definitely a feature of the portfolio of Italian households, the trend suggests that the weight of foreign securities in financial wealth is bound to increase even more in the future. Finally, the indebtedness of Italian households has also increased albeit at a slow pace.[1]

In sum, over the past decade the portfolio of Italian households has become much more oriented towards risky assets than it has ever been before. A number of factors contribute to explain the observed trends. Some relate to changes in asset return, others to institutional developments that have increased the incentive to invest in the stock market.

First, the nominal yield on transaction accounts and on short-term bonds has declined significantly over the nineties, while the return on equities, mutual funds, and managed investment accounts has been substantial. The nineties also witness a remarkable development of mutual funds. Introduced in 1984, when only 10 were operating, their number rose to 184 in 1990, 459 in 1995 and over one thousand in 2000. The market value of mutual funds increased especially in recent years, from 7.2 per cent of GDP in 1995 to over 20 per cent by the end of the nineties. Commercial banks have massively entered the sector increasing competition and reducing entry costs and management fees. Fierce advertising campaigns to acquire market shares have contributed to spreading financial information. Financial innovation in terms of packaging of new financial products has been substantial. By offering diversification opportunities not available before and reducing minimum investment constraints, mutual funds have enhanced Italian households' willingness to invest in domestic and foreign risky financial assets.

A second factor has been the privatization of state-owned enterprises and public utilities that has taken place in the 1990s. Starting in 1992, over 25 large state-owned corporations, including public utilities and state-owned banks, were successfully privatized with a total revenue of about 71 trillion euro. The privatization process and the number of firms going public have increased stock market capitalization.[2] The privatization process was accompanied by massive advertising campaigns, which helped households to become acquainted with stocks and their return and risk characteristics.[3] It is likely that this dissemination of information has increased stockholding permanently.

The reform of the social security system and the diminished expectations of pension benefits are urging households to rely increasingly on their own savings for retirement. As a consequence, private pension funds – traditionally negligible items of households' portfolios – have started to increase. Pension funds, in turn, tend to hold riskier portfolios than the representative household, contributing to increased stock market liquidity and thus direct participation. Finally, the lifting of capital controls, which have been in place until 1989, has improved portfolio diversification through acquisition of foreign assets. The marked fluctuations in the exchange rate following the exit of the Lira from the ERM in October 1992 slowed down the process, which has, in fact, accelerated after Italy rejoined the fixed exchange rate agreement in November 1996. With the single currency and the consequent elimination of exchange-rates risk and regulatory standardization in different European countries, we expect a further reduction in the home bias in the coming years.

These developments notwithstanding, the financial portfolio of Italian households – as it results from the financial accounts – retains several features of backwardness. The share of currency and transactions accounts in financial wealth is still relatively high in comparison with other industrialized countries; many financial assets have short maturities. The breadth of the Italian stock market has not yet reached the standards of other industrialized countries. In 1996 the number of listed firms was 3.8 per million inhabitants, while in the EU it was 13.5. Stock market capitalization was 21 per cent of GDP, against 40 per cent in the EU (Cecchetti, 1999). Finally, household debt remains low by international standards, despite deregulation, which has prompted an increase in the supply of loans to households. Low indebtedness reflects mainly supply side factors and financial backwardness. Imperfections in the credit market and limited access to credit have important interactions with portfolio decisions, as investors may be discouraged from holding stock in anticipation of liquidity constraints (Paxson, 1990; Guiso *et al.*, 1996).

Macroeconomic aggregates conceal crucial issues in analysing household portfolio. The aggregate financial accounts cannot establish if the change in asset shares that we observe in the last decade is due to a change in participation or in amount invested conditional on participation. Aggregate data are of no use in assessing whether holdings of stocks and other assets vary systematically with wealth or demographic characteristics (age, education, and demographic characteristics of the household). They also cannot address issues of portfolio mobility: even though an aggregate asset share is constant over time, there can be large and compensating movements in and out the financial markets. To address these issues one must rely on survey data.

6.3 Data on stockownership in Italy

The main microeconomic data source used in this chapter is the SHIW. For most purposes we rely on the last publicly available wave, which refers to 1998; but for comparison we use also some of the previous waves, covering the period 1989–95. The Bank of Italy conducted the 1998 SHIW on a representative sample of 7147 households. The survey collects detailed information on the composition of Italian households' wealth, both real and financial. A special section of the questionnaire addresses crucial issues in the analysis of household portfolios and stockholding, such as knowledge of the various financial instruments and exposure to background risk. Thus, portfolio data are particularly rich. Besides reporting portfolio data, the SHIW contains a comprehensive set of demographic characteristics of all household members. Here we summarize the main characteristics of the data.

Table 6.2 illustrates information available on stockholding in the 1998 SHIW. The survey contains data on direct and indirect stockholding

Table 6.2 Sources and type of information on ownership and amount of stocks, mutual funds and pension funds

The table summarizes the available information that is relevant for describing patterns of direct and indirect stockholding. Data refer to 1998.

	Detail on survey questions	
	Ownership	**Amount**
Stocks, of which	Yes	Yes
Listed shares	Yes	Yes
Non-listed shares	Yes	Yes
Employee share	Yes	Yes, available as a share of the total value of stocks
Shares of privatized companies	Yes	Yes, in brackets and amounts
Foreign shares	Yes	Yes, in brackets and amounts
Number of companies in which respondent owns shares	Yes	Not available for individual stocks
Mutual funds and other managed accounts	Yes, but no information on specific funds	Yes, but no information on specific funds
Defined contribution pension funds (individual and employer-sponsored pension plans)	Yes, with distinction between individual and employer-sponsored plan	Contribution in 1998 is available, cash value of pension fund must be imputed
Life insurance	Yes	Contribution in 1998 is available, cash value of life insurance must be imputed

through mutual funds and other managed investment accounts. It reports data on direct stockholding, both on participation and amounts, separately for listed and non-listed shares. It also has data on the shares of the company where a member of the household works (reported as a fraction of the total value of the stocks) and on the number of companies in which shares are held. These variables offer some guidance on the degree of diversification of risky assets and reasons for participation. Finally, the survey reports information on ownership and amount of foreign stocks and stocks in privatized firms. This level of detail is absent in the previous surveys and has been introduced in the 1998 wave after the privatization programme and the increasing international diversification of the second half of the nineties.

Many investors do not hold stocks directly, but through mutual funds and other managed accounts. The SHIW reports participation and amount invested in mutual funds and participation in pension funds and life insurance (the cash-value of life insurance and pension funds must be imputed). No detail is offered as to the composition of the fund. Considering that all those who invest in mutual funds also invest in stocks overstates stockholding, though it is difficult to say by how much.

Participation and amount invested is elicited with considerable care. For each of the 17 assets, respondents report participation and amount invested. Those who don't report the amount are asked to indicate the bracket where the asset value falls (14 brackets are provided). For these respondents, asset values must therefore be imputed. The problem of bracketing can be handled by assuming that households own the midpoint of the interval or by applying more sophisticated imputation procedures, such as that suggested by Stewart (1983). Imputation requires modeling the responses within each bracket, and its advantage diminishes when the number of brackets is relatively detailed, as in the case at hand, see Miniaci and Weber (2001). We thus proceed with the first alternative.[4]

Though this study uses the best available source to study the portfolio of Italian households, the data are almost surely contaminated by reporting errors and (unavoidable) imputation on our part. The difference observed between the aggregate financial accounts and the survey value of stocks could be traced back to various sources, including non-reporting, underreporting and imputations. Even in the absence of these problems, however, the survey data are bound to underestimate the national aggregate. With the notable exception of the US survey of consumer finances, richer households are largely under-represented in virtually all surveys. Given the high concentration of stocks in the richest segment of the wealth distribution, stock amounts are therefore grossly understated in any representative survey.

This suggests two considerations. First, as explained, reporting errors and imputation affect estimates of asset amounts more than asset participation, so we are more confident about statements on the latter than on the former. Second, if the main source of the difference between the national accounts and the survey information on stocks is that the rich are under-represented, then the survey data remain very useful for understanding differences in participation and amounts invested for the remaining portion of the population.

6.4 Who holds stocks?

In this section we describe stock market participation relying on two definitions of stockownership:

- The first definition is narrow, and considers only shares held directly. Since many households hold stocks through mutual funds, this is an underestimate of total stockholding.
- The second definition is broader, and includes direct and indirect stockholding. The latter includes also mutual funds, managed investment accounts, and pension funds (to the extent that these funds invest at least part of their portfolio in stocks). Due to data limitation we cannot distinguish mutual funds that invest in stocks from those that invest in bonds, or that part of the fund that is invested in stocks. Thus, direct and indirect stockholding is an upper bound for total stockholding.

Table 6.3 reports 1998 summary statistics. Sample characteristics refer to the head of the household. The average age is 54 years, 68 per cent are married and 72 per cent are males. Almost two-thirds of the sample has compulsory education. The remaining third has either high school degrees (27.6 per cent) or college degrees (7.7 per cent). The vast majority of households (72 per cent) have between 2 and 4 members; the proportion of single-earner is about the same as that of two-earners (40 per cent). Pension recipients represent 41 per cent of the sample, 36 per cent are wage earners, 14 per cent are self-employed, and 4 per cent unemployed.[5]

The proportion of households that invest in stock directly is 7.9 per cent, while that investing in mutual funds and other managed investment accounts is 11.1 per cent and that having pension funds is 7.9 per cent. This allows us to place the upper bound of stockholding (direct or

Table 6.3 Summary statistics

The table reports means and standard deviations for the main variables used in the study. All statistics are computed using population weights. Income and wealth are reported in thousand euro. Data are drawn from the 1998 SHIW.

Variable	Sample mean	Standard deviation
Age	54.58	15.76
Education: less than high school	0.647	0.48
Education: high school	0.276	0.45
Education: college	0.077	0.27
Married	0.685	0.46
Male	0.725	0.45
Singles	0.195	0.40
Between 2 and 4 household members	0.718	0.45
More than 4 household members	0.087	0.28
One-income recipient	0.440	0.50
Two-income recipients	0.419	0.49
More than two-income recipients	0.140	0.35
Wage earner	0.360	0.48
Self-employed	0.141	0.35
Unemployed	0.041	0.20
Pension recipient	0.413	0.49
Income	24.93	21.59
Financial assets	24.06	72.97
Real assets	126.96	287.64
Participation		
Proportion investing in stocks	0.079	0.27
Proportion investing in mutual funds	0.111	0.31
Proportion investing in pension funds	0.079	0.27
Proportion investing in stocks, mutual funds or pension funds	0.199	0.31
Amount invested		
In stocks, among stockholders (578 households)	25.38	54.18
In mutual funds, among those who invest in mutual funds (844 households)	45.88	107.70
In pension funds, among those who invest in pension funds (570 households)	11.37	10.26
In stocks, mutual funds and pension funds, among those who invest in these assets (1493 households)	39.96	99.99
Memo: Financial assets among those who invest in stocks, mutual funds or pension funds (1493 households)	70.96	131.82
Total number of households	7 147	

indirect) at 19.9 per cent. It is worth noting that participation has increased considerably in the last decade, from about 8 per cent in 1989 to 19.9 per cent in 1998. However, it is fair to say that even in 1998 only a minority of households invests in stock, and that the share is relatively low by international standards. Recent data from the 2001 BNL Survey on household saving confirms these figures, estimating that direct and indirect participation in 2001 is 21 per cent (Jappelli *et al.*, 2001).

There are at least two reasons for the low stock market participation. First, information, entry, and management costs are not trivial. Second, historically the Italian stock market has been extremely volatile, a consequence of a small and illiquid stock market.[6] In the last four decades, the standard deviation of the real growth rate of stock prices was 35 per cent, as opposed to standard deviations ranging from 16 to 19 per cent in France, Germany, the United Kingdom and the United States. The increased participation in mutual funds has been favoured by the appearance of mutual funds leading to lower transaction costs and better risk diversification.

However, entry costs remain high, particularly at low wealth levels. Minimum investment requirements further prevent entry. Transaction costs can explain why stock market participation is low compared to other countries at a similar stage of economic development. However, they cannot account fully for cross-sectional differences between stockholders and non-stockholders. We now turn to examine some of these characteristics in detail.

6.4.1 Age and stockownership

Table 6.4 reports the age profile of stockholding separately for direct holding, mutual funds and other investment accounts, pension funds, and for the total. In all cases, participation is hump shaped. With the exception of pension funds, at the beginning and at the end of the life cycle the proportion of stockholders is about the same. Participation peaks in the age class 50–59. At peak, the proportion of direct stockholders is 10.2 per cent (2 points above average), that of mutual funds is 13.9 per cent (3 points above average), and that of pension funds is 8.9 per cent (1 point above average). For total stockholding, the peak is at 24 per cent.

Figure 6.1 plots the age profile of the three categories (stocks, mutual funds and pension funds) and total (direct plus indirect) stock market participation. The raw data are smoothed by a probit regression with a third-order age polynomial. The figures confirm graphically a marked hump in participation. With pure cross-sectional data it is not possible

Table 6.4 Participation in stocks, mutual funds and pension funds, by age

The table reports the fraction investing in stocks by age. Data are drawn from the 1998 SHIW. All statistics use population weights.

	< 30	30–39	40–49	50–59	60–69	≥ 70	Total
Stocks	0.041	0.095	0.083	0.102	0.074	0.050	0.079
Mutual funds	0.055	0.149	0.125	0.139	0.109	0.052	0.111
Pension funds	0.049	0.148	0.112	0.089	0.050	0.009	0.079
Stocks, mutual funds or pension funds	0.121	0.284	0.240	0.243	0.169	0.088	0.199
Proportion of households	0.033	0.161	0.218	0.223	0.187	0.177	1.000

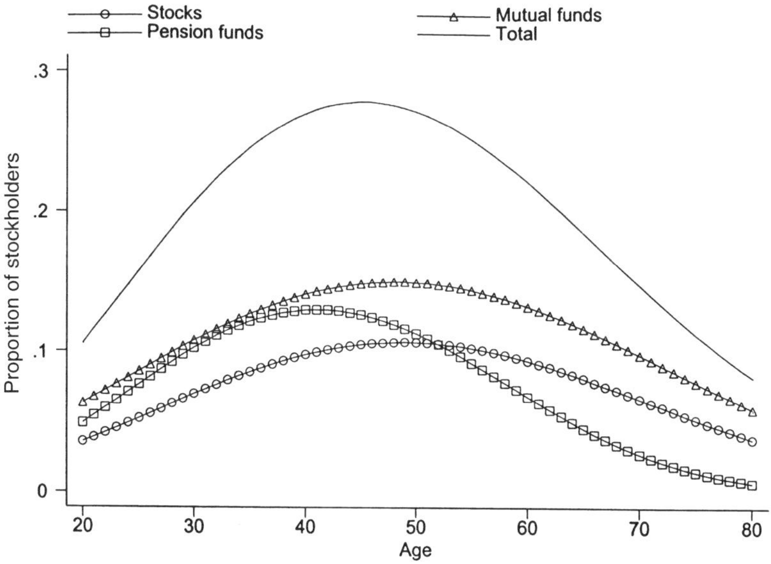

Figure 6.1 Participation in stocks, mutual funds and pension funds, by age

The figure plots the actual and estimated age profiles of the fraction of households that invest in stocks, mutual funds or defined contribution pension funds. Data are drawn from the 1998 SHIW. The estimated profile is obtained by a probit on a third order age polynomial.

to distinguish a pure age profile from cohort effects, that is, it might well be that older households in Figure 6.1 invest less in stocks because they belong to a different generation, and not because of a genuine age effect. Repeated cross-sectional data can be used to purge the cross-sectional age-profile from cohort effects. We thus use the 1989, 1991, 1993, 1995 and 1998 data to explore if cohort effects contaminate the cross-sectional profile.

Given the collinearity between age, time and cohort, with repeated cross-sectional data we can identify only two of these effects. In principle, there are two plausible identifying assumptions. One is to explain the raw data in terms of cohort and age effects. This decomposition disregards time effects, or assumes that they reflect idiosyncratic macro shocks that sum to zero and are orthogonal to a time trend (Deaton and Paxson, 1994). The other is to interpret the data as a combination of age and unrestricted time effects. We experimented with both to see which provides a more plausible description of the data. The decomposition in terms of cohort dummies (or polynomials), age dummies (or polynomials) and restricted time effects produces an increasing age profile (from 10 per cent at age 20 to 80 per cent at age 80), and offsetting and declining cohort effect and absence of time effects. Since the theory of portfolio choice provides no strong reason for including cohort effects in participation, we believe that the implausible combination of increasing age effects and decreasing cohort effects simply reflects a trend in participation. Financial innovations and increased competition among financial intermediaries (see Section 6.2) supports such an interpretation of the data, so we conclude that the age-profile in Figure 6.1 is a valid description of the data.

The hump in the age-profile of participation suggests the presence, at all ages, of significant fixed costs in purchasing stocks, and that investors consider investing in stocks only after they have accumulated substantial wealth. This effect is even more apparent if one considers that the incentive to invest in stocks is stronger for the young, as suggested by several theoretical models, see Heaton and Lucas (2000) and Haliassos (2002). Yet, in the data we observe a humped shape.

6.4.2 Education and stockownership

Table 6.5 breaks down stockholding by the educational attainment of the head. Education can affect portfolio choice for at least two reasons. It is correlated with a person's permanent income and wealth. Education also correlates with an investor's ability to acquire and process information, and with financial sophistication in general. Both

Table 6.5 Participation in stocks, mutual funds and pension funds, by education
The table reports the fraction investing in stocks by education. Data are drawn from the 1998 SHIW. All statistics use population weights.

	Less than high school	**High school**	**College**	**Average**
Stocks	0.042	0.125	0.222	0.079
Mutual funds	0.063	0.176	0.285	0.111
Pension funds	0.055	0.114	0.151	0.079
Stocks, mutual funds or pension funds	0.127	0.304	0.436	0.199
Proportion of households	0.617	0.295	0.087	1.000

reasons suggest a positive correlation between education and stockholding. We classify education into three groups: compulsory education (corresponding to 8 years of schooling), high school degree (5 additional years of schooling) and college degree or higher. Table 6.5 indicates that in the group with college degree participation is more than twice the average, while in the group with compulsory education it is about half the average. The effect of education on indirect stockholding is even stronger than that on direct stockholding. Interestingly, in the group with a college degree (8.7 per cent of the total sample) total stockholding is 43.6 per cent.

If the age profile of stockownership is plotted by educational attainment, one observes for each group the same humped shape in participation that we document in Figure 6.1 for the whole sample (for brevity these graphs are not reported). In particular, for investors with a college degree the profile of participation is steeper early in life and peaks later than for the less well educated.

6.4.3 Wealth and stockownership

Portfolio models with fixed participation costs into the stock market (due to information costs, participation fees, or other types of entry costs) imply that investment in stocks is optimal once the investor's wealth exceeds a given threshold. The theoretical prediction is therefore that stock market participation is an increasing function of wealth. Minimum thresholds for purchasing listed stocks also act as a barrier to entry and lead to a positive correlation between wealth and stockholding even in the absence of fixed participation costs. In Italy, in the past decade the threshold level was about euro 5000 (slightly higher than median financial wealth in 1998).

Table 6.6 shows the proportion of direct and indirect stockholders by financial assets quartile and for the top 5 and 1 per cent of the financial wealth distribution. Direct investment in stocks is virtually absent in the first quartile (0.4 per cent have stock, 1.2 per cent mutual funds, 0.3 per cent pension funds) and very low even in the second. Thus, in below median financial wealth virtually no household invests in stocks. This finding is confirmed even if one considers direct and indirect stockholding (only 1.5 per cent of those in the first quartile and 5.3 per cent in the second quartile invest in stocks). Even in the third quartile the proportion of households investing in stocks is only 4.6 per cent, about half the sample average. Stock market participation is much higher in the fourth quartile (26.8 per cent), and even higher in the top 5 and 1 per cent of the wealth distribution (50.5 and 60.9 per cent, respectively).

Indirect stockholding is higher than direct stockholding, above the third quartile of the wealth distribution, consistent with the fact that direct entry in the stock market is more costly than purchasing stocks indirectly through mutual funds. Overall, about 53.8 per cent of those in the fourth quartile invest in stocks, either directly or indirectly. The proportion rises to 76.7 and 78.3 per cent for households in the top 5 and 1 percentiles, respectively. Sorting the data by disposable income reveals a similar pattern. Participation is virtually absent in the two bottom income quartiles. Significant stockholding appears in household portfolios only for those with income above the median. For brevity, these results are not reported.

It is worth pointing out that even in the top percentiles of the wealth and income distributions there is a non-negligible fraction of households that do not invest in stocks or in mutual funds. This is hard to explain with the presence of fixed costs alone and suggests that features

Table 6.6 Participation in stocks, mutual funds and pension funds, by financial asset quartiles

The table reports the proportion of investors by gross financial asset quartiles. Data are drawn from the 1998 SHIW. All statistics use population weights.

	Quartile I	Quartile II	Quartile III	Quartile IV	Top 5%	Top 1%	Average
Stocks	0.004	0.013	0.046	0.268	0.505	0.609	0.079
Mutual funds	0.012	0.014	0.082	0.358	0.591	0.671	0.111
Pension funds	0.003	0.027	0.122	0.174	0.206	0.238	0.079
Stocks, mutual funds or pension funds	0.015	0.053	0.224	0.538	0.767	0.783	0.199

other than monetary participation costs are relevant in explaining stockownership.

6.4.4 Characteristics of stockholders and non-stockholders

The descriptive evidence shown thus far suggests that the typical stockholder is middle-aged, with relatively high level of financial assets and possibly a high level of education. Here, we extend the comparison between stockholders and non-stockholders to a richer set of household characteristics. Table 6.7 displays sample means of demographic and economic characteristics for households that invest in stocks directly, indirectly through mutual funds and pension funds, for those that invest in either stocks, mutual funds and pension funds, and for those who do not invest in stocks.

Compared to non-stockholders, stockholders are more likely to be married (especially for indirect holding), male, and have households of 2 to 4 members with more than two-income recipients. Being a wage earner does not seem to affect the decision to invest in stocks. The self-employed are twice more likely to invest in stocks. One explanation for this finding, which is common to other countries as well, is that the self-employed hold a larger share of their wealth in their own business, and invest in stocks in order to diversify their portfolio. In addition, the self-employed are less risk averse and risk aversion increases the propensity to invest in stocks (Guiso and Paiella, 2001). These effects, however, are counteracted by the fact that the self-employed are more exposed to risk, which should discourage them from further investing in risky assets. Needless to say, the unemployed and pension recipients are less likely to invest in stocks, reflecting their low wealth as well as their age.

The last rows of Table 6.7 report also the proportion of respondents that work in small and large business by stock-ownership status. If one reason for stockownership is investing in the company one works for, then the fraction of stockowners should be higher for employees of a large company than for those of a small one. The data are consistent with this hypothesis: the proportion of stockholders among those employed by a company with more than 50 employees is smaller (0.104) than for those employed by firms with more than 50 employees (0.113).

6.4.5 Types, number of stocks and investment in the employer's company

The microeconomic survey allows us to highlight some interesting features of stockownership, such as the type of stocks held, the number of different stocks in the portfolio, and the nature of the equity issuer.

Table 6.7 Demographic characteristics of stockholders and non-stockholders

The table reports demographic characteristics of stockholders and non-stockholders. Data are drawn from the 1998 SHIW. Income and wealth are expressed in thousand euro. All statistics use population weights.

Variable	Stocks	Mutual funds	Pension funds	Stocks, mutual funds or pension funds	Non-stockholders
Married	0.784	0.771	0.833	0.790	0.659
Male	0.818	0.800	0.821	0.807	0.704
Singles	0.117	0.124	0.073	0.110	0.216
Between 2 and 4 household members	0.816	0.813	0.856	0.817	0.694
More than 4 household members	0.066	0.062	0.071	0.072	0.090
One-income recipient	0.270	0.292	0.290	0.294	0.476
Two-income recipients	0.483	0.494	0.455	0.485	0.403
More than two-income recipients	0.246	0.213	0.254	0.221	0.120
Wage earner	0.373	0.381	0.501	0.422	0.344
Self-employed	0.262	0.255	0.281	0.252	0.114
Unemployed	0.016	0.021	0.011	0.017	0.047
Pension recipient	0.318	0.318	0.175	0.279	0.447
Disposable income	50.850	46.418	37.414	41.362	20.843
Gross financial wealth	103.611	90.335	54.943	68.614	12.970
Real wealth	325.803	260.279	189.753	234.229	100.255
Employed in firms with less than 50 employees	0.492	0.489	0.469	0.494	0.529
Employed in firms with more than 50 employees	0.508	0.511	0.530	0.505	0.471
Number of observations	607	876	586	1542	5605

Table 6.8 reports the distribution of stockholding by type of stock in 1998. Among stockholders (direct and indirect) the fraction of those holding listed stocks is 44 per cent. Half of these listed stocks are stocks of privatized companies, consistent with the important role of the privatization process in promoting stockownership.[7] Almost 10 per cent

Table 6.8 Distribution of stockholding, by types of stocks

The table reports the distribution of stockownership by type of stocks. Proportions do not sum to 1 because multiple holdings are possible. Data are drawn from the 1998 SHIW.

	Proportion of holders
Stocks of listed companies	0.447
of which, privatized companies	0.259
Stocks of non-listed companies	0.095
Stocks of limited liability companies	0.032
Stocks of other companies	0.009
Foreign stocks	0.028
Direct stockownership	0.512
Indirect stockownership	0.739
Direct plus indirect stockownership	1.000

Table 6.9 Number of stocks of different companies held by direct stockholders

The table reports the distribution of the number of shares in different companies held by direct stockholders. Data are drawn from the 1998 SHIW. All statistics use population weights. Out of 607 stockholders, 597 report the number of shares.

Number of stocks	**Number of investors**	**As a proportion of those investing in stocks directly**	**Cumulative frequency**
1 stock	256	0.429	0.429
2 stocks	149	0.250	0.678
3 stocks	69	0.116	0.794
4 stocks	49	0.082	0.876
5 stocks	36	0.060	0.936
More than 5	38	0.064	1.000
Total stockholding	597	1.000	—

invest in stocks of non-listed companies and about 4 per cent in other stocks, typically non-listed. A tiny fraction of households (2.8 per cent) invests directly in foreign stocks, a reflection of the extent of the home bias in household portfolios.

Table 6.9 focuses on direct stockholders only. For this group, it reports the distribution of the number of different stocks. Most stockholders (43 per cent) invest in only one company, 25 per cent in two companies, 25.6 per cent in three to five different companies. Very few investors have stocks of more than five companies, suggesting that

Table 6.10 Investing in the employer's company

The first panel reports the number of investors that, among all stockholders, invest in the employer's business. It is obtained from the following question in the 1998 SHIW: '*Among the listed stocks of your family, are there stocks of companies where one member of your household is an employee?*' The second panel reports stocks of the employer's company as a proportion of total stocks. Data are drawn from the 1998 SHIW. Out of 607 stockholders, 599 reply to the question.

Owns employer's stock	Number of investors	Proportion of investors	Cumulative frequency
Proportion investing in one's employer company			
Yes	98	0.164	0.164
No	501	0.836	1.000
Total	599	1.000	—
Stocks in one's employer business as a fraction of total investment in stocks			
Less than 10 per cent	8	0.082	0.082
10–30 per cent	14	0.143	0.225
30–50 per cent	13	0.133	0.358
50–75 per cent	12	0.122	0.480
75–99 per cent	9	0.092	0.572
100 per cent	42	0.428	1.000
Total	98	1.000	—

household portfolios are poorly diversified. Monitoring costs and costs of acquiring information on several companies may limit the number of stocks in the portfolio. This explanation is consistent with the previous evidence concerning low participation in foreign stock markets, which are more costly to monitor.

To complete the picture, Table 6.10 reports the number and proportion of households that own equity in the employer's company (first panel) and the proportion of the value of stocks in the total value of stocks held (second panel). The table focuses again on direct stockholders. About 16 per cent own stocks of the employer's company, on which presumably it is easier to have better and direct information. For about half of them this is the only stock owned directly. For another 20 per cent, stocks in the employer's business account for between 50 and 99 per cent of total direct stockholding.

6.4.6 Econometric estimates

We summarize our exploratory analysis of the determinants of stock-ownership by reporting probit regressions for stockholding. The results are reported in Table 6.11 separately for stocks, mutual funds, pension funds, and overall participation. Results are easy to interpret, because each of the regressors is a dummy variable, and each of the coefficients indicate the effect of the dummy on the probability of investing in a particular asset. The results broadly confirm the descriptive evidence.

Although several of the age dummies are not statistically different from zero, the probits indicate the presence of a humped shape in participation. High school and college degree raise the probability of investing in stocks by 2 and 4 percentage points, respectively. Results for mutual funds, are similar, while for pension funds we do not find a clear association between education and participation. Demographic variables such as married and male are not important determinants of stockownership. Other demographic variables, such as household composition, have been excluded for lack of significance.

Financial and real wealth quartiles are very important determinants of all the probit regressions in Table 6.11. Focusing on the last column (direct and indirect participation) we find that the probability of investing in stocks in the second financial wealth quartile increases by 21 per cent (with respect to the first quartile), 48 per cent in the third quartile, and 68.9 per cent in the third quartile. The effect of real wealth is not as strong as that of financial wealth, and is statistically different from zero only in the fourth quartile.

The last rows of Table 6.11 indicate that residency in the South is generally associated with less participation, and that households resident in provinces with higher unemployment rates invest less in stocks, mutual funds and pension funds. The result for the unemployment rate is particularly interesting, as this variable is a proxy for the overall riskiness of the economic environment in which households make their decisions. This variable may therefore reflect the discouraging effect of background, undiversifiable risk on risky investment (Guiso *et al.*, 1996; Heaton and Lucas, 2000). On the other hand, households resident in provinces with more developed capital markets (as measured by the number of bank branches in the province) invest more in stocks and mutual funds, raising overall participation in the stock market.

6.5 The amount invested in stocks

While age, education and wealth are important determinants of the decision to invest in stocks, mutual funds and pension funds, the asset share invested in stocks, mutual funds and pension funds is much harder to predict. Table 6.12 reports a breakdown of the shares by the

Table 6.11 Probit regressions for participation in stocks, mutual funds and pension funds

The table reports probit regressions for direct stockholding, mutual funds, and pension funds. Income and financial wealth brackets are based on income and gross financial wealth quartiles. Demographic variables refer to the head of the household. The index of financial development is the ratio of loans to GDP in the province of residence. The regressions also include three dummies for city size (between 20 000 and 40 000 inhabitants, between 40 000 and 500 000 inhabitants, and over 500 000 inhabitants). Excluded attributes are: age less than 35, less than high school, non married, female, singles, non self-employed, non pension recipient, first income bracket, first wealth bracket. Data are drawn from the 1998 SHIW (7145 households). *z*-values are reported in parenthesis.

Variable	Stocks	Mutual funds	Pension funds	Stocks, mutual funds or pension funds
Age				
30–39	0.033 (2.21)	0.019 (1.56)	0.035 (2.73)	0.085 (3.27)
40–49	0.016 (1.27)	0.009 (0.84)	0.020 (1.81)	0.048 (2.08)
50–59	0.025 (1.88)	0.009 (0.79)	0.007 (0.74)	0.038 (1.68)
60–69	0.022 (1.62)	0.011 (0.95)	− 0.001 (− 0.76)	0.022 (0.99)
70 +	0.019 (1.37)	− 0.003 (− 0.25)	− 0.023 (− 3.19)	− 0.023 (− 1.11)
High school	0.019 (5.31)	0.016 (4.29)	− 0.001 (− 0.02)	0.033 (4.26)
College	0.041 (6.49)	0.036 (5.66)	0.007 (1.42)	0.079 (6.00)
Married	0.006 (1.60)	− 0.001 (− 0.08)	0.010 (2.69)	0.017 (1.84)
Male	0.003 (0.69)	− 0.001 (− 0.15)	− 0.004 (− 0.96)	− 0.007 (− 0.77)
II financial wealth quartile	0.050 (2.77)	0.093 (2.98)	0.100 (4.33)	0.217 (6.20)
III financial wealth quartile	0.125 (5.39)	0.263 (5.87)	0.253 (7.75)	0.487 (12.01)
IV financial wealth quartile	0.305 (9.02)	0.509 (8.69)	0.286 (8.28)	0.689 (0.033)
II real wealth quartile	0.010 (1.70)	0.004 (0.68)	0.001 (0.19)	0.013 (1.17)
III real wealth quartile	0.023 (3.82)	0.014 (2.59)	0.001 (0.25)	0.035 (3.27)
IV real wealth quartile	0.034 (5.36)	0.023 (4.07)	0.001 (0.33)	0.059 (5.23)
Resident in the South	− 0.005 (− 0.91)	− 0.024 (− 3.95)	− 0.021 (− 3.60)	− 0.072 (− 5.68)
Number of bank branches in the province of residence	− 0.011 (− 0.69)	0.008 (0.49)	0.041 (2.58)	0.036 (0.99)
Index of financial development	0.009 (2.34)	0.001 (0.49)	0.001 (1.85)	0.020 (2.15)
Unemployment rate in the province of residence	− 0.067 (− 1.92)	− 0.088 (− 2.25)	− 0.022 (− 0.61)	− 0.107 (− 1.34)

Table 6.12 Asset shares invested in stocks, mutual funds and pension funds, by age

The asset shares are computed in the group of households that reports investing in stocks, mutual funds or pension funds (1493 observations).

	<30	30–39	40–49	50–59	60–69	≥70	Total
Stocks	0.062	0.082	0.101	0.116	0.127	0.146	0.107
Mutual funds	0.175	0.201	0.197	0.254	0.338	0.304	0.242
Pension funds	0.203	0.246	0.197	0.146	0.100	0.046	0.169
Stock, mutual funds or pension funds	0.441	0.529	0.495	0.516	0.564	0.496	0.518

Table 6.13 Asset shares invested in stocks, mutual funds and pension funds, by education

The asset shares are computed in the group of households that reports investing in stocks, mutual funds or pension funds (1493 observations).

	Less than high school	High school	College	Total
Stocks	0.090	0.115	0.132	0.107
Mutual funds	0.230	0.247	0.263	0.242
Pension funds	0.199	0.158	0.120	0.169
Stocks, mutual funds or pension funds	0.519	0.519	0.514	0.518

age of the household head. Each share is computed in the group of households that invest in stocks, mutual funds, or pension funds (1493 observations). This way the different shares can be more easily compared.

In the total sample, the asset share of stocks is 10.7 per cent, 24.2 per cent for mutual funds, and 16.9 per cent for pension funds, with a total investment of 51.8 per cent in these assets. While for stocks and mutual funds the share is slightly increasing in age, the pattern of pension funds is opposite, reflecting much higher contribution rates for the young. Thus, the overall profile of the share is rather flat, ranging from 44.1 per cent for the youngest group to 49.6 per cent for the oldest.

Asset shares by education are reported in Table 6.13. As with age, the education profile is rather flat (and even decreasing for pension funds).

Table 6.14 Asset shares invested in stocks, mutual funds and pension funds, by financial asset quartiles

The asset shares are computed in the group of households that reports investing in stocks, mutual funds or pension funds (1493 observations).

	Quartile I	Quartile II	Quartile III	Quartile IV	Top 5%	Top 1%	Total
Stocks	0.149	0.108	0.069	0.123	0.154	0.187	0.107
Mutual funds	0.058	0.104	0.167	0.288	0.367	0.481	0.242
Pension funds	0.257	0.384	0.314	0.087	0.032	0.018	0.169
Stocks, mutual funds or pension funds	0.465	0.596	0.550	0.498	0.553	0.687	0.518

Finally, grouping households by financial asset quartiles (Table 6.14), reveals that the asset share invested in stocks by investors in the lowest quartile (14.9 per cent) is similar to that invested by investors in the fourth quartile or top 5 per cent of the wealth distribution. The total share (stocks, mutual funds, and pension funds) is 46.5 per cent in the lowest quartile, and 55.3 per cent in the top quartile. Clearly, age, education and wealth matter for the decision to invest in stocks, and much less for the amount invested in each of these assets. This insight is confirmed by regressions analysis.

Estimation of asset shares with microeconomic data requires careful econometric modeling. To clarify, let's consider the case of the asset share invested in stocks. OLS estimates of the share invested in stocks on the entire sample are inconsistent, because not all households invest in stocks. OLS estimates of the share on the restricted sample of households who invest in stocks are also inconsistent because they are subject to selection bias. Miniaci and Weber (2002) explain that the best strategy is to model the demand for stocks as a two-stage decision process, where the first step is a probit regression for the probability of investing in stocks, and the second step consists in estimating the conditional demand of stocks, using the first stage probabilities to correct for selectivity bias.

In practice, we posit that households choose first whether to invest in stocks or not, and then how to allocate financial wealth between stocks and other assets. To identify the demand for stocks, one must consider different sets of explanatory variables in the first and second stage regressions. The identification restriction in the empirical analysis is

Table 6.15 Regressions for the asset shares invested in stocks, mutual funds and pension funds

The table reports second stage regressions for the asset share invested in stocks, mutual funds and pension funds. Data refer to 1998. *t*-statistics are reported in parenthesis. Income and financial wealth brackets are based on income and gross financial wealth quartiles.

Variable	Stocks	Mutual funds	Pension funds	Stocks, mutual funds or pension funds
Age				
30–39	0.143 (1.39)	0.037 (0.14)	− 0.047 (− 0.63)	0.054 (0.96)
40–49	0.148 (1.49)	0.069 (0.26)	− 0.059 (− 0.81)	0.052 (0.94)
50–59	0.162 (1.60)	0.113 (0.43)	− 0.048 (− 0.65)	0.088 (1.60)
60–69	0.172 (1.69)	0.194 (0.72)	− 0.066 (− 0.86)	0.124 (2.21)
70+	0.107 (1.04)	0.190 (0.56)	− 0.005 (− 0.06)	0.116 (1.97)
High school	0.070 (1.99)	− 0.013 (− 0.14)	− 0.021 (− 0.95)	0.007 (0.43)
College	0.112 (2.32)	− 0.014 (− 0.10)	0.009 (0.31)	0.032 (1.39)
Married	0.062 (1.78)	− 0.005 (− 0.06)	− 0.036 (− 1.14)	0.011 (0.49)
Male	− 0.051 (− 1.46)	− 0.012 (− 0.12)	− 0.028 (− 0.97)	− 0.027 (− 1.22)
II financial wealth bracket	0.029 (0.17)	0.145 (0.01)	0.211 (1.26)	0.054 (0.42)
III financial wealth bracket	0.049 (0.26)	0.140 (0.01)	0.113 (0.65)	− 0.046 (− 0.34)
IV financial wealth bracket	0.048 (0.21)	0.072 (0.01)	− 0.177 (− 1.01)	− 0.165 (− 1.15)
II real wealth bracket	0.041 (0.78)	− 0.037 (− 0.19)	− 0.052 (− 1.57)	− 0.046 (− 1.61)
III real wealth bracket	0.057 (1.08)	− 0.051 (− 0.33)	− 0.064 (− 2.09)	− 0.065 (− 2.51)
IV real wealth bracket	0.109 (1.88)	− 0.021 (− 0.13)	− 0.058 (− 1.93)	− 0.030 (− 1.15)
Number of uncensored observations	578	844	570	1493

that information and transaction costs affect the decision to invest in stocks, but not the amount purchased. In the first stage (the probit regression), these costs are proxied by the number of bank branches in the province, region of residence, the index of financial development, and the provincial unemployment rate. These variables are therefore excluded from the second stage regressions. We model the demand for mutual funds and pension funds and the overall share invested in stocks, mutual funds and pension funds in a similar way.

The results of the second stage estimation are reported in Table 6.15. Overall, the regressions indicate that it is hard to predict conditional asset shares on the basis of standard economic and demographic variables. None of the age coefficients is statistically different from zero. With the exception of the 'college' dummy in the equation for stocks, the education categories are also not statistically different from zero. The asset share of stocks increases with wealth but, again, the coefficients of the dummies for financial wealth are not statistically different from zero.

6.6 Information and transaction costs

In 1998, direct stock market participation was about 8 per cent. Including also indirect participation through mutual funds and pension funds raises participation to about 20 per cent. Participation is limited or absent below median financial wealth, and even in the fourth quartile of the wealth distribution it is only slightly above 50 per cent. On the other hand, the correlation between the amount invested in stocks and financial wealth is weak at best.

The strong correlation between wealth and stock market participation points to the importance of fixed participation costs as a crucial element in understanding the portfolio choice of Italian investors. These costs take various forms, from minimum investment requirements, to transaction costs in purchasing stocks and mutual funds, to information costs.

Currently, typical entry costs or exit fees for equity funds are still generally in the order of 3 per cent for investment under 5000 euro. A significant reduction in costs applies only to very large investments, above 500 000 euros. Sometimes mutual funds do not charge at entry but impose an exit fee that varies with the amount invested and the timing of disinvestments. Even these fees vary between 2 and 3 per cent for investment of 5000 euros withdrawn after 1 year. The finding that the index of bank diffusion – which we regard as a good proxy for financial transaction costs – correlates positively with participation lends indirect support to the importance of these costs in Italian financial markets.

Managing a portfolio requires effort and knowledge of transaction costs, asset returns, volatility, and covariances with other assets. In this respect, in Italy many households lack not only sophisticated financial information, but also basic knowledge of financial assets. A set of questions in the 1998 SHIW asks respondents to report knowledge of each of the 17 popular assets. About one-third of the sample does not know of the existence of equities; over 50 per cent are ignorant of the existence of mutual funds. About half of the sample is unaware of the existence of certificates of deposit and corporate bonds.

These results are confirmed by a recent survey carried out by Filippa and Franzosi (2001) for the Italian Stock Exchange. The survey indicates that most investors lack financial information: about two-thirds of the investors do not even know how much time they spend on collecting portfolio-relevant information and managing their assets (implying that it must be a marginal activity). This proportion becomes 75 per cent for women, the elderly and resident in the South. Of those who know, median time dedicated to personal finance is less than 30 minutes per week. The results of this survey are even more telling considering that the sample is a highly selected group of investors that own stocks listed at the Milano Stock Exchange. This type of investor is not only more educated and wealthier than the median investor, but should also be particularly interested in gathering financial information and following stock market developments.

Even more striking is the finding by Filippa and Franzosi that among the selected group of investors with listed stocks, only about two-thirds know the existence of mutual funds and less than 50 per cent the existence of certificates of deposits and of non-listed shares. The evidence from the SHIW and from the survey of investors in the Milano Stock Exchange represents therefore strong evidence that Italian investors lack basic financial information, and that informational barriers represent a significant obstacle to stock market participation.

6.7 Conclusions

In this chapter we provide a thorough analysis of the trends in the portfolio of Italian households and of their propensity to invest in stocks. We study the determinants of the decision to invest in the stock market and of the amount invested, and identify the main variables that explain household heterogeneity in the propensity to invest in stocks. Our main source of data is the survey of household income and wealth. The survey is particularly well suited for the purpose at hand because it collects detailed information on the composition of household financial wealth and on demographic variables.

We find that direct stock market participation is about 8 per cent. Including also indirect participation through mutual funds and pension funds raises participation to about 20 per cent. The age profile of participation is hump shaped, with a peak around the age of 50, and participation is generally correlated with education. Participation is limited or absent below median financial wealth, and even in the fourth quartile of the wealth distribution it is only slightly above 50 per cent.

On the other hand, the correlations between the amount invested in stocks and age, education, and financial wealth are generally weak.

The strong correlation between wealth and stock market participation points to the importance of fixed participation costs (minimum investment requirements, transaction costs, and information costs) as a crucial element in understanding the portfolio choice of Italian investors.

Appendix

In this Appendix we report detailed information on the 1998 survey of household income and wealth and on the characteristics of portfolio data used in this chapter.

The 1998 survey of household income and wealth

The 1998 Bank of Italy survey of household income and wealth (SHIW) collects detailed data on demographics, households' consumption, income and balance sheets. The survey covers 7147 households. The SHIW surveys a representative sample of the Italian resident population. Sampling is in two stages, first municipalities and then households. Municipalities are divided into 51 strata defined by 17 regions and 3 classes of population size (more than 40 000, 20 000 to 40 000, less than 20 000). Households are randomly selected from registry office records. The net response rate (ratio of responses to contacted households net of ineligible units) is 43 per cent. Households are defined as groups of individuals related by blood, marriage, or adoption and sharing the same dwelling. If the head is a female, and the spouse is a male, we define the household head to be the male. A CD-ROM containing the entire historical SHIW archive can be obtained by writing to: The Research Department, Banca d'Italia, Via Nazionale 91, 00186 Roma, Italy.

Stock market participation and amount invested

Respondents report participation in 25 financial assets categories: transaction accounts, two categories of saving accounts, certificates of deposit, repurchasement agreements, postal accounts, postal bonds, five categories of government bonds (BOT, CCT, BTP, CTZ, other government bonds), corporate bonds, mutual funds, listed stocks, three categories of unlisted shares, three categories of managed investment accounts, three categories of foreign assets (corporate and government bonds, stocks, other foreign assets), loans to cooperative societies. For each of the 25 assets, respondents are first asked:

Do you invest in [this particular asset]?
If the answer is yes, the interviewer gives the respondent a list of 14 brackets, and asks him to report the interval:

- Up to 2 million lire
- Between 2 and 4 million
- Between 4 and 8 million
- Between 8 and 12 million

- Between 12 and 16 million
- Between 16 and 24 million
- Between 24 and 36 million
- Between 36 and 70 million
- Between 70 and 140 million
- Between 140 and 300 million
- Between 300 and 600 million
- Between 600 million and 1 billion lire
- Between 1 and 2 billion
- Above 2 billion

The respondent is then asked:
Could you tell me the approximate amount you invest in [this particular asset]?
If the respondent refuses to answer, the interviewer asks for each asset:
Could you at least tell me if the amount is closer to the upper interval, to the lower interval, or in the middle of the interval?

Imputation of stock amounts

The problem of bracketing can be handled either by assuming that all households own the mid-point of the interval or by applying more sophisticated imputation procedures, such as that suggested by Stewart (1983). The advantage of the second procedure falls with the number of brackets. Since we have 14 brackets, we proceed with the first alternative.

Financial assets are the sum of the 25 asset categories, plus the cash value of life insurance and the cash values of defined contribution pension funds. These must be imputed separately on the basis of the yearly contribution and on the number of years of contributions and then added to the other financial assets.

Total financial assets come to only about half of the corresponding financial account aggregate. The items that are more seriously underestimated are corporate bonds, stocks, mutual funds, life insurance, private pension funds, and foreign assets. This is partly due to under-sampling and under-reporting by the wealthy, which own a disproportionate share of these financial instruments.

References

Cecchetti, S. G. (1999) 'Legal structure, financial structure, and the monetary policy transmission mechanism', NBER Working Paper 7151.

Cesari, R. and F. Panetta (1998) 'Style, fees and performance of Italian equity funds', Bank of Italy, *Temi di Discussione* no. 325.

Deaton, A. and C. Paxson (1994) 'Saving, growth and aging in Taiwan', in D. Wise (ed.), *Studies in the Economics of Aging*, Chicago: University of Chicago Press.

Filippa, L. and A. Franzosi (2001) 'Investitori retail e borsa: risultati di un'indagine presso i risparmiatori italiani', *BIT Notes* no. 3, Milano: Borsa Italiana.

Guiso, L., T. Jappelli and D. Terlizzese (1996) 'Income risk, borrowing constraints and portfolio choice', *American Economic Review*, **86**: 158–72.

Guiso, L. and M. Paiella (2001) 'Risk aversion, wealth, and background risk', *CEPR Discussion Paper* no. 2728.
Haliassos, M. (2002) 'Stockholding: recent lessons from theory and computations', this volume, Chapter 2.
Heaton, J. and D. Lucas (2000) 'Portfolio choice in the presence of background risk', *The Economic Journal*, **109**: 1–25.
Jappelli, T., Ch. Julliard and M. Pagano (2001) 'La diversificazione del portafoglio delle famiglie italiane', in *XIX Rapporto BNL-Centro Einaudi sul risparmio e i risparmiatori in Italia*, Roma: BNL Edizioni, Guerini e Associati.
Miniaci, R. and G. Weber (2002) 'Survey design and estimation of portfolio models', this volume, Chapter 3.
Pagano, M., F. Panetta and L. Zingales (1998) 'Why do companies go public? An empirical analysis', *The Journal of Finance*, **53**.
Paxson, C. (1990) 'Borrowing constraints and portfolio choice', *Quarterly Journal of Economics*, **105**: 535–43.
Stewart, M. B. (1983) 'On least squares estimation when the dependent variable is grouped', *Review of Economic Studies*, **50**: 737–53.

7
Stockholding in the Netherlands

Rob Alessie and Stefan Hochguertel

7.1 Introduction

This chapter details the trends in (in)direct stockownership and in portfolio shares of different types of risky assets conditional upon ownership in the Netherlands over much of the past decade, and tries to identify some of the main driving forces of household investment behaviour. We use descriptive evidence from macro data sources to show overall trends in household sector portfolio composition. To identify the economic and demographic characteristics of the average household we use a recent micro data set that follows individual households over time. This CentER Savings Survey (CSS), administered in close cooperation with economists and other academics studying saving behaviour, is an extraordinary rich source of information that not only reflects the major trends in financial markets for the private household sector, but also allows inference on which household characteristics are associated with level and composition of financial portfolios.

Like in other European societies, stocks in the Netherlands were traditionally in the hands of a few. Typically, listed shares were owned either by other businesses and financial institutions or institutional investors such as pension funds or life insurance companies. The vast majority of households was not much exposed to direct stockholding, but somewhat more through indirect channels such as pensions and life insurances. This picture held until the early 1990s but has changed considerably in recent years. In particular, mutual funds became very attractive forms of saving for the average household, since stock returns were high during the 1990s, and participation and transaction costs were reduced (not least owing to increased competition in this market sector and technological developments such as phone and internet banking). Holding stocks via mutual funds has however seen much higher growth rates in the recent past than holding stocks directly. Much of the increase in overall financial risk taking has been accompanied by a reduction of traditional savings accounts and related investment vehicles. At the same time, households have invested more in housing.

The Netherlands differs in important respects from other European economies such as Italy, France, or Germany, when it comes to household finances. Unlike in other countries, bond holding is not widespread among consumer households. Instead, traditional savings accounts are of much higher importance. The institutional economic framework also differs in the Netherlands. For instance, the Dutch Guilder had established itself as a strong currency, latest since the 1980s, when regulatory exchange controls and other restrictions in financial markets were abolished. Monetary policy pursued a tight link to the German Deutschmark using interest rates as the main instrument, and the country was well prepared to enter the European Monetary Union. So, the immediate effects of joining the Euro zone on household finances will not have been as pronounced as in some other countries. Likewise, privatization will not have contributed much to direct stockholding, in particular, since among large former state-owned companies only the shares of KPN (telecommunications) are traded on the stock market.

Rather, competitive forces in the banking and insurance industry have led to innovation in financial products. Coupled with a period of stable economic growth and a booming stock market this is presumably the main reason why households appear to be more risk taking than before. But also policy changes with respect to the old-age retirement system may have induced private households to use high-return assets with the long run in mind.

We begin Section 7.2 by introducing basic macro facts and institutional settings. Section 7.3 contains a brief description of the household-level data on asset ownership and amounts. Section 7.4 presents summary statistics and cross-tabulations on stockholders versus non-stockholders. In this section, we also discuss results from regression analyses, conducted on our micro data, explaining ownership. In Section 7.5 we pay attention to the portfolio shares of different types of risky assets conditional upon ownership. Section 7.6 reflects back on particular issues relevant for the Netherlands that are possibly not shared by other countries, and Section 7.7 concludes. An Appendix contains details on the micro data source and on questions posed to the respondents.

7.2 The household portfolio in the Netherlands: macroeconomic indicators[1]

Table 7.1 shows figures from the National Account Statistics. Financial data for the household sector became available as of 1995. In the Netherlands, the asset category 'defined benefit pensions and contribution pensions and other life insurance assets' is an important part of the household portfolio: more than 50 per cent of all financial assets are held in this form, which is very high by European standards. In Germany, for instance, the share of life insurance and pension plans in total financial assets is about 22 per cent (see Deutsche Bundesbank, 1999), in Italy only 10.5 per cent (in 1998). The high share in the Netherlands is largely due to the compulsory occupational pension system of the defined benefit type, which covers most employees (about 90 per cent) and ex-employees.[2] Moreover, the category is rather broadly defined, and also includes (non-compulsory) whole life insurance and annuities. These include assets that are popular because of their tax-preferred nature. Also note that in some cases premiums of the insurance policies can be invested in risky assets. However, in this case

Table 7.1 Composition of household financial wealth: aggregate financial accounts

The table reports the composition of household financial wealth from National Account Statistics. The definition of the household sector includes 'non-profit institutions serving households'. Bonds cover all types of bonds. Stocks and mutual funds cannot be distinguished from the data. The data refer to beginning-of-year amounts.

Financial assets	**Asset shares**	
	1995	**1998**
Cash	2.5	1.8
Transaction and saving accounts	18.1	15.9
Certificates of deposit	2.9	2.2
Bonds	3.0	2.5
Stocks and mutual funds	18.8	22.6
Defined benefit and defined contribution pensions and other life insurances	52.0	52.6
Other financial assets	0.3	0.2
Trade credits and residual	2.3	2.2
Total financial assets	100.0	100.0
Total financial assets (in billion €)	674.2	935.1
Total number of households (in million)	6.49	6.66

we are not able to distinguish between assets that entail (substantial stockholding) risk and those that do not.

Within the short period of observation, households have transformed their portfolio composition in a substantial way. For instance, we see that the share of rather safe assets (like cash, transaction and saving accounts, CDs and bonds) has decreased (from a total of 26.5 per cent in 1995 to 22.4 per cent in 1998). Stocks and mutual funds, on the other hand, have seen a surge of about equal size. It is fairly safe to say that stocks and mutual funds are of the risky asset type. Most assets of the mutual funds were held in equity (about 50 per cent in 2000), followed by real estate (about 25 per cent) and bonds (10 per cent). The importance of equity and real estate in the portfolio of mutual funds has increased considerably during the nineties at the expense of deposits and bonds (De Nederlandsche Bank, 2001a).

While direct stockholding may have been reduced when stock markets displayed negative returns in 2000 and 2001, the fast growth in mutual funds also continued beyond 1999. The Dutch Central Bank reports that the number of registered mutual fund schemes has increased from 318 in 1997 to 558 in 2000 (i.e. by more than 20 per cent annually).[3] Also, the total investments in these funds were increasing at high rates, from about €44 billion (ultimo 1994) to about €117 billion at the end of 2000 (29 per cent of GDP). In terms of geographical diversification one sees that only about 14 per cent of funds were purely domestic in 2000. Much of the rest was internationally diversified owing to the popularity of industry-specific and other specialized funds (De Nederlandsche Bank, 2001a). In Section 7.6, we pay attention to the question why participation in mutual funds has increased so much.

Macroeconomic data can give an impression about overall trends, but they mask important developments at the level of the individual household. Important for an understanding of consumer households' portfolio behaviour is the issue of participation in the stock market. We know from the available evidence on microeconomic data that the majority of households do not hold stocks at all. Likewise, distributional aspects concerning the cross section of households cannot be addressed with aggregate statistics (Poterba and Samwick, 2001). Also, it should be stressed that the Dutch Financial Accounts definition of households differs from the definition of a consumer household or family in that certain non-profit organizations serving households are included, which may blur the picture.

For all these reasons, the remainder of the chapter will focus on an analysis based on household-level data.

7.3 Data on stockownership in the Netherlands

We now describe our micro data source, a rich panel data set launched in 1993. The CSS is an annual household survey targeted at the structure of individual and household wealth and at saving behaviour. It has been designed in close cooperation with an international research network of economists and other social scientists at Tilburg University.

The domain of the questionnaires extends to general demographic and economic characteristics of the household and its members, to income of all sources, health, and accommodation. The core parts consist of questions regarding asset and liability ownership and amounts, and a module on economic-psychological concepts. The Appendix contains more detail on the data.

At the time of writing, six waves of the CSS were available at annual frequency, until 1998. The panel consists of two samples. One is designed to be representative of the Dutch population. The other sample is drawn from the upper decile of the income distribution. For the representative sample, which contains around 2000 households in each wave, refreshment samples are drawn each year to correct for attrition. The high-income sample covers initially around 900 households, but is eroded due to attrition. It is virtually not available anymore in 1998, which is the reason why we focus on the 1997 wave for presenting cross-sectional results. The main virtue of the high-income panel is that it yields more insight into financial behaviour of rich households due to the higher asset level and more diversified portfolios. In the present chapter, we use both samples and sampling weights in all descriptive statistics to correct for non-representativeness.[4]

For most of the about 40 asset and debt categories in the survey, all respondents in the household of 16 years and over, were first asked to indicate whether they owned assets or debts of a particular type. If they did, a series of questions concerning amounts and the precise nature of each asset in that category was probed. For wealth held in accounts, amounts were probed for each single account per respondent. Respondents were requested to look up information from account statements, as far as possible. If exact amounts were unknown, a bracket value was probed.[5]

The data collection setup thus ensures that there is virtually no nonresponse in the ownership questions. Item-nonresponse on asset amounts can be substantial, however. On average, over the years, about 20 per cent of those who own stocks do not know or refuse to report the value of their stocks.[6] Mutual funds are somewhat better reported with an average non-response rate of around 13 per cent per year.[7]

For our purposes we need to aggregate wealth items first to respondent level, then to the household level, and finally to larger wealth aggregates. Since we have four sublevels of household wealth (asset, respondent, household, and household wealth aggregate), item-nonresponse is a particular problem. Missing values would be passed on to the next level. To deal with this problem, we adopt the procedures of Alessie *et al.* (2001b). Unknown asset amounts were imputed where ownership was known. Imputed values are based upon midpoints of brackets, amounts held in adjacent years, and on the use of panel regression models which relate the observed amounts to household characteristics. In this way, we have imputed the expected amount invested in the different types of assets. By imputing only expected amounts, one underestimates the dispersion in the asset distribution and the correlation over time in the portfolio distribution. In order to address these problems we have used in the imputation procedure the estimated distributions of the error terms of the panel regression models mentioned above. Basically, errors are drawn from the estimated error-term distributions, taking the covariance structure of errors over time fully into account.

Table 7.2 gives a short account of what type of information is available in the CSS, relevant to the present chapter. We distinguish direct stockholding from indirect stockholding. Direct stockholding comprises information on stocks and shares, and on shares of substantial holding. The latter concern ownership of more than 5 per cent of a company's equity and differ from other shares with respect to tax-treatment.[8]

The survey data do not explicitly distinguish the nature of stocks and shares. Respondents are simply asked to report any of them, irrespective of them being stocks or shares, listed or non-listed, domestic or foreign, or of privatized companies.

For shares, the questionnaire asks with how many different companies shares are held, and asks for identification of the company name. The public release data are purged of this sort of information, so without access to the original data it is not possible to assess the importance of foreign-company shares or non-listed shares in Dutch households' portfolios. The questionnaire does ask whether or not the respondents held any shares in the private limited company that they work(ed) for (in their current or last job or before retirement). The value of these shares is not probed directly.[9] Instead, amounts of all shares held are asked, separately for all different companies with whom shares are held.

Indirect stockholding includes holding of mutual funds (mutual fund accounts) and defined contribution plans (single premium annuity insurance policies).

Table 7.2 Data on direct and indirect stockholding

The table summarizes the available information that is relevant for describing patterns of direct and indirect stockholding. Data refer to the 1997 questionnaire, but are similar (if not identical) for other years.

	Detail on survey questions	
	Ownership	**Amount**
Direct stockholding		
Stocks and shares	Yes	Yes
Listed shares	Not separately	Not separately
Non-listed shares	Not separately	Not separately
Employers' shares	Not separately	Not separately
Shares of privatized companies	Not separately	Not separately
Foreign shares	Not separately	Not separately
Shares of substantial holding	Yes	Yes
Number of companies in which respondent owns shares (diversification)	Yes	n.a.
Indirect stockholding		
Mutual funds and mutual fund accounts	Yes	Yes
Retirement accounts (individual and employer-sponsored)	n.a.	n.a.
Individual defined contribution plans (single premium annuity life insurance)	Yes	Yes
Employer-sponsored defined contribution plans[10]	No	No

For mutual funds, a similar list of questions is asked as for stocks and shares. That is, one knows the number of mutual fund (accounts), and the financial institution with which the account is held, and what the name of that product is. Again, the latter information is not available in the public release data, which precludes a precise investigation on the nature of mutual funds (i.e. equity, debt, real estate, mixed, general or industry-specific, etc.) at the micro level.

Single premium annuity insurance plans are also queried with a similar degree of detail. There is no information whatsoever on how much of this will be invested in stocks, since this is at the discretion of the issuing insurance company. Our measure of 'indirect stockholding' should therefore be interpreted as an upper bound on indirect stockholding.

Alessie *et al.* (2001b) compare in some detail the CSS data with national accounts statistics and other available statistics that are based on micro data. Although the comparison is hampered by various incongruities in definitions of households and certain wealth components, the general conclusions from this exercise are that the CSS panel seems to overestimate home values and may underestimate balances on checking and savings accounts. It is also suggested that the CSS considerably underestimates average amounts in stocks, bonds, and mutual funds, *conditional* on ownership. As a result, the CSS does not capture very well the extreme right tail of the wealth distribution, despite its high-income component. The CSS does, however, adequately reflect many important trends in the data. In sum, its quality is certainly comparable with other carefully designed surveys elsewhere, with the exception of the US Survey of Consumer Finances (SCF). Underreporting is also observed in the SCF, but the SCF makes a special attempt to identify the content of mutual funds, thus helping figure out indirect stockholding more accurately.

7.4 Who holds stocks?

Table 7.3 displays weighted summary statistics on household and head of household characteristics that may be correlated with stockownership or non-ownership. All figures refer to the 1997 wave of the CSS data. The average age of the head of household in the sample is about 51 years. Only 5 per cent have an education less than high school, 54 per cent have high school education, and 41 per cent have at least college education. College in the Netherlands includes universities and other scientific institutions, and vocational colleges. Four out of five (81 per cent) of the heads of household are men, 62 per cent are married and 15 per cent are never-married singles (the rest are divorced, widowed, or live together with a permanent partner to whom they are not married). The majority of households consist of a single income recipient (60 per cent). As income recipient we define everybody whose personal net income is positive (and income includes transfer income and capital income). Almost a third of Dutch households have two-income recipients (32 per cent). The relatively high age of heads of households in the sample is also reflected in the labour market status of the head. Twenty nine per cent are pension recipients, only 54 per cent are wage earners. The fraction of self-employed is 6 per cent, 3 per cent are unemployed.[11] Disposable household income amounted to €25 000 in 1997, accumulated financial assets were on average 55 per cent higher than annual income, €39 000.

About 14 per cent hold stocks and shares directly, while 16.2 per cent have invested some money in mutual funds. About 18 per cent of Dutch

Table 7.3 Summary statistics

The table reports sample mean and standard deviations from the CentER Savings Survey, 1997. All statistics use sample weights.

Variable	Sample mean	Standard deviation
Background variables		
Age	50.59	14.07
Education: less than high school (%)	5.3	22.5
Education: high school (%)	54.0	49.9
Education: college (%)	40.6	49.1
Total financial assets (in €)	38 598	104 685
Married (%)	61.5	48.7
Male (%)	80.7	39.5
Singles (%)	15.4	36.1
Between 2 and 4 household members (%)	64.9	47.8
More than 4 household members (%)	25.5	43.6
One income recipient (%)	59.5	49.1
Two income recipients (%)	32.4	46.8
More than two income recipients (%)	5.2	22.3
Wage earner (%)	54.3	49.8
Self-employed (%)	6.2	24.1
Unemployed (%)	3.1	17.3
Pension recipient (%)	28.8	45.3
Income (in €)	25 016	18 182
Other variables		
Participation		
Proportion investing in stocks (%)	14.4	35.1
Proportion investing in mutual funds (%)	16.2	36.8
Proportion investing in pension funds (%)	17.5	38.0
Proportion investing in stocks, mutual funds or pension funds (%)	33.5	0.472
Amount invested, means		
In stocks, among stockholders (in €)	67 260	210 361
In mutual funds, among those who invest in mutual funds (in €)	17 310	21 371
In pension funds, among those who invest in pension funds (in €)	20 469	41 391
In stocks, mutual funds and pension funds, among those who invest in at least one of these assets (in €)	49 446	150 386
Amount invested, medians	*Sample median*	
In stocks, among stockholders (in €)	10 891	
In mutual funds, among those who invest in mutual funds (in €)	10 104	
In pension funds, among those who invest in pension funds (in €)	6 675	
In stocks, mutual funds and pension funds, among those who invest in at least one of these assets (in €)	14 670	
Number of observations	1 782	

households have at least one defined contribution pension policy in the form of a (single premium) annuity. Finally, it appears that 33.5 per cent of the households invest in either directly held stocks, or mutual funds or pension funds. One could claim that this group consists of direct and indirect owners of shares if one is prepared to assume that at least part of the mutual funds or insurance policies are invested in equity.[12] This allows us to place the upper bound of stockholding (direct or indirect) at 33.5 per cent. In other words, it is safe to say that at least 66.5 per cent of the households do not hold any stocks at all (directly or indirectly).

Among direct stockholders, the average amount invested in stocks equals about €67 000. The median amount is considerably lower (€11 000) indicating that the distribution of stocks is considerably right skewed. The corresponding conditional averages for mutual funds and pension policies are much lower (€17 000 and €20 000). A comparison of medians and means suggests that the distributions of the amounts invested in mutual funds and pension policies are less right skewed than that of stocks: the median amount invested in mutual funds (pension policies) is equal to €10 000 (€6700). This is not a surprising result because, among other things, investment in stocks requires more financial knowledge than investment in other types of assets. The cost of acquiring and of maintaining financial information may be substantial especially for the small investor. Moreover, mutual funds and defined contribution plans can provide a level of diversification that would require a large number of different stocks. These saving vehicles seem therefore very attractive for the small, non-expert investor who wants to invest a limited amount with relatively low transaction costs. On the other hand, since, contrary to mutual funds, investments in stocks does not require payments of management fees, holding individual stocks may be more attractive for the large investors.

Table 7.4 provides a breakdown of stockownership patterns by age class. Direct stockholding is increasing in age, throughout. Ownership of mutual funds also increases with age up to age 50. Thereafter, the ownership rate remains fairly constant at a level of about 20 per cent. The age–ownership profiles are possibly contaminated by time and cohort effects. Analysis by Alessie *et al.* (2001a,b) suggests that generation (cohort) effects are presumably not important in explaining ownership of risky assets. Time effects, however, are important. Due to a surge in the stock market and the introduction of new financial products, ownership of risky assets became more common between 1993 and 1998 (see Section 7.6).

Table 7.4 Direct and indirect stockholding by age

The table reports the fraction investing in stocks by age. Data refer to 1997. All statistics use sample weights.

	<30	30–39	40–49	50–59	60–69	≥70	Total
Stocks	4.7	6.8	13.4	18.4	17.8	21.2	14.4
Mutual funds	6.3	11.8	13.0	21.1	19.6	20.6	16.2
Pension funds	7.2	15.8	22.9	23.6	15.6	4.0	17.5
Stocks, mutual funds or pension funds	12.1	25.6	33.7	40.1	38.6	35.9	33.5
Sample proportion of households	5.3	19.4	25.1	21.9	17.3	11.0	100.0

The results reported in Table 7.4 differ somewhat from the age profiles found, for instance, in Italy. King and Leape (1987), however, have found a similarly increasing age pattern. Their explanation is that, other things equal, financial knowledge about information-intensive assets (such as stocks) accumulates with age. Another explanation for the strong positive age gradient of direct stockownership lies in the Dutch Social Security and occupational pension system. In comparison with other countries Dutch elderly households receive in general a rather generous pension especially if one takes into account that their children typically have left the house. Moreover, the elderly do not face much income risk because their occupational (defined-benefit) pensions typically depend on last earnings and not on stock market returns. Given the generous pension system and the limited amount of labour income risk, elderly people are more tempted to invest directly in stocks than, say, Italian households and younger households in the Netherlands who have to finance the expenditures of their children. We should however qualify somewhat the explanation given above: since elderly may have difficulty borrowing or adjusting their labour supply in bad times, they may choose to invest less in risky assets.

Table 7.4 also suggests that the age–ownership profile of defined contribution pension plans is hump shaped. As a result, the age–ownership profile of all risky assets together is also slightly hump shaped. Figure 7.1 confirms these patterns. Here, we have regressed stockownership (direct and indirect) on a third-degree age polynomial using a probit model. The figures plot predicted values of ownership probability.

There are also interesting correlations between stockholding and education. Table 7.5 provides this breakdown. The college-educated (22.5 per cent) are more than four times more likely to hold stocks directly than

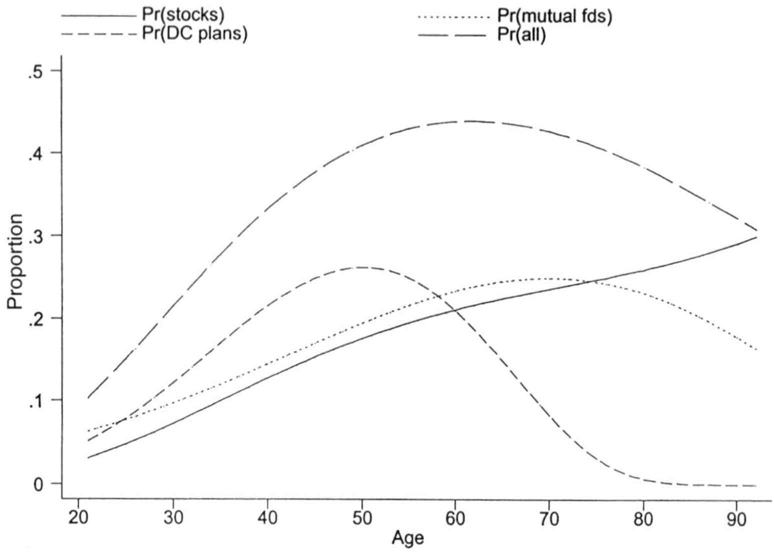

Figure 7.1 Proportion of households investing in stocks, mutual funds, or pension funds, by age

The figure plots four estimated age profiles: the fraction of households that invest in stocks, mutual funds, pension funds, and the fraction investing stocks, mutual funds or pension funds. Each profile is obtained by a probit on a third order age polynomial.

Table 7.5 Direct and indirect stockholding by education

The table reports the fraction investing in stocks by education. Data refer to 1997. All statistics use sample weights.

	Less than high school	**High school**	**College**	**Total**
Stocks	5.2	9.1	22.5	14.4
Mutual funds	8.7	11.8	23.0	16.2
Pension funds	19.9	13.7	22.2	17.5
Stocks, mutual funds or pension funds	26.6	25.0	45.6	33.5
Proportion of households	5.3	54.0	40.6	100.0

the low-educated (5.2 per cent). Also, the prevalence of mutual funds is highest among the high-educated although its education gradient is much less pronounced than that of direct stockholding. Rather surprisingly, we do not observe a monotonic relation between ownership of defined contribution pension plans and education.

Table 7.6 Proportion of households investing in stocks, by financial asset quartiles

The table reports the proportion of investors by gross financial asset quartiles. Data refer to 1997. All statistics use sample weights.

	Quartile I	Quartile II	Quartile III	Quartile IV	Top 5%	Top 1%	Total
Stocks	0.5	3.7	13.0	40.4	77.1	100.0	14.4
Mutual funds	0.4	4.7	16.0	43.7	49.0	44.9	16.2
Pension funds	3.6	10.1	17.3	38.9	42.0	32.6	17.5
Stocks, mutual funds or pension funds	4.4	16.9	36.8	75.9	92.3	100.0	33.5

A relatively high fraction (26.6 per cent) of low-educated families holds at least one type of risky assets. Ownership of risky assets reaches 46 per cent within the high-educated group. The fact that the education gradient of directly held stocks is most pronounced does not come as a surprise. Education will also be highly correlated with financial knowledge and may pick up the effect that direct stockholding requires more financial knowledge than indirect holding. Another explanation for our results is that education proxies human capital and consequently total wealth, which is quite strongly related to stockownership.

Stockholding has a very strong asset gradient. In Table 7.6 we show sample proportions according to the financial asset quartile. Only half-a-per cent of households in the lowest quartile hold any stocks directly. Similarly, only 0.4 per cent of the same households own some mutual funds while only 3.6 per cent of the asset-poor participate in defined contribution pension funds. These numbers should be compared to the percentages in the highest financial asset quartile: 40 per cent for stocks, 44 per cent for mutual funds and 39 per cent for pension funds. Not much to our surprise, we find even more stockholders in the right tail of the distribution. It should be noted, however, that the data underestimate wealth components in this tail by a considerable margin.

Are stockholders different from non-stockholders? A first answer to this question can be obtained by redisplaying the characteristics of Table 7.3 according to stockowner status. Table 7.7 presents this breakdown. The most pronounced differences can be observed between non-stockholders and direct stockholders. We will therefore first focus on a comparison between these two groups. Direct stockholders are on average 6 years older than non-stockholders and much higher educated. The ratio of high-school-to-college education among direct stockholders is 1 : 1.8 and 1.8 : 1 among non-stockholders. These are reflections of the patterns

Table 7.7 Demographic characteristics of stockholders

The table reports demographic characteristics of stockholders and non-stockholders. Data refer to 1997. All statistics use sample weights.

Variable	Stocks	Mutual funds	Pension funds	Stocks, mutual funds or pension funds	Non-stockholders
Age	55.3	53.9	48.9	52.8	49.5
Less than high school (%)	1.9	2.9	6.1	4.2	5.9
High school (%)	34.4	39.3	42.3	40.4	60.9
College (%)	63.7	57.8	51.7	55.4	33.2
Gross financial wealth	142 967	93 833	75 522	88 419	13 519
Age					
30–39 (%)	9.2	14.2	17.5	14.8	21.7
40–49 (%)	23.4	20.2	32.9	25.3	25.0
50–59 (%)	28.0	28.5	29.5	26.2	19.7
60–69 (%)	21.4	21.0	15.4	19.9	16.0
>70 (%)	16.3	14.1	2.5	11.8	10.6
Second financial wealth bracket (%)	6.4	7.2	14.5	12.6	31.2
Third financial wealth bracket (%)	22.6	24.8	24.8	27.5	23.8
Fourth financial wealth bracket (%)	70.2	67.4	55.6	56.6	9.0
High income panel (%)	32.1	27.2	24.8	24.3	6.2
Unemployed (%)	0.6	1.5	1.9	1.5	3.9
Retired (%)	32.8	33.5	14.3	28.1	20.5
Disabled (%)	3.5	3.1	3.2	2.9	7.1
No paid job (%)	1.3	2.7	2.9	2.4	5.8
Other employment (%)	1.2	1.7	3.4	2.3	3.6
Self employed (%)	18.3	8.8	12.0	12.1	3.1
Risk aversion: high (%)	29.2	39.9	37.4	37.4	37.7
Risk aversion: medium (%)	54.1	46.4	40.9	45.3	27.3
Risk aversion: does not know (%)	5.3	4.7	10.9	8.5	26.1
Financial interest: low (%)	9.6	14.5	24.8	19.7	57.0
Financial interest: intermediate (%)	51.9	50.3	45.1	49.6	36.7

reported earlier in Tables 7.4 and 7.5. Among the direct stockholders we find a very high percentage of self-employed (18 per cent), and a very low percentage of unemployed (0.6 per cent). The reverse holds true for non-stockholders (3 per cent and 4 per cent, respectively). The high number of retirees among the direct stockholders will be (partly) caused by the higher average age of this subsample. Furthermore, stockholders are less risk averse, have more interest in financial matters, and have more financial wealth than non-stockholders.[13]

Generally speaking, mutual fund owners resemble direct stockholders more closely than non-stockholders. Compared to stockholders, mutual fund holders tend to be holding less financial assets and are slightly younger and slightly lower educated, have a higher degree of risk aversion and a lower interest in financial matters. Also the fraction of self-employed is much smaller than among direct stockholders. Defined contribution pension plan holders are again younger, less educated, less financially interested, and asset-poorer than stock and mutual fund holders, but still much wealthier than non-stockholders. There are much fewer retirees among them compared to both stock- and non-stockholders.

Much of these tabulations will be similar for other years of the survey since characteristics tend to change slowly if they change at all. It is interesting to point out some trends in ownership over the years, though. Alessie *et al.* (2001a) report household ownership rates of stocks and of mutual funds over the years 1993–98, using the same data. Their figures show that in 1993 about 11.4 per cent of households held stocks, and 11.8 per cent held mutual funds (with a cross-sectional correlation of about 22 per cent). These ownership rates rose to 15.4 per cent (stocks) and 18.4 per cent (mutual funds), respectively, in 1998 (and a correlation of about 28 per cent).

To complete our analysis of participation behaviour, we now turn to estimating ownership as a function of a multivariate vector of characteristics. This way, we isolate the impact of certain characteristics while holding others constant. The resulting probit regressions are displayed in Table 7.8. This reveals important differences with the univariate analysis above.

Consider, for instance, education. In Table 7.5 we have seen that college households are more often owners of stocks than other households. This finding may, however, be explained by college graduates being richer or more interested in financial matters than other households.[14,15] Indeed, Table 7.8 suggests that education level is not an important explanatory factor in explaining direct stockownership once we control for financial wealth and interest in financial matters.[16] This finding makes a lot of sense. Education should be relevant for stockholding (once we control for income and wealth) insofar as it helps the household understand financial matters and how to handle them.

In Tables 7.4 and 7.7 we have seen that older people are more often direct stockowners than other households. This result is however not entirely confirmed in the probit analysis: presumably due to the limited amount of observations, the age dummies are only significant at the

Table 7.8 Demographic characteristics of stockholders and non-stockholders

This table presents estimated marginal effects, that is, the changes in the ownership probability if explanatory variables change by one unit, *ceteris paribus*. To be precise, for continuous variables, the derivative of the estimated probability is evaluated; for dummy variables (like education), the change from 0 to 1 is considered and the corresponding change in probability is reported.

Variable	**Stocks**		**Mutual funds**		**Defined contribution pension funds**		**Stocks, mutual funds and pension funds**	
	estimate	**s.e.**	**estimate**	**s.e.**	**estimate**	**s.e.**	**estimate**	**s.e.**
Test joint sign age dummies,	$P = 0.094$		$P = 0.306$		$P = 0.002$		$P = 0.793$	
Ref group: age <30								
Age								
30–39	0.053	0.124	−0.074	0.042	0.031	0.084	0.003	0.114
40–49	0.105	0.134	−0.081	0.047	0.028	0.081	0.026	0.113
50–59	0.104	0.139	−0.045	0.053	0.034	0.083	0.072	0.117
60–69	0.141	0.162	−0.054	0.053	−0.036	0.074	0.082	0.129
>70	0.256	0.216	−0.038	0.057	−0.138	0.033	0.065	0.136
Test joint sign educ dummies	$P = 0.089$		$P = 0.757$		$P = 0.032$		$P = 0.123$	
Ref group: less than high school								
High school	0.059	0.048	0.009	0.046	−0.118	0.045	−0.043	0.070
College	0.091	0.055	0.021	0.047	−0.105	0.042	0.023	0.071

Test joint sign fin wealth dummies	$P = 0.000$		$P = 0.000$		$P = 0.000$		$P = 0.000$	
Ref group: first fin wealth bracket								
Second financial wealth bracket	0.090	0.059	0.158	0.077	0.141	0.055	0.220	0.064
Third financial wealth bracket	0.169	0.063	0.311	0.082	0.252	0.058	0.383	0.059
Fourth financial wealth bracket	0.318	0.070	0.490	0.080	0.410	0.060	0.642	0.045
High income panel	0.055	0.026	0.029	0.025	0.059	0.031	0.074	0.047
Test joint sign labour market status dummies	$P = 0.004$		$P = 0.404$		$P = 0.145$		$P = 0.146$	
Ref group: employee								
Unemployed	−0.038	0.052	0.122	0.100	0.055	0.076	0.076	0.106
Retired	0.007	0.032	0.046	0.040	−0.037	0.038	0.024	0.066
Disabled	0.025	0.054	−0.014	0.049	−0.049	0.045	−0.064	0.085
No paid job	−0.022	0.055	0.045	0.080	0.026	0.074	0.004	0.100
Else job	−0.003	0.058	0.058	0.086	0.179	0.103	0.120	0.115
Self employed	0.152	0.049	−0.028	0.027	0.002	0.036	0.172	0.067
Test joint sign risk aversion dummies	$P = 0.000$		$P = 0.017$		$P = 0.521$		$P = 0.023$	
Ref group: risk aversion low								
Risk aversion: high	−0.081	0.026	−0.040	0.030	−0.032	0.033	−0.104	0.055
Risk aversion: medium	−0.024	0.026	−0.015	0.030	−0.037	0.033	−0.009	0.057
Risk aversion: does not know	−0.074	0.021	−0.092	0.024	0.001	0.043	−0.083	0.063

Table 7.8 (cont.)

Variable	**Stocks**		**Mutual funds**		**Defined contribution pension funds**		**Stocks, mutual funds and pension funds**	
	estimate	**s.e.**	**estimate**	**s.e.**	**estimate**	**s.e.**	**estimate**	**s.e.**
Test joint sign fin interest dummies	$P = 0.000$		$P = 0.000$		$P = 0.000$		$P = 0.000$	
Ref group: financial interest high								
Financial interest low	−0.154	0.021	−0.138	0.022	−0.122	0.025	−0.354	0.037
Financial interest medium	−0.058	0.018	−0.025	0.020	−0.062	0.024	−0.161	0.040
Log likelihood	−441.33		−497.32		−550.18		−634.74	
Pseudo R^2	0.297		0.258		0.180		0.307	
No. of observations	1380		1380		1380		1380	

10 per cent level (see Table 7.8). The following variables contribute in a significant way to the explanation of direct stockownership: financial wealth, risk aversion and interest in financial matters. The regression coefficient corresponding to these variables all have the expected sign. For instance, according to Table 7.8, the very risk averse invest, *ceteris paribus*, less often in stocks than people who are not risk averse.

Table 7.8 also suggests a very strong positive effect of being self-employed on direct stockownership: *ceteris paribus*, the probability of being stockowner is 15.2 per cent higher for self-employed people than for employees (the reference group). In interpreting this result, one should realize that shares from a substantial holding are included in the definition of stocks (see Table 7.2). Self-employed are often owners of this type of stocks, which may explain the strong positive impact of being self-employed on the probability of being a stockowner. Alessie *et al.* (2001a) have experimented with the definition of stocks by removing shares from a substantial holding. It appears, however, that the effect of being self-employed remains positive and very strong.

Like direct stockownership, the main explanatory factors of mutual fund ownership are financial wealth, interest in financial matters, and the level of risk aversion. In comparison with stocks, the marginal effects of the dummy variables indicating the different financial wealth quartiles are even somewhat bigger for mutual funds. The main difference with the probit results for stocks is the fact that self-employment does not predict ownership of mutual funds.

Alessie *et al.* (2001a) also investigate the joint decision to hold mutual funds *vis-a-vis* stocks and find only limited substitutability between the two asset categories, despite their rather high contemporaneous correlation at the household level. Their results suggest that there is no generic 'learning effect' in the sense that exposition to holding one type of risky assets increases the likelihood of holding other risky asset types.

In comparison with stocks and mutual funds, the ownership structure of defined contribution plans are explained by other characteristics. For instance, age is an important factor in explaining ownership of defined contribution pension plans. It appears that, *ceteris paribus*, the age profile of ownership of defined contribution pension funds has an inverted U-shape. In this respect, the probit analysis confirms the results reported in Table 7.4. Especially people older than 70 years less often own defined contribution plans.

Rather surprisingly and contrary to the evidence presented in Tables 7.5 and 7.7, Table 7.8 suggests that *ceteris paribus* college-educated households own less often defined contribution pension plans. Apparently, the positive education gradient observed in Table 7.5 should be explained by other factors like financial wealth and interest in financial matters. It is interesting to note that the level of risk aversion does not explain ownership of defined contribution pension plans. One should realize that these pension plans are only partially reflecting indirect stockholding.

7.5 The amount of stocks held

So far, we have analysed the ownership structure of different types of risky assets. No attention is paid to the question of how much money is invested in stocks, mutual funds, and defined contribution plans conditional upon ownership. In this section we explain the share of gross financial assets invested in stocks, mutual funds, and defined contribution plans. Table 7.9 summarizes the distribution of these so-called conditional asset shares: for different asset types we present the average asset share among owners of any risky assets (i.e. holding either stocks, mutual funds, or defined contribution pension plans). According to the table, owners of risky assets hold 14.1 per cent of their financial assets in stocks, 11.5 per cent in mutual funds, and 14.5 per cent in defined contribution pension funds. Table 7.9 shows that the conditional asset shares of stocks and mutual funds are U-shaped in age (with a minimum around age 40). In case of defined contribution pension plans, the age profile of the conditional asset share is however hump shaped.

Table 7.10 presents for different types of risky assets the education gradient of the conditional asset shares. Given the explanations presented in Section 7.4, it does not come as a surprise that for mutual funds and stocks college-educated people have a higher conditional asset share than other people. Table 7.10 also suggests that the education gradient of conditional asset shares is steepest for stocks. In case of defined contribution plans, the relation between education level and the conditional asset share is rather weak especially if one takes into account that the analysis is based on rather few observations and that the conditional share is measured with considerable error.

Table 7.11 shows that among owners of risky assets the share of financial assets invested directly in stocks is the highest among the group of households belonging to the highest financial wealth quartile. For owners of risky assets in the lower two financial wealth quartiles it seems that defined contribution pension plans are by far the most important risky asset type.

Table 7.12 reports regressions for the shares of stocks, mutual funds, and defined contribution pension funds. We estimate the relation

Table 7.9 Asset share invested in stocks, mutual funds and pension funds, by age

All rows condition on the group of households that invest in either stocks, mutual funds, or pension funds (this way the group on which we condition each asset share is the same across rows).

	< 30	30–39	40–49	50–59	60–69	≥ 70	Total
	(in percent of total financial wealth)						
Stocks	12.9	9.3	9.4	13.8	16.2	27.0	14.1
Mutual funds	11.2	10.2	8.0	11.7	12.8	17.9	11.5
Pension funds	3.2	15.2	15.8	18.7	16.1	1.0	14.5
Stock, mutual funds or pension funds	27.3	34.7	33.2	44.2	45.1	45.9	40.1

Table 7.10 Asset share invested in stocks, mutual funds and pension funds, by education

All rows condition on the group of households that invest in either stocks, mutual funds, or pension funds (this way the group on which we condition each asset share is the same across rows).

	Less than high school	High school	College	Total
	(in percent of total financial wealth)			
Stocks	9.4	12.7	15.4	14.1
Mutual funds	7.0	10.7	12.4	11.5
Pension funds	14.4	15.5	13.8	14.5
Stocks, mutual funds or pension funds	30.8	38.9	41.7	40.1

Table 7.11 Asset share invested in stocks, mutual funds and pension funds, by financial asset quartiles

All rows condition on the group of households that invest in either stocks, mutual funds, or pension funds (this way the group on which we condition each asset share is the same across rows).

	Quartile I	Quartile II	Quartile III	Quartile IV	Top 5%	Top 1%	Total
	(in percent of total financial wealth)						
Stocks	7.2	7.3	11.7	17.1	38.3	58.2	14.1
Mutual funds	2.5	7.4	12.1	12.6	8.0	2.7	11.5
Pension funds	41.0	18.4	12.4	13.2	11.6	8.9	14.5
Stocks, mutual funds or pension funds	50.6	33.0	36.2	42.9	58.0	69.9	40.1

Table 7.12 Regressions for the asset share invested in stocks, mutual funds and pension funds

Variable	Stocks		Mutual funds		Defined contribution pension funds		Stocks, mutual funds and pension funds	
	estimate	s.e.	estimate	s.e.	estimate	s.e.	estimate	s.e.
Test joint sign age dummies, Ref group: age < 30	$P = 0.022$		$P = 0.103$		$P = 0.077$		$P = 0.053$	
Age								
30–39	0.383	0.301	0.039	0.135	0.133	0.152	0.207	0.133
40–49	0.238	0.297	0.131	0.135	0.157	0.150	0.198	0.131
50–59	0.311	0.295	0.172	0.133	0.234	0.150	0.283	0.132
60–69	0.363	0.298	0.137	0.141	0.280	0.160	0.287	0.138
> 70	0.518	0.303	0.193	0.145	0.113	0.205	0.333	0.142
Test joint sign educ dummies Ref group: less than high school	$P = 0.861$		$P = 0.101$		$P = 0.101$		$P = 0.197$	
High school	−0.058	0.184	0.001	0.082	0.164	0.083	0.111	0.071
College	−0.076	0.185	0.061	0.082	0.178	0.083	0.127	0.071
Test joint sign fin wealth dummies Ref group: first fin wealth bracket	$P = 0.445$		$P = 0.474$		$P = 0.293$		$P = 0.156$	
Second financial wealth bracket	−0.184	0.193	−0.047	0.163	−0.116	0.119	−0.146	0.095
Third financial wealth bracket	−0.254	0.187	−0.010	0.170	−0.197	0.138	−0.212	0.102
Fourth financial wealth bracket	−0.207	0.201	0.058	0.185	−0.295	0.174	−0.202	0.122
High income panel	0.026	0.047	−0.063	0.033	−0.005	0.044	0.023	0.032

Test joint sign labour market status dummies	$P = 0.389$		$P = 0.303$		$P = 0.131$		$P = 0.404$	
Ref group: employee								
Unemployed	−0.225	0.294	−0.071	0.116	0.149	0.109	0.070	0.106
Retired	0.035	0.073	0.084	0.058	0.127	0.069	0.056	0.051
Disabled	0.138	0.119	0.076	0.086	−0.003	0.101	0.097	0.080
No paid job	0.084	0.227	−0.019	0.109	0.088	0.125	0.054	0.110
Else job	0.018	0.154	0.123	0.100	0.077	0.114	0.138	0.090
Self employed	0.150	0.068	−0.076	0.052	0.127	0.053	0.086	0.045
Test joint sign risk aversion dummies	$P = 0.767$		$P = 0.921$		$P = 0.121$		$P = 0.273$	
Ref group: risk aversion low								
Risk aversion: high	−0.002	0.080	−0.008	0.049	−0.001	0.055	−0.055	0.047
Risk aversion: medium	0.038	0.062	0.006	0.048	0.066	0.055	−0.004	0.045
Risk aversion: does not know	−0.046	0.125	−0.049	0.103	0.107	0.073	0.008	0.068
Constant	0.103	0.460	−0.157	0.235	0.170	0.299	0.239	0.209
Mills ratio	0.083	0.090	0.162	0.070	−0.068	0.107	−0.047	0.062
Rho	0.282		0.691		−0.269		−0.166	
Sigma	0.293		0.235		0.254		0.286	

between the financial portfolio share of a given asset and household characteristics for those households that hold any wealth in this form, and correct for the fact that owners are a self-selected subgroup of the underlying population. In order to identify the parameters of such a selection model, we need to have at least one variable at our disposal that determines the choice of owning versus not owning and not the decision of how much to invest. We have experimented with different variables (e.g. the degree of urbanization), which could serve as 'exclusion restrictions'. We settled to rely on the dummies indicating interest in financial matters. Preliminary analysis on the 1997 data suggests that on statistical grounds we can use these variables as exclusion restrictions: they do explain the ownership decision (cf. Table 7.8), but do not contribute to explaining conditional shares.

As we said before, the amount invested in (risky) financial assets is measured with considerable error. Moreover, the analysis summarized in Table 7.12 is based on quite a few observations (for instance the Heckman regression explaining the conditional asset share of stocks is based on 234 observations). Due to these two factors, it is very difficult to find variables that explain in a statistically significant way the shares of risky assets. Table 7.12 suggests that age is the most important factor explaining the asset shares: In case of stocks and mutual funds the asset share increases with age whereas we observe a hump-shaped age profile for defined contribution pension funds. The other variables do not appear to be significant.

7.6 Issues specific to the Netherlands

As we have documented in the previous sections, direct and indirect stock market participation in the Netherlands have substantially increased during the 1990s. Reasons are not only a prosperous economic climate and a booming stock market in the second half of the 1990s. Important changes in the banking industry also have had their impact on households' investment behaviour. Large-scale mergers and acquisitions led to a concentration in the banking industry around four leading firms, which are active on the Dutch market: ING, ABN-AMRO, Rabobank, and Fortis.[17] The conglomerates ING and Fortis are not banks in the strict sense but they also supply life insurance products through insurance firms like Nationale Nederlanden (part of ING) and AMEV (part of Fortis). Rabobank took over Robeco in 1996, the dominating provider of mutual funds in the 1980s. Apart from these four financial conglomerates, some big insurance companies are active on the Dutch market, notably AEGON and direct writers such as OHRA and Centraal Beheer. These insurance companies increasingly supply banking services (e.g. saving accounts, mutual funds).

Competition between the financial conglomerates has however driven much of the observed technological and market changes that eased the penetration and dissemination of risky financial products. We list four main, interconnected factors that accompanied increased competition: advertising and information, reduced transaction fees, product innovation and exploitation of tax-arbitrage, and linkages between a booming housing market and financial products.

First, both established and new financial institutions entered the market for risky assets.[18] In the early 1980s Robeco supplied only a few (less than 10) mutual funds. Gradually, the other financial conglomerates and other companies started to enter the market of mutual funds. This increased competition has led to massive advertising of new or newly packaged products and increased media attention that in turn increased consumers' exposure to financial information. This in turn can also have had effects on households' direct stock market participation. Advertising new emissions of stocks from privatization of large public enterprises, as has been the case in Italy or Germany, for instance, has presumably not played a large role in boosting direct stock holding during the nineties.[19]

Second, banks have slashed their transaction fees for buying and selling stocks and mutual funds by introducing new cost effective transaction channels like Internet and phone banking.[20] The latter technologies circumvent the intermediation through an account manager but do not offer individual financial advice. Typical transaction fees for buying or selling stocks for a value of €10 000 are as follows: about €50 in case of Internet, €70 in case of phone banking, and €110 through an account manager. Apart from transaction costs, mutual funds also charge yearly management fees and partly administration costs. According to Morningstar (2001), an independent firm that surveys mutual funds, the average yearly management fee of Dutch mutual funds is with 0.75 per cent relatively low by international comparison. There is, however, not much transparency in the fee structure, which caused the Central Bank to announce certain measures that help increase cost transparency (De Nederlandsche Bank, 2001b).

Third, increased competition has stimulated banks and other financial institutions to develop new financial products. Many of the new products exploit some features of the tax system and link traditional asset and liability types with mutual funds. Examples are investment whole life insurances, where the periodic payments made by the individual are invested in mutual funds, promising a higher expected return at the expense of a higher risk. In order to understand the tax-preferred nature of such 'unit link' insurance products, one should realize that until recently premiums paid were not tax deductible. Instead, under some conditions concerning time span and amount, benefit payments were tax-free. These rules imply that if the premiums of such life insurance policies are invested in, say, mutual funds, both the capital gains and the dividend payments on the mutual fund policy are untaxed. If one directly invests in mutual funds, dividend payments are liable to be taxed (capital gains are untaxed, see e.g. Alessie *et al.* (2001b) for more details of the Dutch tax system). Mutual funds are also often linked with single premium annuities where the premium is tax deductible and benefits are taxed. The comprehensive tax reform act of 2001, however, abolishes a number of tax advantages for certain assets, and sizeable effects on portfolio behaviour of households can be expected. The most important change in the tax law is the fact that interest and dividend payments are not liable to income tax anymore. Instead, the wealth tax rate has been increased (from 0.7 to 1.2 per cent) and its base has been broadened: for instance, money invested in life insurances was not taxed but under the new law it will be taxed. This may result in unit link life insurance products becoming less popular. Another example of abolished tax advantages concerns financial lease products in which the acquisition of shares and/or mutual funds is financed by a loan. Since the new tax law curtails the tax deductibility of interest payments on consumer loans, repercussions for risky asset ownership are to be expected.

Fourth, developments in the housing market are of importance since they had spill-over effects on the market for mutual funds. Whereas the homeownership rate rose only slightly (from 48 per cent in 1993 to 51 per cent in 1999), mortgage interest rates fell during the period, and mortgage qualification constraints were relaxed.[21] This led to a mortgage boom and rocketing house prices. New mortgages, however, are not only effected in order to purchase a house. In the third quarter of 1999 about 60 per cent of the new mortgages were used to exploit the increase in the house value to buy other durable goods and to finance stock market operations (Statistics Netherlands, 1999). From 1997 onwards, banks and insurance companies have marketed the investment mortgage rather heavily for this purpose. This is another unit link product exploiting tax arbitrage: the mortgage repayments are locked in a mutual fund account whose proceeds are used to redeem the mortgage, and the interest paid on the mortgage is fully tax deductible.[22] Under the new tax law, the tax deductibility of mortgage interest payments is not abolished if the mortgage is used for purchasing a new primary residence.

Apart from the bull market and the consequences of increased competition between banks, a further source of increased mutual fund participation is due to the restructuring of the early retirement benefit system. Following the abolition of the rather generous, pay-as-you-go early retirement system (see e.g. Kapteyn and De Vos, 1999), some pension funds (e.g. the civil servant pension fund ABP) offer their employees supplementary private pensions that can be used for early retirement. These are again unit-link annuity policies and may have fueled demand for mutual fund and other indirect stock market participation. Until recently, annuity insurance premiums were tax deductible, which again left room for some tax arbitrage. Under the new tax law, however, the tax deductibility of annuity insurance premiums has been heavily curtailed.

7.7 Conclusions

Dutch consumers have experienced a higher exposure to the stock market during the 1990s, both directly and indirectly. We have investigated the relationship between investment in risky assets and background characteristics of households such as age and education that determine households' participation choice. One of the interesting results is that contrary to other countries direct stock market participation increases with age. Of course, with micro data from just a single year we are not able to identify macroeconomic factors that will undoubtedly contribute to explaining the overall trend. We have pointed to changes in relative asset returns (booming stock market), and increased competition in the financial sector that eased the penetration and dissemination of risky financial products.

As recently as 2000–01, stock prices have fallen, however, and possibly seeded some mistrust against stockholding for people that have made quick losses instead of quick gains. As the *Economist* (2001) asks: 'Will the slump in share prices kill this emerging equity culture?' Another question is how risky investment behaviour will be affected by the introduction of the new tax law in 2001 that curtails the possibilities of tax arbitrage. It remains a task for future research to answer such questions. At the time of writing, household-level data until 1998 (referring to end-of-year balances in 1997) were available for the Netherlands. In order to see if the reversal in share prices has had any effects, we need at least four more waves of data. We need much more in order to see if the stock price reversal was continuing over a longer period, and if it triggered any long-range effects at the household level. Presently, this is open to speculation, and the beginning equity culture may just have learned a lesson, as the *Economist* concludes: 'If the bear market reminds "experts" and amateurs alike that risk and return go together, it will have served a useful purpose.'

Appendix

This appendix provides additional information on the data used and the construction of variables.

Data collection and content

The interview was carried out online, as every participating household had been equipped with a PC or other terminal device and modem. General questions on the demographic background of the household and its members were probed, as was labour market status of adult household members, health status, and details on income from all sources. The core parts of the questionnaires relevant for the present chapter are a detailed section on assets and debts, and a module referring to economic-psychological concepts. Income and other flow information refer to the year preceding each wave (i.e., year 1992 for the 1993 wave, and so on). Asset information was requested as end-of-year information (31 December 1992 for the 1993 wave, etc.).

Some of the questionnaires have not been fielded for the entire sample but only for new panel entrants in 1994, because the 1993 wave had been completed only with considerable delay. Nyhus (1996) discusses survey design, sampling frame, and response rates. Even though the questionnaires have undergone various revisions, the structure and content of the survey and details on question have only changed slightly over the years. The bulk of information is consistently and comparably available for all survey years.

Measurement of asset items

To illustrate the degree of detail that is available in the data, we present the following questions on shares from the 1997 questionnaire:[23]

By owning SHARES you participate in the capital of a company. In a way, all shareholders together are the owners of the company. Shareholders receive dividends dependent on the profits made by the company.

BZ14 Did you, on 31 December 1996, own any SHARES? If relevant: do NOT include shares of your own private limited company here. Also, do NOT include bonds through MUTUAL FUNDS here. These have already been reported.
1 yes AAN2
2 no BZ15

AAN2 With how many Dutch and/or foreign companies did you have SHARES on 31 December 1996? If relevant: do NOT include shares of

your own private limited company here. Also, do NOT include bonds through MUTUAL FUNDS here. These have already been reported.
answer > 10 .... AAN2A
answer < 11 .... AAN301

AAN2A How much was the total estimated market value of all your SHARES with [NUMBER AAN2] companies on 31 December 1996? If you really don't know, type 0 (zero).
0 .... AAN2D
> 0 .... AAN301

AAN2D Into which of the categories mentioned below did the total value of your shares go on 31 December 1996?
1 less than Dfl. 2000 .... AAN301
2 2000–5000 .... AAN301
[3... etc.] AAN301
14 300000 or more AAN301
0 unknown AAN301
The following questions are repeated for a maximum of ten investments in shares. When answering these questions, please keep in mind the ten – to you – most important INVESTMENTS.

The following questions concern your (most important) investments in SHARES.

AAN301 thru AAN310
What is the name of the [1st thru 10th] company with which you had SHARES on 31 December 1996?
[List of 16 company names; suppressed for brevity] AAN501
17 other AAN401

AAN401 thru AAN410 (string)
What is the name of the [1st thru 10th] company with which you had SHARES on 31 December 1996? If you don't know, type a question mark.
any answer AAN501

AAN501 thru AAN510
How many shares did you have on 31 December 1996 with [NAME OF COMPANY MENTIONED WITH AAN301 THRU AAN310]?
any answer AAN601

AAN601 thru AAN610
How much was the TOTAL market value of these shares with [NAME OF COMPANY MENTIONED WITH AAN301 THRU AAN310] on 31 December 1996? If you really don't know, type 0 (zero).
0 .... AAN81
> 0 .... BZ15

AAN801 thru AAN810
Into which of the categories mentioned below did the value of your shares with [NAME OF COMPANY MENTIONED WITH AAN301 THRU AAN310] go on 31 December 1996?

1 less than Dfl. 2000 .... BZ15
2 2000–5000 .... BZ15
[3... etc.] BZ15
14 300000 or more BZ15
0 unknown BZ15

Head of household definition; constructed variables of interest

Aggregates of financial wealth and household size relate to the entire household. Most of the other demographic characteristics, such as age, education, and so on, relate to the head of household. The head of household in our data set is self-defined by respondents. We adjust the respondents' evaluation of who is head of household in cases where there are either multiple or no heads, so as to obtain a unique head per household. If there are several heads of households we consider the one that is most often referred to as head in the panel. If this leaves several options, we consider the oldest male. The status of heads of household in our panel data can change over time due to changes in family composition (divorces, break-ups, deaths, marriages, etc.).

We use the total amount of financial assets at the household level as one of the regressors. This is defined as the sum of all financial assets, excluding liabilities. It includes checking accounts, deposit books, savings or deposit accounts, and saving certificates; stocks and shares (including shares of substantial holding), bonds, mutual funds and/or mutual fund accounts; defined contribution plans, cash value of life insurance, employer-sponsored savings plans, growth funds, and other financial assets.

Financial interest and attitudes to risk

The module on economic-psychological concepts probes various measures of financial expertise and financial attitudes. Among these are a measure pertaining to the interest of the respondent in financial matters, and one that can proxy risk aversion. In both cases, respondents were asked to indicate their agreement with a statement presented to them. The degree of agreement had to be expressed on a seven point scale with labeled endpoints ('1' indicating total disagreement, and '7' indicating total agreement).

The two statements were:

- 'I am very interested in financial matters (insurance, investments, etc.)' and
- 'I think it is more important to have safe investments and guaranteed returns, than to take a risk to have a chance to get the highest possible returns.'

The first of these statements has been presented to all participants of the economic-psychological module, the second to those whose total net household income amounted to 20000 Dfl. (€9076) or more. We coded the answer into dummy variables as follows:

Low financial interest	answers 1 or 2
Intermediate financial interest	answers 3, 4, or 5
High financial interest	answers 6 or 7
Low risk aversion	answers 1 or 2

Intermediate risk aversion	answers 3, 4, or 5
High risk aversion	answers 6 or 7
Don't know or not applicable	answer 'don't know' or income below 20 000 Dfl.

Note that for reasons of statistical identification we dropped those that answered 'don't know' to the financial interest question from the sample (instead of creating a separate dummy variable).

References

Aldershof, T., R. Alessie and A. Kapteyn (1997) 'Female labour supply and the demand for housing', CentER for Economic Research, Tilburg University, Discussion Paper No. 9746.

Alessie, R., S. Hochguertel and A. van Soest (2001a) 'Ownership of stocks and mutual funds: a panel data analysis', CentER for Economic Research, Tilburg University, Discussion Paper No. 2001-94.

Alessie, R., S. Hochguertel and A. van Soest (2001b) 'Household portfolios in the Netherlands', in L. Guiso, M. Haliassos, and T. Jappelli (eds), *Household Portfolios*, Cambridge, MA: MIT Press, 340–88.

De Nederlandsche Bank (2001a) 'Recordinleg bij Beleggingsinstellingen in 2000', Central Bank of the Netherlands, *Statistisch Bulletin*, March, 17–22.

De Nederlandsche Bank (2001b) 'Circulaire met betrekking tot transparantie van kosten en nauwe banden', Central Bank of the Netherlands, mimeo.

Deutsche Bundesbank (1999) 'Changes in households' asset situation since the beginning of the nineties', *Deutsche Bundesbank Monthly Report*, January.

Economist (2001) 'Waking up to equity risk', *Economist*, March 8.

Juster, T. F. and J. P. Smith (1997) 'Improving the quality of economic data: lessons from the HRS and AHEAD', *Journal of the American Statistical Association*, **92**: 1268–78.

Kapteyn, A. and K. De Vos (1999) 'Social security and retirement in the Netherlands', in J. Gruber and D. A. Wise (eds), *Social Security and Retirement Around the World*, Chicago: University of Chicago Press, 269–303.

King, M. A. and J. I. Leape (1987) 'Asset accumulation, information, and the life cycle', *NBER Working Paper*, No. 2392.

Kleijn, J. de (1999) 'Vermogensverdeling 1997', *Sociaal-Economische Maandstatistiek*, **6**: 24–7.

Morningstar (2001) 'Lage kosten doen ertoe', press release, 14–6–2001; http://www.morningstar.nl.

Nyhus E. K. (1996) 'The VSB-CentER savings project: data collection methods, questionnaires and sampling procedures', VSB-CentER Savings Project, Progress Report, No. 42, Tilburg University.

Poterba, J. M. and A. A. Samwick (2001) 'Household portfolio allocation over the life cycle', in S. Ogura, T. Tachibanaki and D. A. Wise (eds), *Aging Issues in the United States and Japan*, Chicago: University of Chicago Press, 65–103.

Statistics Netherlands (1999) 'Hypotheekmarkt overtreft alle records', *CBS Press Release* PB99-285, November 4.

Vazquez-Alvarez, R. (2001) 'A nonparametric approach to the sample selection problem in survey data', PhD dissertation, Tilburg University.

8
Stockholding in the United Kingdom

James Banks and Matthew Wakefield

8.1 Introduction

This chapter provides empirical evidence on the portfolios of UK households.[1] We give particular attention to holdings of stocks and shares and differentiate between direct holdings that can be self-traded and indirect holdings in unit trusts and mutual funds and in tax favoured personal equity plans (PEPs), and also holdings in private personal pension accounts. We argue that household portfolios in the United Kingdom share many features with those of other countries included in this analysis. Across households with different characteristics there are wide differences in ownership rates for stocks held directly and stocks held indirectly. But within the group of stockholders we find little evidence of systematic variations in the proportion of household wealth that is accounted for by stocks held either directly or in direct and indirect forms. Age, income and education are important factors in describing the level of financial wealth that households have, and the various assets that they hold.

We estimate age, education, and wealth profiles for the direct and indirect ownership of stocks and for conditional portfolio shares accounted for by stockownership. These show that, as in other countries, and the US and Italy in particular, the ownership profile displays more of a pronounced 'hump shape' across age groups than does the conditional share. As might be expected, both educational attainment and wealth have a positive impact on stockownership rates and on the share of wealth that is held in stocks. In both cases, the relationship to ownership seems to be stronger than that to portfolio share. To summarize, our analysis suggests that the typical UK stockholder is middle-aged, well educated and wealthy and has about half of his or her wealth in stocks.

We begin with two sections that provide some background information on stockownership in the UK. The first of these discusses some recent institutional changes that are likely to have affected the shareholding behaviour of UK households, and the second outlines aggregate data on how these institutional pressures altered the portfolio of the UK household sector between 1990 and 1998. Section 8.4 then describes the main dataset we use to analyse stockholding in the UK at a microeconomic level. Section 8.5 provides a univariate analysis of factors that affect the decision of whether or not to hold stocks and Section 8.6 extends this to present a multivariate analysis. Section 8.7 describes why a supplementary dataset was needed in order to analyse the portfolio share of households' wealth that is held in stocks, and presents a univariate analysis of this question. Section 8.8 presents our multivariate analysis of the same issue. The final section concludes by summarizing our findings and arguing that if better data were available then institutional changes in the UK could have provided interesting case studies through which to analyse some of the issues raised in our chapter. Even without such analysis our chapter provides new data on stockholding in the UK that is particularly interesting when viewed alongside the data on other countries that is provided in this volume.

8.2 Background: institutional changes that have affected stockholding in the UK

In comparison to the other countries considered in this analysis, the UK is seen to have high rates of direct and indirect stockownership. There are several key episodes that help to explain why this has come to be the case. The first is the experience of the UK in the 1980s. This was a decade that saw dramatic, and rapid, changes in the levels of ownership of stocks and shares, both directly and via ownership of private pensions. In addition, increases in the level of home ownership, coupled with the increasingly common use of endowment policies to finance mortgage borrowing, will also have increased exposure to the stock market.[2] In all cases, government 'supply side' policies were fairly critical in driving the changes. Most notably, these came in the form of the introduction of personal pensions, the 'right-to-buy' policy which sold off public housing to tenants at considerably less than the market rate, and the privatization of previously nationalised industries. In the case of share ownership the proportion of households owning shares more than doubled during a four-year period in the mid-1980s coinciding with the privatization of British Telecom and British Gas. The extensive advertising provided by the government for its privatization programme appeared to have been successful in attracting new shareowners from younger and less well-educated groups (although not typically from middle or lower-income groups). There is some evidence that the privatization experience – as well as reductions in transactions costs – had the effect of raising the level of share-ownership more generally. Households who were too young to have experienced privatization directly are more likely to own shares than were older cohorts at the same age. But it is difficult to reconcile the argument that the privatization process may have played an educational role in teaching people about share-ownership, with the fact that a large proportion of shareowners at the end of the 1990s only hold shares in privatized industries or the recently demutualized building societies.

A second key feature of the UK policy environment is the government's use of tax incentives to try to encourage saving – through private pensions and through designated 'tax-free' savings schemes such as tax exempt special savings accounts (TESSAs) and PEPs, which were introduced in the late 1980s and subsequently replaced with Individual Savings Accounts (ISAs) in the late 1990s. At least some of the funds in personal pension accounts are likely to be invested in stocks and shares, and PEPs and ISAs are tax-advantaged savings accounts that typically have a substantial component invested in stocks and shares.

In this chapter, we provide analysis of micro-data on saving and share-ownership, and we present descriptive evidence for comparison with the other countries represented in this study. For reasons of brevity, we do not describe the system or institutional factors in the UK in particular detail apart from where necessary. Useful summaries of these issues include Budd and Campbell (1998) and Disney *et al.* (2001) on pensions, and Banks and Blundell (1994) on savings institutions more generally.

8.3 Background: aggregate data

Table 8.1 reports portfolio shares for different assets calculated using aggregate data for 1990 and 1998. These aggregate statistics also give an insight into some of the key changes that have occurred in wealth holding in the United Kingdom in recent years. As in other countries, there has been a reduction in the importance of cash, transactions, and savings accounts in household portfolios and an increase in the importance of mutual funds, life insurance, and other risky assets during the 1980s and the 1990s.

One category of financial assets, National Savings, is peculiar to the United Kingdom. National Savings is a government agency providing

Table 8.1 Composition of household financial wealth: aggregate financial accounts

This table presents aggregate statistics on what proportion of the financial wealth held by households in the UK is held in each of several different types of asset.

Financial assets	Asset shares (as proportion of total financial assets)	
	1990	**1998**
Currency, transaction and savings accounts *Currency and deposits: total*[a]	0.307	0.215
Government bonds[b]	0.008	0.010
Other bonds[c]	0.009	0.004
Shares and other equity (excluding mutual funds)	0.167	0.161
Mutual funds	0.006	0.038
Defined-contribution pension funds	not available	not available
Cash value of life insurance[d] *Insurance technical reserves: total* (includes net equity in insurance and pension funds)	0.451	0.542
Other financial assets[e]	0.051	0.030
Total financial assets	£1 174 298 mn	£2 652 340 mn
Total financial assets (1998 pounds)	£1 494 473 mn	£2 652 340 mn
Total financial assets (Euro)	2 207 038 mn[f]	3 916 976 mn[f]
Average financial assets per household		163 919
Total number of households		23 895 690

Notes

[a] Italicized names are taken directly from *Financial Statistics*.

[b] Including local authority bonds, which are a small proportion of the total.

[c] Other bonds include bonds issued by private enterprises, Special Credit Institutions, and foreign bonds.

[d] Cash value of life insurance includes assets held by domestic and foreign insurance companies as a counterpart to life insurance policies sold to residents.

[e] Calculated as a residual. Includes securities other than bonds and shares, loan assets, and assets held in other accounts.

[f] Calculated using 1998 annual average pound/euro exchange rate of 1.4768.

Source: *Financial Statistics* (Office for National Statistics), Table 8.12.1N: 'Financial Balance Sheet: households and non-profit institutions serving households'.

savings and investment vehicles that are used to finance national borrowing. But the agency provides a wide range of different assets, most of which do not have the characteristics of traditional government bonds. For example they provide short and medium-term deposit accounts paying fixed rates of interest, some instant access products, and various types of bond: that is, they represent a very heterogeneous part of the portfolio.[3] In the official aggregate statistics reported in Table 8.1 it is not possible to distinguish between the amounts of wealth held in each of these forms, so in this table we simply treat such assets as savings accounts. In the microeconomic analysis that follows we are able to distinguish between different forms of National Savings products and group them with assets of similar characteristics.

The table shows that between 1990 and 1998 the proportion of household financial wealth that was held in shares and equities remained approximately constant at 16 per cent. Since real household financial wealth increased by over 75 per cent during this period, this did represent a significant increase in the amount of wealth held in equities. More strikingly, the amount of wealth held in mutual funds increased significantly as a proportion of the total as well as in real terms. The most likely factor underlying this growth was the expansion in mutual fund based PEPs over this period.

Data on aggregate portfolio shares do not tell us much about the asset holdings of the majority of people. Given the inequality in the distribution of wealth, only a relatively few people account for most of the total. For example, in 1995 the top 1 per cent of the wealth distribution owned 19 per cent of total personal sector wealth, the wealthiest 5 per cent owned 39 per cent of total marketable wealth and the bottom half of the wealth distribution accounted for only 7 per cent of total wealth (Inland Revenue, 1999).[4] Although this distribution is equalised somewhat by the inclusion of occupational pension rights, it is still the case that the top half of the wealth distribution account for 89 per cent of the total. It follows that changes in the aggregate statistics could be driven by changes in the behaviour of a very few very wealthy individuals. For a more representative guide to the stockholding patterns of the majority of the population, we turn to micro data sources.

8.4 Microeconomic data: description

Unfortunately, in the United Kingdom, micro data on wealth and asset holding are currently not of particularly high quality. Indeed, there is a distinct lack of official detailed data on household wealth, such as the survey of consumer finances in the United States. Table 8.2 summarizes the available information that is relevant for describing patterns of direct and indirect stockholding. The table refers to the family resources survey (FRS), which is the primary source of official data for

Table 8.2 FRS data on direct and indirect stockholding

This table summarizes what information the UK family resources survey provides on which financial assets households own and on the amounts held in each of the various asset types.

Direct stockholding	**Detail on survey questions (family resources survey)**	
	Ownership	**Amount**
Stocks	Yes	No
Listed shares	No	No
Non-listed shares	No	No
Employers' share	No	No
Shares of privatized companies	No	No
Foreign shares	No	No
Number of companies in which respondent owns shares (diversification), if available	No	No
Mutual funds and other managed investment accounts	Yes	No
Defined contribution pension funds and other retirement accounts (individual and employer-sponsored pension plans)	Yes	No

Source: UK family resources survey (FRS) 1998/99.

Table 8.3a Summary statistics for characteristics of adults in the FRS 1998/99

Tables 8.3a and 8.3b list the sample mean and standard deviation for various characteristics of adults and households in the FRS 1998/99. The variables that are considered in the tables are those that will be used in the analysis of sections five and six of this chapter.

Variable (individual characteristics)	**Household heads**		**All adults**	
	Sample mean	**Standard deviation**	**Sample mean**	**Standard deviation**
Average age	51.1	17.5	46.8	18.0
Education: less than high school*[a]	0.053	0.224	0.052	0.223
Education: high school*	0.638	0.455	0.617	0.486
Education: college*	0.309	0.462	0.329	0.470
Married*	0.516	0.500	0.567	0.495
Male*	0.743	0.437	0.489	0.500
Singles*	0.419	0.493	0.360	0.480

Table 8.3b Summary statistics for characteristics of households in FRS 1998/99

Variable (household characteristics)	Sample mean	Standard deviation
Between 2 and 4 household members*	0.645	0.478
More than 4 household members*	0.067	0.251
One earner*	0.290	0.454
Two earners*	0.235	0.424
More than two earners*	0.050	0.218
Head is a wage earner*	0.466	0.499
Head is self-employed*	0.084	0.278
Head is unemployed*	0.039	0.193
At least one pension recipient*[b]	0.361	0.480
Average household income (£/week)[c]	347.6 (€494.8)[d]	349.7 (€497.8)
Proportion of direct stockholders*	0.279	0.448
Proportion investing in mutual funds*[e]	0.169	0.374
Proportion investing in personal pensions*	0.202	0.402
Proportion of direct and indirect stockholders*	0.449	0.497
Total financial assets	not available	not available
Number of observations (adults)	40 498	
Number of observations (adults, grossed)	43 783 069	
Number of observations (households)	22 858	
Number of observations (household, grossed)	23 895 690	

Notes: All statistics are for sample grossed up to the number of adults or households in the population.

* Discrete (0/1) nature of variable means that the 'sample mean' measures the proportion of the sample who fall into the relevant sub-group

[a] Less than high school is education to less than compulsory school leaving age, high school is education up to exactly this age and college education is education beyond this age. The proportion given is the proportion of households with a head with the particular education.

[b] Proportion of households with at least one adult receiving income from the basic state pension or from an occupational pension.

[c] Household income is unequivalized, measured before housing costs and expressed in January 1999 prices.

[d] Since FRS values are expressed in January 1999 pounds, they are converted to Euros at the rate prevailing in January 1999, which was £1: €1.4236 (source: Bank of England).

[e] 'Mutual funds' includes holdings in unit or investment trusts and in personal equity plans (PEPs).

Source: FRS 1998/99, authors' calculations.

the analysis of income and assets in the UK. For the majority of the remainder of this chapter we will use data from the 1998 FRS cross-section – for which the sample period is April 1998 to March 1999 – to describe patterns of share ownership. As the table shows, the FRS contains detailed information on ownership of assets but no information on the amounts held for the majority of the sample. Consequently, for the analysis of amounts held in stocks we will then turn to the British Household Panel Study, which has a wealth module in wave 5 (1995), from which we can estimate the proportion of wealth held in stocks and shares.

Tables 8.3a and 8.3b present summary statistics from the 1998 FRS cross-section, both on a household and a per-adult basis. As the tables show, around 28 per cent of households own shares directly, and 44 per cent own shares either directly or indirectly.

We also produce estimates for stockholding excluding holdings in Defined Contribution (personal) pension schemes from the definition of indirect stockholdings. This is done to aid comparability between our findings and the findings on other countries considered in this project: for several of the countries considered, institutional factors or issues of data availability make it difficult to count such DC pension holdings as a form of stockownership. It should though be noted that, in the United Kingdom, excluding such holdings might be thought to imply an inappropriate definition of indirect stockholding since a decision to own a DC personal pension certainly represents a decision to hold an asset that is subject to stockmarket risk. The grossed up figures from Table 8.3b indicate that 27.9 per cent (6.7 million) of households hold stocks directly and 16.9 per cent (4.0 million) hold stocks in a PEP or a unit or investment trust. Taking these two together, 34.8 per cent (8.3 million) of households hold stocks either directly, or in a PEP, or a fund, or both. As a marker for comparison, in 1995/6 FRS the corresponding figures were 21.3 per cent (5 million) holding stocks directly and 11.8 per cent (2.8 million) holding stocks in a PEP or fund. In total, 26.8 per cent (6.3 million) held stocks in one or other (or both) of these forms.

8.5 Univariate analysis of asset ownership rates

Table 8.4 begins our analysis of stockownership rates by presenting a simple unconditional univariate tabulation of stockownership rates by age band. The table reports the fraction of households investing in stocks. The population is split into age bands according to the age of household head, and all statistics are computed using population

Table 8.4 Direct and indirect stockholding by age of head of household

For age bands defined according to the age of the head of the household, the table reports the fraction of households that invest in stocks. Stocks held directly are those that can be self-traded. All statistics are computed using population weights in an effort to make them representative for the UK population.

	Age						Total
	< 30	30–39	40–49	50–59	60–69	≥ 70	
Stocks (held directly)	0.171	0.252	0.317	0.349	0.329	0.228	0.279
Mutual funds	0.067	0.134	0.175	0.242	0.248	0.129	0.169
Pension funds	0.157	0.278	0.300	0.296	0.128	0.021	0.202
Stocks or mutual funds or pension funds	0.310	0.467	0.538	0.565	0.477	0.292	0.449
Proportion of households	0.113	0.197	0.179	0.180	0.144	0.186	1

Source: FRS 1998/99, authors' calculations.

Table 8.5 Direct and indirect stockholding by education

The table divides the population of households into groups according to the years of education of the head of the household and lists the proportion of households in each education group that holds stocks. All statistics are computed using population weights in an effort to make them representative for the UK population.

	Less than high school	High school	College	Average
Stocks (held directly)	0.136	0.228	0.407	0.279
Mutual funds	0.070	0.123	0.280	0.169
Pension funds	0.138	0.196	0.226	0.202
Stocks or mutual funds or pension funds	0.260	0.396	0.590	0.449
Proportion of households	0.053	0.638	0.309	1

Source: FRS 1998/99, authors' calculations.

weights. The table shows the familiar hump shaped profile for share ownership by any of the definitions. Peak ownership rates are for households with the head aged 50–59.

In Table 8.5 we present similar gradients, this time splitting the population according to the education of the household head. Although the education categories are not the most appropriate way to group the data, given the UK educational system, we construct groups on the basis of comparability to other countries in the analysis by choosing those where the head received full time education for less than 12 years, 12–15 years, and over 15 years, respectively. Clearly, the most educated households are by far the most likely to be observed holding shares. Pensions are held more evenly across groups. The proportion of the most educated group that hold a DC pension is less than twice that in the least educated group. The equivalent ratio is around three for shares held directly and four for shares held in mutual funds.

Table 8.6 reports the proportion of households who have stocks, by gross financial asset quartiles. Since we do not observe total levels of assets or wealth in the FRS data, quartiles are generated using data on interest income and will be accurate under the assumption that the average rate of return on assets is either constant or increases with wealth, which does not seem unreasonable. Those with no financial assets (approximately thirty-two per cent of the grossed up sample) are ranked according to overall household income. As would be expected, and as in other countries, stock holding is concentrated in the upper part of the financial wealth distribution, with six out of ten households in the upper quartile owning stocks directly and over three quarters holding stocks in some form or other, whether directly or indirectly.

Table 8.6 Proportion of households investing in stocks, by financial asset quartiles[5]

The table ranks the population of households into quarters according to their financial wealth (proxied by asset income as discussed in the main text) and then lists the proportion of households in each quarter who hold stocks. Similar statistics for the wealthiest five per cent and one per cent and across the population as a whole, are also provided. All statistics are computed using population weights in an effort to make them representative for the UK population.

	Quartile I (lowest wealth)	**Quartile II**	**Quartile III**	**Quartile IV (highest wealth)**	**Top 5%**	**Top 1%**	**Average**
Stocks (held directly)	0.016	0.117	0.387	0.595	0.735	0.808	0.279
Mutual funds	0.015	0.058	0.168	0.434	0.593	0.654	0.169
Pension funds	0.068	0.229	0.260	0.251	0.279	0.316	0.202
Stocks or mutual funds or pension funds	0.091	0.340	0.588	0.776	0.890	0.944	0.449

Source: FRS 1998/99, authors' calculations.

Similar patterns of stock holding are observed across the income distribution and presented in Table 8.7. The observed gradients are, however, slightly less steep than those across the wealth distribution, as would be expected.

To conclude the descriptive analysis, in Tables 8.8a and 8.8b we present sample summary statistics corresponding to Tables 8.3a and 8.3b, this time focussing on just those households who own stocks and shares by the various definitions. All in all, stockholders are more likely to be married, from larger households with more earners and

Table 8.7 Proportion of households investing in stocks, by income quartiles

The table ranks the population of households into quarters according to their income and then lists the proportion of households in each quarter who hold stocks. Similar statistics for the richest five per cent and one per cent and across the population as a whole, are also provided. All statistics are computed using population weights in an effort to make them representative for the UK population.

	Quartile I	Quartile II	Quartile III	Quartile IV	Top 5%	Top 1%	Average
Stocks (held directly)	0.129	0.183	0.314	0.488	0.590	0.708	0.279
Mutual funds	0.070	0.102	0.175	0.327	0.480	0.521	0.169
Pension funds	0.068	0.135	0.256	0.349	0.436	0.513	0.202
Stocks or mutual funds or pension funds	0.210	0.325	0.534	0.725	0.843	0.930	0.449

Source: FRS 1998/99, authors' calculations.

Table 8.8a Demographic characteristics of stockholders and non-stockholders

Tables 8.8a and 8.8b list the sample mean for various characteristics of adults and households who are stockholders and non-stockholders in the FRS 1998/99.

Variables (individual characteristics)	Direct stockholders		Mutual fundholders		Personal pension holders		All with stocks, mutual funds or pensions		Non-stockholders	
	Household head	All adults	Household head	All adults	Household head	All adults	Household head	All adults	Household head	All adults
Married*	0.659	0.665	0.673	0.681	0.706	0.663	0.656	0.656	0.402	0.481
Male*	0.854	0.510	0.854	0.510	0.914	0.527	0.859	0.513	0.650	0.465
Single*	0.280	0.273	0.278	0.268	0.204	0.252	0.276	0.274	0.535	0.442
Age	52.0	47.7	53.4	49.2	45.1	41.5	50.2	46.0	51.9	47.6

Table 8.8b Demographic characteristics of households by stockholders status

Variable (household characteristics)	Direct stockholders	Mutual fundholders	Personal pension holders	All with stocks, mutual funds or pensions	Non-stockholders
Between 2 and 4 household members*	0.731	0.735	0.781	0.732	0.575
More than 4 household members*	0.057	0.053	0.092	0.066	0.069
One earner*	0.307	0.313	0.366	0.325	0.262
Two earners*	0.315	0.285	0.368	0.318	0.167
More than two earners*	0.070	0.063	0.098	0.074	0.030
Head is a wage earner*	0.563	0.529	0.628	0.573	0.378
Head is self-employed*	0.107	0.113	0.260	0.141	0.038
Head is unemployed*	0.012	0.010	0.017	0.014	0.059
At least one pension recipient*	0.382	0.447	0.144	0.328	0.388
Number of households	6269	3785	4423	10052	12806
Number of households (grossed)	6657346	4028104	4829369	10719674	13176016
Number of adults	12114	7282	9212	19601	20897
Number of adults (grossed)	13289476	8007170	10381569	21589076	22193993
Employed in low-risk firms	n.a.	n.a.	n.a.	n.a.	n.a.
Employed in high-risk firms	n.a.	n.a.	n.a.	n.a.	n.a.
Low-risk occupations	n.a.	n.a.	n.a.	n.a.	n.a.
High-risk occupations	n.a.	n.a.	n.a.	n.a.	n.a.

Notes: All statistics are for sample grossed up to the number of adults or households in the population.

* Nature of variable means that 'sample mean' measures the proportion of the sample that have the relevant characteristic.

Source: FRS 1998/99, authors' calculations.

with a household head who is less likely to be either unemployed or self-employed. Unfortunately, in the FRS data there is no satisfactory question asked to respondents by which one could classify employees into whether they are in high- or low-risk firms or occupations.

8.6 Multivariate analysis of asset ownership rates

Table 8.9 reports the marginal effects from probit regressions for the various forms of direct and indirect stockholding. Income and financial wealth brackets are based on income and financial wealth quartiles. Other variables refer to the head of the household. All estimates are in comparison to the base household which has a head aged less than 35

Table 8.9 Probit regressions for direct and indirect stockholding

Variable	Direct stockholding	Mutual fundholders	Personal pension holders	All stockholders
Age				
30–39	0.028**	0.042***	0.049***	0.084***
40–49	0.051***	0.054***	0.035***	0.091***
50–59	0.036**	0.081***	0.038***	0.072***
60–69	0.021	0.048***	−0.015	0.004
70+	0.032**	−0.026**	−0.114***	−0.133***
High school	0.032**	0.021*	0.024**	0.063***
College	0.084***	0.085***	0.009	0.126***
Married	0.029**	0.015*	0.022***	0.073***
Male	0.034***	0.014*	0.044***	0.067**
Between 2 and 4 household members	−0.053***	−0.035***	0.009	−0.094***
More than 4 household members	−0.079***	−0.041***	−0.014	−0.163***
Two earners	0.022**	−0.009*	0.043***	0.073***
More earners	−0.002	−0.0270***	0.088***	0.082***
Head self-employed	−0.005	0.004	0.344***	0.279***
Any pension recipients	−0.001	0.052***	−0.074***	−0.010
Second income bracket	0.049***	0.036***	0.048***	0.105***
Third income bracket	0.097***	0.074***	0.064***	0.167***
Fourth income bracket	0.146***	0.142***	0.067***	0.222***
Second wealth bracket	0.213***	0.067***	0.100***	0.218***
Third wealth bracket	0.528***	0.211***	0.151***	0.478***
Fourth wealth bracket	0.676***	0.415***	0.180***	0.638***
Number of observations	22858	22858	22858	22858

Notes
*** Significant at 1 per cent level.
** Significant at 5 per cent level.
* Significant at 10 per cent level.

Source: FRS 1998/99, authors' calculations.

with less than high school education, who is non-married, female and single and is a non-self-employed, non-pension recipient, in the first income bracket and the first wealth bracket.

Many of the gradients identified in the previous univariate analysis remain present in this multivariate context. Direct stockownership is hump shaped in age and increasing in education and income and increasing sharply in wealth, with all effects strongly statistically significant. Given that personal pensions have only been available in the UK since 1988 they are concentrated in the lower part of the age distribution so when these are either analysed in isolation (column 3), or included in the definition of stockholders in the final column, the familiar hump-shaped age-profile is not present.

8.7 Univariate analysis of portfolio shares

To move beyond this analysis of who holds stocks and examine the degree to which there is variation in the amounts of stocks held by stockholders, one requires detailed information on the amount held in each of the various asset types. Unfortunately, as mentioned above, only limited such information is available from the financial resources survey. Values of balances held in each of the asset types are only collected for that part of the wealth distribution that has between £1500 and £20 000 in financial wealth. This represents only around 30 per cent of the sample. The information is collected only for these people because the primary aim of the wealth questions in the survey is to understand asset tests which qualify or disqualify households from certain state benefits, and balances outside this range do not affect eligibility. In order to try to continue using this dataset for the remaining analysis we experimented with imputing asset balances for the whole distribution using the balance information for this group, coupled with the asset-ownership information and the interest-income information for the distribution as a whole. This method does not provide accurate information, however, since (as we will see in what follows) the relationship between amounts held in stocks and other household characteristics is much weaker than the relationship between those characteristics and stockownership as defined in the previous sections. As a result, imputing values from a subset of around 30 per cent of the data is unsatisfactory. Equally, it is not sufficient to focus just on the subset of the data for which we have asset values, since it is not a random subset of the data. Hence, we are forced to turn to a different dataset for the remaining analysis.

In 1995, the British Household Panel Study fielded a wealth module for every household in their sample. This module asked much less detailed questions about asset ownership but did collect balances in the broadly defined categories of 'savings' and 'investments'. The latter category corresponds almost exactly to what we define in this chapter as stocks plus mutual funds, that is, our measure of indirect share ownership (excluding DC pensions, for which there is no survey in the UK which collects information on balances). Some questions on the ownership of assets within the 'investment' category also allow the proportion of wealth held as 'direct' holdings of shares to be estimated. This wealth data has been described and analysed in detail elsewhere as well as being compared to the panel survey of income dynamics, which has similar information for the United States.[6]

Tables 8.10–8.12 correspond to Tables 8.4, 8.5 and 8.6, and present univariate analysis of the asset share invested in stocks by age, education, and wealth respectively. The asset share invested in stocks is defined as the amount held in stocks – either directly or indirectly – divided by total net financial wealth. Only those households who report to holding some stocks, either directly or indirectly, are included in calculations of asset shares across population groups. That is, for the second row of each table (asset shares invested in stocks held either directly or indirectly) this variable will never take the value of zero, whilst for the first row of the table there will be some values of zero in the data which will correspond to those households who hold stocks in mutual funds but do not own shares directly. In both cases, however, the zero values corresponding to households that do not own stocks at all are removed from the calculations.

As is immediately apparent from the tables, the patterns in how asset shares invested in stocks vary with other household characteristics, are much less uniform than those in stockownership rates. Conditional on owning stocks in some form, there is no particular relationship of the amount held to the age of the head of the household with the exception that the oldest households do seem to have less of their portfolios in stock, which would seem to accord with the predictions of portfolio theory. This is true whether one looks at direct holdings of stock only, or at the broader definition of direct and indirect holdings together. Additionally, the average asset shares for direct holding of

Table 8.10 Asset share invested in stocks, and mutual funds, by age of head of household

The table reports the fraction of financial wealth that is held in stocks by stock- or mutual fund-holding households in each of several age bands, where households are allocated to bands according to the age of the household head. All statistics are computed using population weights in an effort to make them representative for the UK population.

	Age						
	<30	30–39	40–49	50–59	60–69	≥ 70	Total
Stocks	0.33	0.35	0.29	0.34	0.26	0.18	0.28
Stocks and mutual funds	0.61	0.53	0.50	0.50	0.52	0.40	0.49

Source: British Household Panel Survey (BHPS), 1995 wealth data; authors' calculations.

Table 8.11 Asset share invested in stocks and mutual funds, by education of head of household

The table reports the fraction of financial wealth that is held in stocks by stock- or mutual fund-holding households in different educational groups, where households are allocated to groups according to the education of the household head. All statistics are computed using population weights.

	Less than high school	High school	College	Total
Stocks	0.21	0.30	0.37	0.28
Stocks and mutual funds	0.43	0.51	0.55	0.49

Source: BHPS, 1995; authors' calculations.

Table 8.12 Asset share invested in stocks and mutual funds, by financial asset quartiles

The table ranks the population of households into quarters according to their financial wealth and then lists the proportion of financial wealth held by stock- and mutual fund-holding households in each quarter that is held in stocks. Similar statistics for the wealthiest 5 per cent and 1 per cent and across the population as a whole, are also provided. All statistics are computed using population weights.

	Quartile I (lowest wealth)	Quartile II	Quartile III	Quartile IV (highest wealth)	Top 5%	Top 1%	Average
Stocks	0.04	0.19	0.28	0.34	0.39	0.48	0.28
Stocks and mutual funds	0.86	0.43	0.41	0.54	0.64	0.68	0.49

Source: BHPS, 1995; authors' calculations.

stock are considerably lower than those for the broader definition as a result of the inclusion of the zero-values for the fairly substantial fraction of stock holders who only hold their stocks in the form of mutual funds.

There is evidence of a more uniform pattern in the relationship between the portfolio share that is invested in stocks and the education level of the head of household (with education groups defined to be comparable to those used in the other data earlier in this chapter). Even conditional on asset ownership, the proportion of household portfolios invested in stocks rises with education although maybe not as steeply as might be expected.

When looking across wealth groups the expected pattern – with portfolio shares rising with levels of wealth – emerges as one moves into the top half of the wealth distribution. In the low wealth region of the data there are only a very few households who are observed to hold shares in any form. This table shows that even these do not hold very many shares directly but in contrast have an extremely high fraction of their portfolio in mutual funds. This particular statistic should be interpreted with caution, however, since the large majority of the bottom wealth quartile (around 92 per cent in the BHPS data) are excluded from this group as a result of our exclusion of non-stockholders from the reference group.

8.8 Multivariate analysis of portfolio shares

In the final analysis of this chapter we investigate portfolio shares on a multivariate basis, taking account of the fact that only certain types of households typically hold any shares at all. To do this, we estimate a simple selectivity model that, in the first stage, models the probability of being a share holder (akin to the probit estimation presented in Table 8.9 above) and then estimates a linear regression for the amount of the portfolio invested in stocks that controls for the conditional probability of being a shareholder as well as for other conditioning variables. To identify this model, we need to find a factor that determines the probability of share ownership but not the actual amount invested in stocks (conditional on all the other covariates) and we choose to use voting preferences. There is some evidence elsewhere that attitudes to capital markets and institutions differ by political preferences,[7] and since the BHPS data asks all adults which of the political parties they most closely support, we are able to construct two dummy variables taking the value 1 if the household head is a strong supporter of Labour or the Conservatives, respectively. The remaining households (who support some other party, or do not associate strongly with any party) form the base group. Confirming the results of other studies, conditional on other observables, Labour voters are less likely to own stocks and Conservative voters are more likely, than the base (non-affiliated) group.

With political preferences added to the probit it is possible to construct the conditional selection probability terms and estimate the regression for the share of the portfolio held in stocks that controls for selection into the group of stock holders.[8] Table 8.13 presents the results of this analysis. Probit estimates and the selection probability parameter are not presented for brevity. Broadly speaking, however, the univariate patterns presented in Tables 8.10–8.12 are borne out in the

Table 8.13 Regressions for the asset share invested in stocks and mutual funds

Variable	**Stocks**	**Stocks and mutual funds**
Age		
30–39	−0.113***	−0.111***
40–49	−0.100**	−0.108***
50–59	−0.099**	−0.100***
60–69	−0.085*	−0.116***
⩾70	−0.158**	−0.221***
High school	0.003	0.054**
College	−0.006	0.062**
Second financial wealth bracket	−0.236	−0.271***
Third financial wealth bracket	−0.386	−0.220*
Fourth financial wealth bracket	−0.365	0.003
Other variables		
Household size	−0.045***	−0.033***
Number of children	0.073***	0.060***
Head employed	−0.039*	−0.010
Home owner	0.010	0.030
Number of observations	4303	4303

Notes
*** Significant at 1 per cent level.
** Significant at 5 per cent level.
* Significant at 10 per cent level.

Source: BHPS, 1995, authors' calculations.

multivariate modelling, particularly when one looks at the broader definition of stockownership. Asset shares are fairly flat with respect to age, although they are lower for the oldest households, and increase with education. Note however, that the statistical significance of many of the parameters is less than in the probit analysis presented earlier, and in general the model fits the data less well. Basically, the table shows that there is much less (uniform) variation in asset shares for stockholders than in stock holding probabilities themselves.

8.9 Conclusions

This chapter has presented empirical evidence on patterns of stockholding and asset ownership in the United Kingdom. Unfortunately, unlike for income or expenditure, the household-level data that is required to undertake such analysis adequately is relatively sparse and of fairly poor quality at present. With the data available to us, we have been able to describe asset holding patterns in some detail. These patterns correspond to those observed in other countries, with asset ownership rates varying substantially and significantly by age, education, wealth and income, both in univariate and multivariate analysis. Looking at the portfolio shares of investors in the stock market, around one half of their portfolios are seen to be in the form of shares, again broadly in accordance with other countries. This fraction varies less systematically with other characteristics than does the likelihood of being a stockholder, and the fact that this is true even at the bottom of the age and wealth distributions is suggestive of transactions costs in owning and trading shares. It is important to note that two significant forms of institutional share holding (life insurance and DC pensions) have been excluded from much of our analysis. This is done for the sake of international comparability and because of data availability issues. When such accounts are included the exposure of UK households to the stock market would be considerably higher (albeit in a fairly diversified way).

The liberalization of stockmarket trading and ownership in the 1980s could provide a potentially interesting case study through which to investigate the effects of transactions costs. A detailed analysis of UK household share-ownership over this period could also shed considerable light over the role of 'demand and supply' factors, along with the role of government intervention, in driving share-ownership rates. However, to our knowledge there are no good data covering this period in sufficient detail to allow a full investigation of the episode. One lesson that can be drawn from the analysis presented in this chapter is a clear need for more, and better, microeconomic data on household wealth and share-ownership in the United Kingdom.

References

Bank of England (2001) *Monetary and Financial Statistics.*

Banks, J., R. Blundell and J. P. Smith (2000) 'The distribution of wealth in the US and the UK', IFS Working paper 2000/20, IFS: London, forthcoming in *Journal of Human Resources*

Banks, J. and R. Blundell (1994) 'Household saving in the UK', in J. Poterba (ed.), *International Comparisons of Household Saving*, Chicago: Chicago University Press.

Budd, A. and N. Campbell (1998) 'The roles of the public and private sectors in the UK pension system', in M. Feldstein (ed.), *Privatising Social Security*, Chicago: University of Chicago Press.

Davies, T. and A. Shorrocks (2000) 'The distribution of wealth', in A. B. Atkinson and F. Bourguignon (eds), *Handbook of income Distribution*, Amsterdam: North-Holland.

Disney, R., C. Emmerson and M. Wakefield (2001) 'Pension reform and saving in Britain', *Oxford Review of Economic Policy*, **17**(1): 70–94.
Inland Revenue (1999) *Inland Revenue Statistics 1999*, London: The Stationery Office.
Johnson, P. and S. Tanner (1998) 'Ownership and distribution of wealth', *Political Quarterly*, **69**: 365–77.
National Statistics (various years) *Financial Statistics*, London: The Stationery Office.

Notes

1 Stockholding: A European Comparison

1 An exception is the United States, where sometimes individuals designate their accounts as predominantly stocks or bonds. In this case, we rely on a definition of direct and indirect stockholding available in the 1998 Survey of Consumer Finances, which defines total financial assets invested in stocks as (1) directly-held stock, (2) stock mutual funds (full value if described as stock mutual fund, 1/2 value of combination mutual funds, (3) IRAs/Keoghs invested in stocks (full value if mostly invested in stock, 1/2 value if split between stocks/bonds or stocks/money market, 1/3 value if split between stocks/bonds/money market, (4) other managed assets w/equity interest (annuities, trusts, MIAs) (full value if mostly invested in stock, 1/2 value if split between stocks/MFs & bonds/CDs, or 'mixed/diversified', 1/3 value if 'other', (5) thrift-type retirement accounts invested in stock full value if mostly invested in stock, 1/2 value if split between stocks and interest earning assets).

2 Table 1.2 and all subsequent Tables are based on the datasets described in Section 1.3 and summarized in Table 1.1. Data refer to 1998 and all statistics are calculated using the population weights provided in the surveys.

3 The only exception to this seems to be the United Kingdom, where the positive relationship between income deciles and participation appears to be more or less linear.

4 Perhaps the most visible effect is that inclusion of mutual funds makes the hump in United States participation rates much more pronounced. This is consistent with evidence that most of the spread of equity culture in the United States took the form of indirect stockholding through mutual funds and individual retirement accounts (Bertaut and Starr-McCluer, 2002).

5 Recall that asset shares are not available in the United Kingdom. In Germany, we have information only on the asset share of directly held stocks, preventing the calculation of the total asset share invested in stocks.

6 In European countries (but not in the United States), there is not enough information on the portfolios held by mutual funds to assess which part of the mutual fund investment declared by the household actually represents investment in stocks. Thus, the portfolio shares we report represent overestimates of the conditional portfolio shares of stocks in European countries.

7 As noted in Section 1.3 and in Table 1.1, part of the difference between the United States and European countries rests on the different definition of total assets invested in stocks.

8 For example, Carroll (2002) shows that such findings are consistent with a model in which households are less risk averse with respect to the size of their bequests than to the level of their consumption, and bequests are a luxury good. The rich tend to accumulate more for bequest purposes and to be less concerned about the riskiness of assets accumulated for this purpose.

2 Stockholding: Lessons from Theory and Computations

1 Gollier (2001 a,b) provides an excellent discussion of the portfolio implications of models that can be solved exactly using analytical methods, which complements the analysis in this paper. Campbell and Viceira (2002) provide a very useful, in-depth discussion of various aspects of portfolio theory, including lessons from models using analytical approximations.

2 An early statement of this result is in Arrow (1974).

3 If there is negative correlation between labour incomes and stock returns, then this provides an additional reason to hold stocks, namely as an insurance against earnings fluctuations. The case of positive correlation poses subtler issues, and we will return to it below.

4 It should be stressed that this discussion refers to constraints on *net* wealth. We will see below that borrowing constraints of other types can justify zero stockholding.

5 See Quiggin, 1982; Yaari, 1987; Epstein and Zin, 1990; Haliassos and Hassapis, 2001; Donkers, 2000.

6 Technically, indifference curves under such specifications exhibit kinks, thus making it possible for an investor to be 'stuck' at one of those kinks for a range of slopes of the budget line.

7 In the example, the two relevant states with ambiguous ranking are (r^H, Y^L) and (r^L, Y^H), where r is the return on stocks, Y is labour income, H denotes the high realization, and L denotes the low realization. Reversal in the rankings does not occur at zero stockholding, but at that (positive) level of stockholding for which the difference in portfolio income exactly offsets the difference in labour income across the two states. Ranking reversals for other states can be ruled out through a more sophisticated argument.

8 Technically, the imposition of two separate short sales constraints, one on stocks and the other on bonds, breaks the symmetry of treatment between bonds and stocks by allowing the shadow values of these two constraints to differ.

9 Cash on hand is defined as the sum of current wealth and of labour income, and it is normalized by either current labour income or by the permanent component of labour income.

10 Cocco, Gomes and Maenhout offer a possible intuitive explanation for why this ratio matters so much for portfolio composition. Future labour income, though risky, has a positive minimum value in each future period. This value is guaranteed without risk, in the sense that the household will receive at least this labour income in each future period. Thus, it serves as a surrogate riskless asset, displacing (some of) the riskless asset that the household would otherwise include in its portfolio and encouraging the household to devote more of its financial wealth to stocks. As age progresses and the household gets closer to retirement, the importance of this labour income floor diminishes and households are predicted to shift their portfolios more into the riskless asset and away from stocks.

11 It is worth noting that household perceptions relevant for the participation choice are not confined to perceptions about entry costs alone. They notably include household perceptions as to the size of the equity premium. The larger the perceived premium on the expected return on equity, the more

likely is the household to participate in the stock market for any given level of perceived entry costs. Econometric research has shown that the size of the equity premium is difficult to estimate, even with full access to available historical data (Cochrane, 1997). Moreover, full knowledge of the equity premium is unlikely for households that have never invested in the stock market and are contemplating entry for the first time. The formation of perceptions and their influence on both the decision of households to enter and the threshold costs computed by researchers are useful areas for future research.

12 While the assumption of infinite horizons is clearly unrealistic, it has been found in computations that policy functions for the infinite-horizon problem are essentially the same as those derived from a finite-horizon model for young households.

13 Technically, this refers to households with rate of time preference equal to 10 per cent.

14 These are assumed to have rate of time preference equal to 4 per cent.

15 The empirical chapters in this book present the available evidence on portfolio shares of various forms of stockholding. The contributions in Guiso *et al.* (2001) show how stocks are combined with other assets in household portfolios.

16 See Cocco *et al.* (1999), and Haliassos and Michaelides (2001).

17 Technically, the size of the Lagrange multipliers on the two constraints is not the same.

18 For a technical discussion of this point, see Haliassos and Michaelides (1999).

19 Haliassos and Michaelides (1999) also show that it remains optimal for households with positive correlation between their earnings and stock returns to borrow at the (lower) riskless rate than at the (higher expected) risky rate for plausible parameter values when both short-sales constraints are binding. Thus, portfolio specialization in stocks continues to be observed for small savers, unless we are willing to assume very high positive correlation.

20 The same effect could be observed in less extreme cases of ignorance, namely when households do not themselves know how to rebalance their portfolios but know that they can purchase financial advice or brokerage services (including participation in a mutual fund). High perceived costs of acquiring reliable financial advice or brokerage services could deter portfolio rebalancing, even if these cost perceptions are not accurate.

4 Stockholding in France

1 Data of 2000 come from the survey EPCV, INSEE (Dumontier *et al.*, 2001).

2 According to the degree of risk, the various types of financial assets listed in Table 4.1 can be divided into three classes: *clearly safe financial assets* include currency, transaction and saving accounts; *fairly safe financial assets* include government bonds, other bonds and cash value of life insurance; *risky financial assets* include stocks, mutual funds and managed investment accounts.

3 Among the main State-owned companies which have been privatized: BNP-Paribas, Aventis, Usinor, Total-Fina Elf, Pechiney, Renault, Altadis, CNP, Air France, Crédit Lyonnais, EADS, France Telecom, Thomson Multimédia.

4 In 1997, after the privatization of France Telecom, 12.5 per cent of direct stockholders did not hold stocks directly or indirectly, a year before.

5 Data of 2000 come from the survey EPCV, INSEE (Dumontier *et al.*, 2001).

6 The 'game' consists in determining, sequentially, whether the interviewee would accept to give up his present income and to accept other contracts in a lottery form: she has one chance in two to double her income, and one chance in two for it to be reduced by one third (contract A), by one half (contract B), and by one fifth (contract C). This procedure allows to obtain a range of measures of relative risk aversion under the assumption that preferences are strictly risk averse and utility is of the CRRA type. The degree of relative risk aversion is less than 1 if the individual successively accepts contracts A and B; between 1 and 2 if she accepts A but refuses B; between 2 and 3.76 if she refuses A but accepts C; and finally more than 3.76 if she refuses both A and C. Among the 4633 respondents to the recto–verso questionnaire, 3483 individuals participated in the lottery game.

7 More precisely, the 'Patrimoine 1997' survey records only about 20 per cent of the amount of stocks registered in National Account. We obtain the same values with the previous survey (Arrondel *et al.*, 1996).

8 The difference between this amount and those of Table 4.1 issued from national accounts comes from (1) a different definition, (2) a different evaluation method and (3) the under-evaluation of asset demands in survey. With similar definition, the amount evaluated in the 'Patrimoine 1997' survey represents around 40 per cent of the evaluation in national account (Talon, 1999).

9 Intuitively, households take more risk in their portfolio if they could increase their income to compensate bad investments (see also Section 5.1).

10 Income, measured in brackets, has also a positive, but smaller effect on stockholding: less than 5 per cent of households in the first income quartile own direct stockholding (respectively 4.5 per cent for indirect stockholding) when almost 30 per cent of households in the fourth quartile hold this asset (resp. 26 per cent). At the level of the top 5 per cent of the income distribution, 45.5 per cent of the households have direct stockholding (resp. 37 per cent). This proportion is almost 60 per cent for the top 1 per cent of the income distribution (resp. 36 per cent).

11 This gender-specific risk behaviour is also obtained by Jianakoplos and Bernasek (1998) or Sundén and Surette (1998) but is in contrast with the results of Schubert *et al.*, 1999.

12 If the consumer has labour income, her 'wealth' is assumed to include both assets and the present value of her human capital. These two kinds are perfect substitutes because capital market is assumed to be perfect.

13 If the prices of assets are distributed according to a log-normal distribution, the demands for assets are the same as those found in the static model of Tobin-Markowitz (Merton, 1971)

14 Apart from the characteristics of the assets (risk and return), this myopia is related to consumers' risk tolerance (the inverse of absolute risk aversion) which must be a linear function of wealth (Mossin, 1968). Hence, Gollier (2001) shows that if the investor's absolute risk tolerance is convex, then the share of risky assets in wealth will decrease as age increases and that it is a positive linear function of wealth.

15 Szpiro (1995) introduces an additional constraint on fixed transaction costs: the investor buys an asset *i* if, and only if, the sum of its discounted expected returns is higher than its holding costs. The higher the sum of the discounted expected returns, the easier it is to exceed fixed costs. Moreover, the longer the horizon of the investment, the higher the likelihood of removing constraints. Favourable taxation increases the expected returns and makes it easier to exceed the fixed costs.

16 The effect of uninsurable and unavoidable earning risk on consumption and portfolio choice was first studied by Drèze and Modigliani (1972). They show in a two-period model that if absolute risk aversion is decreasing, portfolio choice and saving decisions are not separable (Drèze and Modigliani 'substitution effect'): an endogenous decrease (increase) in demand for risky assets decreases (increases) precautionary saving.

17 Eeckhoudt *et al.* (1996) propose a synthetic approach of all these concepts. 'Standarness' implies that every loss-aggravating risk aggravates every undesirable risk. 'Properness' is more restrictive: an undesirable risk can never be made desirable by the presence of an independent undesirable risk. 'Risk vulnerability' (an undesirable risk can never be made desirable by an independent unfair risk) includes proper risk aversion and standard risk aversion as particular cases.

18 Similarly, they should tend to buy more insurance against risks that are insurable (Eeckhoudt and Kimball, 1992).

19 For more details about estimation of household portfolio models, see Miniaci and Weber (2001).

20 As there are only two categories of assets used in regressions, it is also possible to handle the selection bias by estimating a simple Tobit model on the share of risky assets (with a lower limit of zero holding). However, Tobit estimation constrains the determinants of the probability of ownership and of the demand of risky assets to depend on the same set of variables.

21 Moreover, gains or losses on the stock exchange and the mode of portfolio management have been introduced only in demand equation.

22 This effect is also true everything being equal (Lollivier, 2001).

23 This effect could be explained by the influence of the supply of stocks (more important in town) or/and by a price (higher in big urban area) effect of main residence.

24 For more details on the characteristics of this sample, the questionnaire on risk attitudes and the econometric results, see Arrondel (2000).

25 Only some recent papers study the impact of income uncertainty and precautionary motives on the composition of households' portfolio. On Italian data, households facing uninsurable risk and future liquidity constraints will reduce their share of risky assets (Guiso *et al.*, 1996) and increase coverage against the risks that can be avoided (Guiso and Japelli, 1998). Vissing-Jorgensen (1999) also finds evidence that background risk reduces stock market participation in the United States. Hochguertel (1998) results for the Netherlands are inconclusive and those of Alessie *et al.* (2001) for the same country did not find significant effect of income uncertainty on the demand for risky assets.

26 However, there may be a non-negligible error in the measurement of the income variance (e.g. some of the zeros in the self-reported measure of earnings variance may be artificial). In this case, the coefficients of the

variance of earnings are biaised. Additionally, there could be an endogeneity bias due to occupational choice. To account for these facts, we instrument these variables in the wealth equations (Arrondel, 2000). In addition to the set of exogenous variables, we include in the instrumental set parent's social status and portfolio composition. The partial R^2 for the included instruments in the first stage regressions is quite low (1.15 per cent) but F-test (2.69) is significant. Moreover, tests of over-identifying restrictions do not reject the model specification and the chosen instruments. But in the two cases (for direct and indirect stockholding), the test of exogeneity allows us to reject the endogeneity of the variable measuring income variance variable in Heckman's two-stage procedure (Robin, 2000).

27 From a theoretical point of view, two conclusions could be drawn from these facts. First, the positive effect could be due to a negative correlation between risky portfolio risk and income risk (Heaton and Lucas, 2000; Haliasos, 2002). So households could insure themselves against income risk by buying stocks. Second, household have not DARA + DAP utility function. The only measure of correlation between human capital and non-human capital risk for France is those of Bottazzi *et al.* (1996). This correlation is negative and so, could explain the previous econometric result.

28 How do French households manage their portfolio of stocks? Among direct stockholders, 38 per cent hold their portfolio without specific management, 24.5 per cent manage their portfolio personally, 23 per cent follow their financial advisor to reallocate their portfolio and 15 per cent with managing of portfolio of stocks.

29 For indirect stockholding, there is no variable that is statistically significant.

30 When we consider the sub-population of respondents to the questionnaire on risk attitudes (Table 12bis), we obtain the same conclusions.

5 Stockholding in Germany

1 Life insurance can be a vehicle for indirect stockholding. Traditionally, however, the share of stocks in a typical German life insurance portfolio was small and restricted by various laws. Life insurance companies rather have placed their investments directly. Section 5.2 will show that all this is currently changing.

2 Deutsche Bundesbank (1992, 1993b, 1999b), Euler (1985, 1990, 1992), Kim (1992), Börsch-Supan (1994a,b), Schönig (1996), Schnabel (1999), and Börsch-Supan *et al.* (2001).

3 Schlomann (1992), Grimm (1998), and Lang (1998) have used waves 1983, 1988, and 1978, 1983, 1988 of the Income and Expenditure Survey, respectively, to analyse the socioeconomic determinants of household portfolio choice. Börsch-Supan and Stahl (1991), Brunsbach and Lang (1998) and Walliser and Winter (1999) have focused on specific assets, that is building society savings ('*Bausparverträge*') and life insurance contracts, to analyse the effect of tax incentives and policy changes on asset choice. Himmelreicher (1999) has used the German Socioeconomic Panel for a cohort study of wealth and portfolio choice, yet had to rely on reported income from interest and dividends and highly aggregated indications as to asset ownership in order to determine household wealth levels.

4 World Development Indicators, table 1.5.2.
5 In the late eighties, the average lag between the EC directive and the respective legal adjustments was five years.
6 Börsch-Supan and Winter (1999).
7 The difference-in-difference is about the same for lower marginal tax rates.
8 Deutsche Börse (1999), table 1.2.3.
9 Deutsche Börse (1999), table 1.10.4.
10 Classified according to socioeconomic household properties this data is presented in the Fachserie 15 'Wirtschaftsrechnungen', income and expenditure sample 1993, by the Federal Statistical Office.
11 The relative small fraction of unemployed depends on the fact that statistics refer to the household head. The incidence of unemployment among spouses and adult dependents is much larger.
12 Cf. Guiso *et al.* (1996), Bertaut (1998), Hochgürtel *et al.* (1997), Börsch-Supan *et al.* (1999), or Vissing-Jørgensen (1999).
13 A maximum subsidy of €100 on a maximum contribution of €500.
14 Börsch-Supan (1994c).
15 Life insurance contracts are a noteworthy exception to this rule. The tax treatment of interest and capital gains favours the rich. Moreover, contributions to life insurance contracts are (partly) tax exempt for civil servants and the self-employed (cf. Brunsbach and Lang, 1998).
16 For a survey of loopholes in Germany cf. Lang *et al.* (1997).
17 Börsch-Supan and Brugiavini (2001) discuss the preponderance of evidence.
18 Börsch-Supan and Brugiavini (2001) project a maximum decline of about 80 basis points. The main reason is that the baby boom retirement entry stretches about 10 years, during which the new pillar does not yet mature. The increase in new accounts therefore compensates for a substantial portion of dissaving among the retired baby boomers. Moreover, an aging economy needs additional productive capital to compensate for the decline in labour supply.
19 See also Lang (1998) for an elaborate critical analysis of the EVS.
20 In order to exclude seasonal effects, the 'Detailed Record Months' are equally distributed across households. Thus, each month, one out of twelve households record in detail.
21 This coarsening was developed in two steps: a one per cent error on each information in these deciles. Moreover, each of the five lowest and highest characteristics were replaced by their mean. See also Helmcke and Knoche (1992) for the method of anonymization.

6 Stockholding in Italy

1 In 1998 the ratio of debt to financial assets was only 8 per cent.
2 Between 1990 and 1997, 71 firms went public. An almost equal number de-listed, so that the number of listed firms has remained unchanged at 244.
3 For instance, the privatization of ENEL – the national electric company – the last to take place in October 1999, featured 3.8 million bookings. To meet all demands the government has raised to 34 per cent the share of ENEL capital on sale from the initial share of 24 per cent.
4 The cash value of life insurance and pension funds is not reported in the survey. In the 1998 wave, we have information only on participation and

annual contributions and on the year in which the household started to contribute. This information is used to impute the cash value of pension funds and of life insurance policies on the assumption that the average years of contributions remained constant over time and that contributions accumulate at the real interest rate of 3 per cent.

5 The relatively small fraction of unemployed depends on the fact that statistics refer to the household head. The incidence of unemployment among spouses and adult dependents is much larger and close to the national average (11 per cent).

6 In turn, stock market illiquidity, can be imputed to a number of factors that act either on the supply of publicly held stock, their demand, or both. Creditors' weak legal protection is often claimed to make investors unwilling to hold shares; lack of transparency and low-quality accounting standards have similar effects, see Pagano *et al.* (1998). On the supply side, ownership concentration can inhibit firms to go public.

7 It also reflects the fact that privatized companies were already listed prior to privatization.

7 Stockholding in the Netherlands

1 This section and parts of the following section draw to some extent on Alessie *et al.* (2001b).

2 Occupational pensions are complementary to the flat rate old-age pension that every citizen of age 65 and above is entitled to.

3 These numbers do not include foreign funds that are active in the Netherlands but not under the supervision of the Central Bank. Including those makes a considerable difference (cf. footnote 11). Likewise unaccounted for are some mutual funds that have been set up by mortgage lenders and life insurers. They may be only accessible to policy (or contract) holders without being subject to Central Bank supervision.

4 These weights are based on home-ownership and income and use external information from a much larger, close to representative survey of Statistics Netherlands (see Alessie *et al.* (2001b) for details).

5 These are 'range cards'. Using bracket information is extremely valuable for reducing item-nonresponse, as shown by Juster and Smith (1997) and Vazquez-Alvarez (2001). See the appendix for more details about the asset and debt questionnaire.

6 This non-response rate falls over time. In the six consecutive waves, the numbers are 30, 22, 23, 23, 15 and 11 per cent respectively.

7 Again, the non-response rate is falling over time, from 17 per cent in 1993 to 7 per cent in 1998. Similar problems exist for the value of life insurances and defined contribution plans (annuity insurances), shares from a substantial holding, and business equity. Even assets whose value seems easy to determine are not free of missings: about 10 per cent of savings account owners report incomplete or missing amounts. Only for the home and mortgage values are non-response rates below 5 per cent.

8 Ordinary shareholders are liable to income tax whereas substantial shareholders are liable to corporate tax. A taxpayer is regarded as having a substantial holding in a corporation if he or she, either alone or with his or her

spouse, holds directly or indirectly 5 per cent of the issued capital. The aggregated value of substantial holdings is rather high: estimates from the income panel survey (IPO) put it at €50 billion at the beginning of 1997 (see de Kleijn, 1999). Yet, only 1.9 per cent of the households own this big amount in this type of stocks.

9 This question is not part of the asset/liabilities questionnaire, but rather asked in conjunction with labour market status and work history. Aggregation of household stockholding must therefore ignore this question, because it otherwise would lead to double-counting.

10 Employer sponsored defined contribution plans are virtually non existing in the Netherlands. Occupational pension plans are typically of the defined benefit type.

11 The survey question asks about the primary occupation, which may underestimate the number of unemployed at a point in time.

12 In case of mutual funds, this is a reasonable assumption: in 1997, more than 50 per cent of the total amount in mutual funds is invested in funds which are specialized in shares. Further, the investment research firm Morningstar that covers about 90 per cent of mutual funds available to the Dutch investor, lists a total of more than 2500 different mutual funds. Among these, Morningstar classifies about two-thirds as equity funds (www.morningstar.nl, accessed on 17 April, 2002).

13 In the appendix, we present the survey questions upon which the dummies reflecting risk aversion and interest in financial matters are based.

14 Instead of parameter estimates, we present in Table 7.8 estimated marginal effects, that is, the changes in the ownership probability if explanatory variables change by one unit, *ceteris paribus*. To be precise, for continuous variables, the derivative of the estimated probability is evaluated; for dummy variables (like education), the change from 0 to 1 is considered and the corresponding change in probability is reported.

15 In the probit analysis we have also experimented with other explanatory variables, for example, income, marital status, other demographic variables and proxy variables, which measure the importance of liquidity constraints and of background income risk. It appears that these variables do not contribute to the explanation of ownership of stocks, mutual funds or pension funds. In Table 7.8, we therefore have removed these variables from the probit model.

16 If we remove the dummy variables reflecting interest in financial matters from the probit regression, we do observe that education level has a significant positive impact on direct stockholding.

17 The conglomerate Fortis consists of some banks and insurance companies from Holland and Belgium. The management is located in Belgium.

18 Postbank (now part of ING) entered this market in the beginning of the nineties. Postbank dominates the market of consumers' checking accounts and uses its market position to cross-sell other financial products, like mutual funds.

19 Privatization of state-owned enterprises such as in the post- and telecommunications sector was phased in already in the late 1980s and completed by the late 1990s. Privatization of the energy market however, has not yet occurred.

20 Bank Labouchere introduced internet broking via its subsidiary ALEX in 1999. This urged the big banks to also supply extra services through Internet.

21 Until 1992 only the income of a mortgage applicant, but not that of his or her spouse was taken into account when calculating the maximum allowable mortgage. From 1992 on, this constraint was relaxed or abolished (see Aldershof *et al.* (1997)).

22 With the tax reform of 2001, the tax deductibility of mortgage interest payments has been abolished for mortgages that are not used for purchasing a new primary residence or for maintenance (renovation) of the existing dwelling.

23 Variable names are indicated in the main column. The routing of the electronic questionnaire depends on the answers given and is indicated to the right.

8 Stockholding in the United Kingdom

1 This study forms part of the Institute for Fiscal Studies research programme into the changing distribution of consumption, economic resources, and the welfare of households funded by the Leverhulme Trust, to which we are very grateful. Co-funding has been provided by OEE to whom we are also grateful. Material from the FRS made available by the Office for National Statistics through the ESRC Data Archive has been used by permission of the controller of Her Majesty's Stationery Office. Data from the British Household Panel Survey were supplied by the ESRC Data Archive. Neither the ONS nor the ESRC Data Archive bear any responsibility for the analysis or interpretation to the data reported here. The authors would like to thank Orazio Attanasio and Sarah Smith for useful discussions surrounding the issues addressed here. The usual disclaimer applies.

2 For further discussion of these changes see Johnson and Tanner (1998).

3 One of these types of bonds, premium bonds, offers a return in the form of a lottery. All premium bond holders are entered into a monthly draw with the chance to win from £50 000 up to £1 million, where the chance of winning depends on total premium bond holdings. Premium bonds are currently held by around one in five households in the United Kingdom.

4 For further discussion of the distribution of wealth in the United Kingdom and other countries, see Davies and Shorrocks (2000).

5 Since amounts of financial asset holding are not available in the FRS, we have used quartiles based on interest income levels. This will be equivalent if interest income is increasing in the level of financial assets.

6 See Banks *et al.* (2000).

7 See Banks *et al.* (2000).

8 Implicit in this analysis is a different treatment of those households who hold stocks indirectly but not directly, so the gradients in the first column of the table will not correspond to those in the earlier tables. As pointed out above, the earlier tables include some households with zero direct stock holdings (but positive indirect stock holdings), which are implicitly excluded from the linear regression part of this analysis.

Index